British think-tanks and the climate of opinion

British think-tanks and the climate of opinion

Andrew Denham and Mark Garnett

First published in 1998 by UCL Press

UCL Press Limited
1 Gunpowder Square
London
EC4A 3DE
UK

and

1900 Frost Road, Suite 101
Bristol
Pennsylvania 19007-1598
USA

The name of University College London (UCL) is a registered
trade mark used by UCL Press with the consent of the owner.

Learning Resources
Centre

1236169 0

British Library Cataloguing-in-Publication Data
A CIP catalogue record for this book is available from the British Library.

Library of Congress Cataloging-in-Publication Data are available

ISBNS: 1–85728–497–6 PB
       1–85728–496–8 HB

Typeset in Classical Garamond
by Graphicraft Typesetters Ltd, Hong Kong
Printed and bound by T.J. International Ltd, Padstow

CONTENTS

FOREWORD

Think-tanks have been proliferating, especially since achieving such a high profile during the Thatcher years when they were credited with all kinds of influence both for good and ill over the policy and strategy of the government. But there have been relatively few systematic studies of their role or influence, and their relationship with pressure groups, political parties, and policy-makers. We are still unsure how to answer the question – do think-tanks make a difference? Think-tanks certainly claim that they do, but then their funding and their image often depends upon it. It has always been a hard claim to test. If there had been no think-tanks at work in the last twenty years would the direction and the substance of policy have been significantly different? But perhaps this is to ask the wrong question. Some argue that the real significance of think-tanks is ideological. They act as ideological entrepreneurs, either sustaining and legitimating an existing "climate of ideas", or acting as the catalysts for a new one.

Andrew Denham and Mark Garnett provide an interesting historical and organisational map of think-tanks in the UK. In doing so they dispel several misconceptions. Think-tanks come in many different shapes and sizes. The origin of the term itself is American, and was first applied in the UK to the CPRS. This was not a good example since in the American usage a think-tank is concerned with blue-skies research as well as with studies and reports which can directly influence the policy process; it has some independence of pressure groups and political parties; and its objectivity and standing derive in part from its ability to deploy relevant academic knowledge and expertise. Denham and Garnett show convincingly that think-tanks in this sense have long existed in Britain – the Fabians and PEP are two examples – but also acknowledge that the term cannot be confined to them. They distinguish between different kinds of think-tank such as contract research organisations and what they call "advocacy tanks".

There are many more think-tanks in Britain and the United States than anywhere else, but the scale and number of think-tanks in the United States is much greater than in Britain. There are several reasons why this should be so. Denham and Garnett cite the greater cohesion of British political parties, the scale of private research funding in the US, and the role of the permanent civil service in the UK which has never relied greatly on external sources of policy advice. But despite this, and while not rivalling the United States, think-tanks appear to have become much more important in the policy process in the UK in the last twenty years.

One explanation argues that the growth and perceived importance of think-tanks is a political phenomenon. The free market think-tanks in Britain played an important role within the political elite in legitimating the key ideas that formed the basis for the Thatcherite reforms of the 1980s. Central to this explanation is the elusive notion of the "climate of opinion". From Dicey to Green-leaf there has always been a strong assumption that the climate of opinion matters, and that the ideas which become the dominant ideas, such as individualism or collectivism, determine the range of feasible policy outcomes, and shape the outlook and basic assumptions of policy actors. Such linkages are notoriously hard to pin down, and the task of characterising a "climate of opinion" is difficult, given the mass of potentially relevant data. What is undeniable, however, is that many of those involved in the Thatcher project saw changing the climate of opinion as one of their fundamental tasks.

What is the future of think-tanks? The new attention which social scientists are paying to them makes possible comparative analysis of how policy advice is provided in different political systems, and the extent to which a role exists for free-standing, relatively independent bodies. The dividing line between think-tanks and pressure groups is often indistinct, especially when a think-tank is an advocacy tank like the Adam Smith Institute. Many kinds of organisations, including trade unions and transnational companies, maintain a research capacity within their organisations, which can be used both to float general ideas, and to assist with a specific lobbying campaign. Another interesting question is the future relationship between think-tanks and universities. Universities are becoming much more integrated into the economy at regional, national, and global levels, and are proliferating research institutes which engage in contract and policy relevant research as well as blue skies research. One scenario is that the role of think-tanks has been to pioneer innovative lines of research, currently not supplied by universities, but that eventually universities will absorb think-tanks. A very different scenario is that the rapid growth of think-tanks is a sign that universities will in future supply a declining share of the market for policy advice. Universities will be one of the casualties of the information revolution, while think-tanks because of their flexibility and ability to innovate, will be one of the gainers.

The heroic age of think-tanks may be over, but study of their role in the market for policy advice as well as their more general role in the political process is likely to grow rather than diminish. What the Thatcher period underlined is the importance of understanding the networks which provide the ideas and assumptions which shape the way in which elites view the world, and form the discourses which construct what is taken as common-sense. In these networks think-tanks in all their different forms have come to play an important part. This book is a valuable exploration of that role.

Andrew Gamble
Political Economy Research Centre
University of Sheffield
April 1998

ACKNOWLEDGEMENTS

In conducting the research for this book we have incurred numerous obligations. Steven Gerrard has been a very helpful (and extremely patient) editor; and we are obliged to all of those at UCL Press who have helped in the production process. For generous financial assistance to Andrew Denham, we are very grateful to the British Academy, and the Research Committee and Department of Politics, University of Nottingham. Among the many individuals who have given up time to discuss particular issues with us, we would like to thank Lord Alport of Colchester, John Blundell, Lord Gilmour of Craigmillar, the late Lord Joseph of Portsoken, Tariq Modood, Sir Ferdinand Mount, Max Nicholson, Rick Nye, Dr Madsen Pirie, Jeremy Shearmur, Frank Vibert, William Wallace and David Willetts. Alexandra Rocca has also unearthed much valuable information and Patricia Denham provided much needed support. Any errors of fact or interpretation, however, are entirely our responsibility.

Andrew Denham
Mark Garnett

1

To our families

Introduction: British think-tanks and the climate of opinion in the twentieth century

Academic interest in think-tanks is growing, but it has not kept pace with their remarkable rise to public prominence on both sides of the Atlantic. The American literature is far more substantial than the British and continues to dominate international discourse on the subject; even so, during the 1970s and 1980s only one article on the subject appeared in any of the major political science journals, and think-tanks are seldom mentioned in standard textbooks on American politics (Dye 1978; Ricci 1993: 2).

In Britain the situation is different; groups such as the Institute of Economic Affairs (IEA), the Centre for Policy Studies (CPS) and the Adam Smith Institute (ASI) are at least mentioned in most discussions of British politics since 1979. Yet references to these bodies is rarely accompanied by any analysis; their influence is assumed, but not investigated. The appearance of a well-publicized book in 1994 was very welcome, however, Richard Cockett's *Thinking the unthinkable* was the story of specific think-tanks, not a systematic account of their development over the present century. Since Cockett wrote his book there have been significant changes, and the publicity surrounding British think-tanks is heavier than ever before. When the findings of an independent body are presented in the media they are almost invariably described as the work of a "think-tank", and there is hardly a day without such findings being published in summary in at least one of the British broadsheets. Clearly there is scope for many more studies of this remarkable phenomenon; the present volume is an attempt to close some of the gaps in the existing literature. In particular, although due attention is paid to

3

the think-tanks discussed by Cockett (usually known collectively as New Right think-tanks), we have extended the scope of this survey to draw in groups which were founded much earlier in the twentieth century, in the hope that this approach will provide the basis for more general conclusions about the origins and development of British think-tanks.

An American phenomenon?

There seem to be three main reasons for the comparative shortfall in academic analysis of British think-tanks. The first is that these groups are widely assumed to be a predominantly, if not uniquely, American phenomenon. Indeed, one American historian has even described think-tanks as "*quintessentially American* planning and advisory institutions" operating on the margins of that country's formal political processes (Smith 1991: xiii; our emphasis). In fact only American think-tanks are "quintessentially American"; as recent studies have shown, even if think-tanks in other countries betray the influence of the US model to some degree, they are all adapted to their diverse national contexts (Stone, Denham and Garnett, forthcoming). However, the *scale* of think-tank development in the United States is certainly unique. In 1991 it was estimated that there were more than 1,000 private, non-profit research institutes operating in the United States, approximately 100 of which were based in and around Washington, DC; more recent calculations put the overall figure at around 1500 (Hellebust 1996; Smith 1991: xiv). Most other western democracies, by contrast, had only a handful of such groups in the 1980s, and despite a recent upsurge in numbers in many countries, there are still far more think-tanks in the United States than elsewhere. Furthermore, American think-tanks tend to be much better-funded than their British counterparts, and to employ far more staff (see Table 1 opposite).

Explanations for the unique scale of think-tank development in the United States point to the "exceptional" features and characteristics of the American political system. Think-tanks, it is argued, "bloom according to the political compost in which they grow" (Hennessy and Coates 1991: 5). The situation in the United States is held to be a reflection of such "elemental political realities" as Amer-

Table 1 Anglo-American Think-tanks: a comparison

Institution	Date	Location	Staff	Budget ($ Million)
Rand Corporation	1946	Santa Monica, CA	950	50–100
Brookings Institution	1916	Washington, DC	220	Over 10
Urban Institute	1968	Washington, DC	220	Over 10
American Enterprise Institute	1943	Washington, DC	125	Over 10
Heritage Foundation	1973	Washington, DC	100	Over 10
PSI (formerly PEP)	1931	London	54	6.5
NIESR	1938	London	43	2.9
IEA	1955	London	19	2.4
CPS	1974	London	4	0.8
ASI	1977	London	7	0.5

Sources: Hellebust (1996); annual reports; private information. The above figures relate to the most recent calendar year for which information was available at the time of writing. Where an organization employs both full- and part-time staff, the overall figure has been adjusted accordingly.

ica's constitutional separation of powers, a party system historically grounded in electoral and political ambitions rather than ideology and "a civil service tradition that gives leeway to numerous political appointees" (Smith 1991: xv). Kent Weaver of the Brookings Institution has described American think-tanks as "policy entrepreneurs" operating in a distinct political system characterized by the "division of powers between President and Congress, weak and relatively non-ideological parties and [the] permeability of administrative elites" (Weaver 1989: 570). Bodies of this sort have grown and continue to flourish in the United States to an extent unknown elsewhere because they fill certain gaps in the American political structure. The fragmentation of the system creates a vacuum, resting as it does on the constitutional separation of powers between the executive and the legislature. Congress does not automatically adopt the President's programme; it, too, initiates legislation. When Congress and the Presidency are controlled by different parties, as they have been for much of the time in recent years, possibilities for independent action and conflict increase, creating multiple audiences for policy analysis and advice (Weiss 1992: 6). This situation cannot arise in Britain, and although private members enjoy the opportunity to introduce legislation of their own the chances of piloting their bills through a parliamentary timetable decided by the government are generally very slim. House of Lords committees are often of a very high standard, but unlike the powerful US Senate the British second chamber has been in decline since the Parliament Act of 1911.

The American system has also produced weak parties in the legislature. In contrast to the situation in Britain, party discipline in the United States is exhibited mainly at the beginning of each new Congress, in matters of organization of the chamber. Thereafter, each member is subject to the pressures of interest groups and constituents, but basically decides on his or her own policy positions. The parties themselves have not undertaken a serious effort at policy development and have few resources at their disposal to help them even if they were to try. Campaign finance reforms have limited the ability of American parties to raise money for such purposes and they have few resources to dispense to candidates or call in past favours as a result. For all these reasons, individual politicians in the US have strong incentives to consult outside policy advisers.

American administrative elites are also exceptionally "permeable" to outsiders. Unlike the British civil service, which despite recent developments still selects the vast majority of its high-flyers through competitive examination, the American civil service tradition is far more welcoming to political appointees, and a high proportion of these are think-tank members who have previously worked with decision-makers. The number of political appointments has increased in recent years:

> . . . since the Nixon presidency, more politically appointed officials have been brought into federal departments. [Whereas] once appointees served only at the level of the office of the secretary, now they also serve in positions two and three levels lower in the departmental structure. Th[is] increasing penetration of political appointments has weakened the standing of line civil servants and downgraded their influence – and perhaps their motivation. Officials at the secretarial level are more likely to turn for advice to other appointees than to career officials (Weiss 1992: 7–8).

American think-tanks, Weiss argues, come to policy questions with a philosophy of "rationality", "logic", "evidence" and "expertise" that is "particularly appealing to the American mind" (Weiss 1992: 8). This seems as sweeping a generalization as the notion that the British are followers of the "cult of the amateur", and instinctively distrust anyone who poses as an "expert". However, there is enough truth in both of these reflections to explain an important difference between the experience of think-tanks in each context.

A final element of American "exceptionalism" is that although Britain has a similar set of rules governing tax-exempt donations, in the United States there is ample private funding available to support the activities of think-tanks (James 1993: 492). The difference in the budgets boasted by American and British groups is largely the result of a much stronger tradition of corporate, foundation and individual donations to private research institutions in the United States. In 1991 the several thousand foundations in the United States had between them assets of more than $150 billion; in no other country have the resources on which all think-tanks ultimately depend been so richly available (Stone 1996: 45). In Chapters 2 and 3 we discuss the initiative to found a research body in Britain on the scale of the massive American Brookings Institution, partly through United States funding. This plan might have sparked off fund-raising for similar large-scale bodies in Britain, but it was finally vetoed in 1979 by Margaret Thatcher (Donoughue 1987: 125–7).

The problem of definition

While these factors indicate why the largest think-tanks are in America rather than Britain, and why they are much more numerous there, circumstances in the latter country have clearly not prevented the emergence of think-tanks. As we have seen, even in America the academic literature has developed relatively slowly. One possible explanation for this which also applies in the context of British politics is the difficulty of establishing a precise definition of a "think-tank" (Ricci 1993: 21). Indeed, the confusion about the nature and role of think-tanks extends beyond academic commentators and is "sometimes shared by the managers, trustees and researchers at these institutions" (Weaver 1989: 564).

Borrowed from Second World War military jargon for a secure room where plans and strategies could be discussed, the term "think-tank" was first used during the 1950s to denote the "contract research organizations" (see later), such as the Rand Corporation, that were set up by the United States military after the war (Dickson 1971; Smith 1991). By the 1960s, the expression had entered popular, as well as political, discourse in the United States, but "think-tank" remains an imprecise term that can and does refer to a wide (and increasingly diverse) range of private research groups (Smith 1991: xiii–xiv). Hames and Feasey have suggested that a broad definition of the term would be "a non-profit public policy research institution with substantial organizational autonomy", but concede that this "hardly reveals much about the character and nature of these entities" (Hames and Feasey 1994: 216).

Indeed, in one sense at least, the problem of defining think-tanks is even *more* complicated in the context of British politics than it is in the United States (Denham and Garnett 1996). This is because the term "think-tank" was first used on this side of the Atlantic to denote the Central Policy Review Staff (CPRS), a "central capability unit" established in the Cabinet Office in 1970–1 by the then Conservative Prime Minister, Edward Heath. This body, staffed mainly by bright graduates and led by Lord (Victor) Rothschild, was designed to help government coordinate its policies across departmental boundaries, and to foster more long-term thinking; in the words of its founder, its main purpose was to ensure that "government strategy could be continuously reviewed and regularly reported on" (Heath and Barker 1978: 382). It attracted unusual publicity, at least in part because of Rothschild's colourful personality, but also because it was just one element of Heath's drive for a more professional approach to the increasingly complex tasks of administration. Even after its abolition by Margaret Thatcher in 1983, the CPRS continued to be popularly known as "*the* Think Tank". Its ability to attract notice had led directly to its downfall; a radical report on the welfare state was leaked in 1982, causing deep embarrassment to a government which was happy for people to "think the unthinkable" when the results of such speculation were either kept quiet or published by groups at arms-length from Whitehall. The CPRS had also annoyed the government by advising it against a near-doubling of Value-Added Tax *on coming to office*; the annoyance did not arise because the CPRS was wrong (Hennessy, Morrison and Townsend 1985; James 1986; Blackstone and Plowden 1988).

Hence, for most of the past 25 years, "think-tank" has usually been synonymous in Britain with one particular "policy planning and research unit" *within* central government (Prince 1983). As the 1980s progressed, however, the phrase acquired a different meaning, closer to American usage; it was increasingly applied to ideologically-charged, free-market bodies which were outside government (and whose conclusions were therefore "deniable"), which supported Margaret Thatcher in her efforts to shift British public policy away from the post-war "consensus". The term was then reflected backwards in time to denote other organizations, like the Fabian Society which had never been called a think-tank in its heyday.

There is a parallel here with Aaron Wildavsky's observation that the term "policy analysis" describes activities that are too wide-ranging to be captured in a single definition. There is nothing more "stultifying", he argues, than "a futile search for Aristotelian essences" (Wildavsky 1979: 15, 410). As with "policy analysis", it seems to us, so it is with those "policy analysis organizations" (Weiss 1992) known collectively as think-tanks. Rather than conducting our own pro-longed search for the "essence" of think-tanks here, we draw on the suggestive work of others to distinguish those bodies with which we are concerned from others that appear similar in structure and functions.

One American scholar has made a useful attempt to resolve the difficulty by identifying, and distinguishing between, three categor-ies of think-tank: "universities without students", "contract research organizations" and "advocacy tanks" (Weaver 1989). The first cat-egory describes large institutions with considerable numbers of staff, working mainly on book-length studies. These institutes differ from universities in at least two important respects. First, staff are not required to teach students in the same way that (most) full-time aca-demics are. Secondly, the subject areas investigated have a stronger policy focus than the research and analysis undertaken in univer-sity departments, which is typically "more academic, theoretical and less palatable for general consumption" (Stone 1991: 201). As Weaver explains, the research output of these two types of organization is usually somewhat different, for two main reasons:

First, university-based researchers face a different set of in-centives: interest in substantive policy issues and in the policy

9

process is rarely rewarded as much in the university as are theoretical contributions to the researcher's discipline. At think tanks, these priorities are reversed. A second reason university-based research may differ from that at think tanks is that university-based researchers are less likely to have contact with policy activists and other policy researchers than those at think tanks. For both of these reasons, the "studentless universities" are more likely than universities to produce research that is attuned to current policy debates. This research is also likely to take a different form – more likely books and pamphlets than articles in refereed academic journals. And it is more likely to include conclusions about how current policy should be modified, even if those conclusions are grudgingly tacked on by the researcher in the last chapter (Weaver 1989: 566).

Groups in this category have long-term horizons focused on affecting opinion, and draw most of their core funding from a variety of corporate, foundation and individual sponsors, diversifying their sources of financial support in order to reduce the risk of client backlash over particular research results (Ricci 1993: 20). The number of American research institutes in this category is small, and members vary in respect of the range of policy issues they deal with. American think-tanks that fit this model include the Brookings Institution and the American Enterprise Institute for Public Policy Research (AEI). One insider has described the ethos and culture at Brookings as "like a university when the students are away and the professors are trying frantically to catch up on research" (Rivlin 1992: 22–3). The great gulf in resources between American and British think-tanks means that there is no comparable UK body, although many of the older groups have aspired to this "ideal" model, and in some cases, like that of the Policy Studies Institute (PSI) and the Institute of Economic Affairs (IEA), staff of British think-tanks are awarded university-style fellowships.

A second type of think-tank identified by Weaver is the *contract research organization*. These institutes, as the name suggests, serve government agencies and/or private sponsors on a contractual basis by executing research solicited in a variety of fields. While any claim to "objectivity" on the part of universities without students (or, for that matter, universities) would raise difficult questions, in the case of the contract research organizations the matter is more clear-cut, because their choice of subjects is strongly affected by the preferences of their clients (and if their conclusions are too much at odds with a client's interests, future research contracts may be awarded to their competitors). Many contract research institutes have especially close ties to a particular agency: the Rand Corporation, for example, works very closely with (and receives most of its core funding from) the US Defense Department.

However, while there are important differences between the universities without students and contract researchers, there is usually significant overlap between the categories. In the 1980s, for example, the Urban Institute won most attention in the United States through its study of changing domestic priorities in the Reagan administration. The findings, published in several volumes, showed the kind of painstaking research characteristic of the universities without students, but since at the time the Institute was dependent on the federal government for most of its resources, Weaver classes it as a contract research organization (Weaver 1989: 566–7). In Britain the contract research organization model fits several think-tanks; examples in the present volume are Political and Economic Planning (PEP – later the Policy Studies Institute (PSI)), and the National Institute for Economic and Social Research (NIESR – see Chapters 1 and 2 respectively). They have been characterized by high-quality research, but their ability to choose their own research topics is strongly affected by funding considerations.

Thirdly, Weaver argues, a distinctive new think-tank model has developed in recent years, alongside the older think-tank models of the studentless university and the contract research institute. While there are many differences between these organizations, they are collectively labelled *advocacy tanks*; the main examples in this book are the Centre for Policy Studies (CPS) and the Adam Smith Institute (ASI) (Chapters 4 and 5; see also Chapter 6) (Weaver 1989: 567). These groups combine a strong policy, partisan or ideological outlook with aggressive salesmanship (either directly through their own publications or through the media) in an attempt to influence current policy debates. It is more usual for advocacy tanks to synthesize and put a distinctive "spin" on existing research, rather than carrying out original research themselves. The format chosen for their output is, typically, short pamphlets and papers, rather than books

11

and monographs. Just as think-tanks in the university without students category resemble academic institutions, advocacy tanks are difficult to distinguish from pressure groups, because their primary motivation is to bring about policy change. An important difference between the two, however, is that while the former tend to operate across a broad range of policy areas (even if they have a primary focus), the latter usually organize their campaigning activities around issues that relate to one particular field. As the number and variety of bodies claiming the status of think-tanks increases, however, even this distinction has already come under strain (Denham and Garnett 1996).

American examples of advocacy tanks include the Heritage Foundation and the Institute for Policy Studies. Heritage, in particular, readily admits that its primary purpose is advocacy, rather than academic research. Staff at Heritage are strongly advised by their employers on arrival that the Heritage Foundation is not an "academic" institution, but one "committed to certain beliefs" (Smith 1991: 205–6). Yet whatever advocacy tanks may be thought to lack in terms of genuine scholarship, they compensate for in their accessibility to policy-makers. The Heritage Foundation, for instance, "aims to make its policy issue papers brief enough to be read in a limousine ride from National Airport to Capitol Hill [and] hand delivers them to congressional offices and other important power centers" (Weaver 1989: 567). However, unlike the other types of institute that can carve out reputations for solid research that make their findings difficult for the media and policy-makers to ignore at any time, advocacy tanks can run into dramatic changes of fortune depending on events in the political world which they might seek to influence but ultimately have no chance of controlling.

This model of three different types of think-tank has some use and validity for organizational purposes, though it should not be interpreted too literally. Weaver himself admits that there are "inherent tensions in any of the three main models" (Weaver 1989: 563). While the three categories outlined above are analytically clear and distinct, the reality is more complicated. For example, the other organization included in the present volume, the Institute of Economic Affairs (see Chapter 3) is very difficult to locate within this scheme; yet it is among the best known of all British think-tanks. In fact, the aims and activities of *individual* think-tanks are diverse.

As Hames and Feasey note, the Heritage Foundation, while primarily an advocacy tank, has also published "some massive pieces of research of a flavour akin to the universities without students model" (Hames and Feasey 1994: 217). Scholars in the United States have concluded that think-tanks do not have a generic form in the same sense as families, armies, churches or industrial corporations. Instead, the term is used to refer to institutions "whose aims may vary across time and whose researchers may associate with one another only temporarily and for personal convenience" (Ricci 1993: 21). This has important implications for the present volume; in particular, it means that when evaluating think-tank performance the differing nature of the various organizations (as well as the changing political background) must be taken into account.

A further problem is that, while many groups that are regarded as think-tanks dislike the term, others (mainly the smaller bodies) frequently invoke it to look and sound important. Bodies regarded as genuine think-tanks consider the term limiting, confusing and even demeaning, on the grounds that it sounds too passive, connotes non-accomplishment (a place where thinking is an end in itself, irrespective of the impact of such thinking on policy and events) and produces confusion as to the goals of such outfits (Dickson 1971: 28) Staff at the Brookings Institution used to disdain the "faintly pejorative" appellation "think-tank", even if they now use it as freely as everyone else (Rivlin 1992: 22). At the other end of the spectrum, meanwhile, it has been argued that the term "think-tank" carries an unmistakable prestige (especially for media pundits) which is sometimes undeserved and that political scientists should be wary of bestowing such accolades without due consideration (Denham and Garnett 1995).

Margaret Thatcher has recently suggested that the Centre for Policy Studies (CPS), a body which she helped to found in the mid-1970s (see Chapter 5), "could not properly be called a think-tank, for it had none of the corporate grandeur of the prestigious American foundations which that term evokes" (Thatcher 1995: 252). While this quotation shows admirable modesty, if followed it would simply make the study of these policy groups even more confusing; it rests on the belief that a body can only qualify as a think-tank if it has a certain number of staff or a large budget, whereas the argument here is that the relevant criterion is its function. One should reinterpret

Lady Thatcher's words to mean that the CPS could not properly fall into the university without students category of think-tanks. In fact, it is a good example of an advocacy tank. As William Wallace has recently observed, the New Right think-tanks that sprang up along-side the IEA in the 1970s were "small, passionately committed and concerned only with providing arguments for those already half-persuaded" (Wallace 1994: 149). Staff at the CPS, for instance, were "already committed to the new economics of the market and mone-tarism" by 1974 and sought merely to change other people's minds (Cockett 1994: 239). For the purposes of the present study Weaver's categories have been adopted as a means of distinguishing think-tanks both from each other and from outwardly similar bodies, with the reservations outlined above. The IEA might not fit snugly into one category, but it has enough in common with two of them (uni-versities without students and advocacy tanks) for us to include this fascinating organization. We discuss problems defining think-tanks of more recent origin in Chapter 6 and the Conclusion. It will be seen that (as has happened in the United States) there has been a gradual historical shift in the character of British think-tanks towards the more partisan advocacy tanks.

What is the role of think-tanks?

The difficulty of establishing a precise definition of think-tank, then, is a second reason for the shortfall in academic analysis of their activities. Establishing a precise boundary between think-tanks and other institutions with a research capacity and a desire to influence policy is frequently problematic. This is true on both sides of the Atlantic. While an exact definition of the term may ultimately be elusive, the role of those groups which are commonly referred to as think-tanks can also present some problems. Wallace (1994: 142–3) has argued that the central functions which all such institutes set out to fulfil, to varying degrees, include:

1   Intellectual analysis of policy issues; using approaches drawn from history, social science, law, or even mathematics, applied to issues relevant to government;

2   Concern with the ideas and concepts which underlie policy; examining, and questioning, the conventional wisdom which shapes day-to-day policy-making;

3   Collection and classification of information relevant to policy, ranging from detailed research to the provision of press reports and documents on which others can draw;

4   A longer term perspective than that which is open to policy-makers, looking at trends rather than immediate events;

5   A degree of detachment both from government and from the immediate partisan political debate;

6   A degree of involvement with government – whether seeking to influence it indirectly through publications and through impact on the policy debate or to engage in discussions with ministers or officials directly;

7   A commitment to inform a wider audience: through publication, through meetings and discussions which involve a wider and more diverse group than government or the academic community alone.

Wallace's list provides an excellent general scheme for evaluating the performance of think-tanks, with the proviso that the emphasis on each item must change in individual cases because think-tanks do not share uniform purposes. As we shall see, the full list represents an ideal of which most bodies called think-tanks fall short, but in different ways; while the first two bodies studied here (PEP/PSI and the NIESR) come close to fulfilling all of the points, some recently founded advocacy tanks seem only to satisfy points 3 and 6 (see especially Chapter 7). The case of the CPRS is the source of further reflections on Wallace's criteria; it was set up specifically to fulfill point 4: but since it was located within Whitehall it was always highly vulnerable on point 5, and it had no chance of fulfilling point 7 (unless inadvertently through leaks). In short, the CPRS fell in a grey area between think-tanks and the civil service; we have not discussed its work at length below because the relevant documents are not yet publicly available. Similar restrictions apply in relation to the Downing Street Policy Unit set up in 1974 by Harold Wilson specifically to advise the Prime Minister, and which in some respects has superseded the earlier body – although it would appear that this body falls quite clearly on the civil service side of the grey area, being more engaged than the CPRS in "hard day-to-day decisions" (Willetts 1987: 445).

Despite the problems associated with any attempt to provide a concrete list of think-tank structure and functions, there do appear to be two main objectives that all think-tanks seek, albeit with varying degrees of emphasis. The first is to influence the "climate of opinion" within which, it is assumed, political actors are bound to operate. The phrase has the great attraction of simplicity, and has often been used by think-tanks when describing what they do, but as we discuss in each chapter it can lead to distortion of what is a highly complex phenomenon. An interesting definition of the climate of opinion was provided by F.A. Hayek in an article of 1949: he regarded it as "essentially a set of very general preconceptions by which the intellectual judges the importance of new facts and opinions" (Hayek 1967: 185). Writing at the beginning of the century, A.V. Dicey referred to the "body of beliefs, convictions, sentiments, accepted principles, or firmly-rooted prejudices" which make up the "dominant current of opinion" at a given time. Dicey believed that this current "determined, directly or indirectly, the course of legislation", and that the dominant opinion is first expounded by a single gifted individual. A group of "apostles of a new faith" spring up; these enthusiasts eventually "make an impression, either directly upon the general public or upon some person of eminence, say a leading statesman, who stands in a position to impress ordinary people and thus to win the support of the nation". At the same time, Dicey allows that "public opinion is itself far less the result of reasoning or of argument than of the circumstances in which men are placed", and he adds an important qualification by writing of cross-currents of opinion which co-exist with the dominant trend and may, in time, overtake it (Dicey 1905: 20–7). More recently, Dennis Kavanagh has written that the climate of opinion "is rather more than what is often called 'political ideas' or 'public opinion'"; yet even from his careful account it is difficult to discern exactly what it is (Kavanagh 1987: 17). We explore the concept of a climate or dominant current of opinion in each chapter of the book; it is sufficient here to suggest that think-tanks either seek to exploit what they perceive as a favourable climate, or, if they believe that it is hostile, to change it – and that their idea of the nature and effect of this climate follows closely the descriptions provided by Dicey and Hayek.

The second objective of think-tanks is to inform public policy decisions more directly, through contact with MPs, government ministers, or officials (Denham and Garnett 1996). The difference between this goal and the first one might seem rather slight, since in both cases the intention is to shape legislation, and the assumption of both Dicey and Hayek is that in a democratic society this can only be achieved on a fairly lasting basis if there is a high (though vaguely defined) level of support from the public. However, an important difference remains; while on the first model a policy is implemented in response to public demands, the second can be seen as something of a short-cut, in which an elected government convinced by think-tank arguments can, in theory at least, introduce legislation even if the general public dislikes the idea, then wait to see how voters respond to the policy in practice. Instead of the wider climate of opinion influencing legislation, in short, this approach depends upon legislation influencing opinion. In a little-noticed passage, Dicey wrote that "the true importance, indeed, of laws lies far less in their direct result than in their effect upon the sentiment or convictions of the public" (Dicey 1914: 42). As a rule, in Britain during the present century it has been easier to make the public acquiesce in existing policies than to persuade it to demand reforms. It will be readily appreciated that this second think-tank objective raises vital questions about the nature of democratic government which do not arise in relation to the first model.

To date the academic literature on think-tanks has generally failed to address the question of how far either of these objectives have actually been achieved. In Britain, this task has become more urgent because of the claims made by and on behalf of New Right groups in recent years (Denham and Garnett 1995). Once again the problem here is that precision in such matters is extremely difficult to attain. This is because think-tanks deal in ideas, whose circulation and impact cannot be measured satisfactorily. Indeed, Ricci argues, this is what makes think-tanks such a frustrating subject from the scholarly point of view:

> Political scientists are intrigued by power, by who has it and who does not [and regard] leaders, parties, bureaucrats and other Washington actors as significant to the extent [that] they are powerful enough to impose their will on other people. It follows

that political scientists would like to know how much power think-tanks exercise. But since ideas are the coin of their realm, there is no way to measure the power think-tanks wield, if any. In which case, their significance, according to scholarly research standards, remains uncertain (Ricci 1993: 208–9).

This pessimism would seem to apply even more starkly to any attempt to evaluate the impact of think-tanks on the climate of opinion, since any evidence relating to opinion is usually itself the subject of fierce contention. An additional problem is that we can rarely be sure exactly *whose* opinion is in question; does the phrase "climate of opinion" refer to the thinking of the whole electorate, a majority of voters, a majority of "thinking" voters (perhaps Hayek's intellectuals), or just a handful of policy-makers, journalists and academics who can easily mistake their private dialogue for a nation-wide conversation? In other words, when examining the relationship between think-tanks and public policy we at least have a known output to work with – i.e. government legislation; when searching for a link between think-tanks and opinion, however, the relevant outputs are open to serious question. Yet this pessimism overlooks the useful work which can be done by social scientists in allied fields (for example in studies of voting behaviour), provided that they retain a properly sceptical outlook. Even so, the methodological difficulties raised by this subject are daunting, and constitute a further reason for the shortfall in analysis of these bodies on the part of British and American political scientists (Stone 1991: 199). We acknowledge that firm conclusions can seem more eye-catching than qualified judgements; but accuracy on this important subject must take priority.

A closed system of government?

As we have seen earlier in this chapter, it is widely assumed that think-tanks in the United States have a ready-made constituency for their activities in the bureaucracy and in Congress, in part as a consequence of the weakness of the American party system. The important differences between Westminster and presidential systems, it is argued, offer different opportunities for think-tanks to influence policy. The depiction of the American political system as "open, permeable and competitive" and of Westminster systems as "insular, closed and bureaucratised" has generated an assumption that think-tanks have fewer opportunities to influence policy in countries such as Britain and Australia than they have in the United States (Stone 1991: 199–200, 209). Hames and Feasey argue that the American political system has always been more conducive to outside "experts" than the Westminster model (Hames and Feasey 1994: 224). Elsewhere, James points out that the policy-making system of the United Kingdom is "largely closed, with decisions formulated in private by ministers, officials and occasional privileged outsiders". Even for Whitehall insiders, he argues, policy-making is an uncertain business; outsiders, such as think-tanks, who feed their ideas into a "closed" system, must expect to experience a high failure-rate (James 1993: 504).

Conversely, however, it is possible to argue that American think-tanks are faced with serious handicaps in their attempts to influence policy or opinion, precisely because the American political system is *so* competitive and "permeable". As Weiss notes, the number of players in the policy game in the United States is legion (Weiss 1992: 7). American think-tanks have to compete not only among themselves, but also with a huge number of other lobbyists in order to persuade policy-makers in both the executive and legislative branches of government to adopt a particular policy or, more ambitiously still, embrace an agenda for policy (Hames and Feasey 1994: 219). British think-tanks – despite recent developments – are still far less numerous and have as their target audience a relatively small and readily identifiable set of political actors, situated, like the think-tanks themselves, in the two to three square miles that contain Westminster, Whitehall, the City and Fleet Street. In short, the "extreme centralisation" of British political and public life means that access to their target audiences is well within the reach of these few, well-located institutions; furthermore, given the near-dictatorial powers normally available to British governments between elections, the potential rewards for those who do win access seem to make the struggle well worth undertaking (Desai 1994: 31).

These characteristics of the British political system compensate, to some degree at least, for the fact that think-tanks on this side of the Atlantic are smaller and poorer than their American counterparts. In addition, those British think-tanks that publish the work of outside contributors from academia, journalism or politics need not find their lack of resources a crippling handicap, because there are clearly sufficient numbers of people in these categories for whom the chance to disseminate their ideas (or, more cynically, to see their names in print), rather than any financial motive, is a sufficient incentive. Oddly enough, this applies with equal (if not greater) force to the economic liberals who have written for New Right think-tanks in recent years, despite the fact that on their own theory it would seem rather eccentric to labour so hard for minimal cash rewards. With the advent of technological innovations, notably the Internet, which facilitate the cheap dissemination of text, the high cost of more traditional forms of publication need not be a handicap.

It would be absurd to rule out British think-tanks as important political actors on the basis of an abstract comparison between the British and American contexts; a closer examination shows that the compost is actually fairly fertile in Britain after all. In recent years it has been assumed that think-tanks (especially those of the New Right) have exercised a profound influence over public policy. Scholars can also consult ministerial memoirs and other sources to compare claims with a reasonable (if inevitably incomplete) picture of reality. Obviously these personal accounts cannot be relied on too far; politicians are not noted for their tendency to give credit to others where they can help it. The British obsession with secrecy continues to prevent access to government documents for 30 years at least, and even where these records are open their evidence needs to be treated with caution and compared with secondary accounts. Yet it is evident that think-tanks are worthy of investigation, and that the question of influence is central to an understanding of their role. The best one can do is to use the available information with a proper degree of scepticism and with a clear analytical framework. As noted earlier, this must vary depending on the nature of each think-tank, although a general picture will build up over the following chapters.

The Fabian Society and the British think-tank tradition

The most surprising aspect of the relative neglect of British think-tanks is that it can be argued that the phenomenon first arose in this country. There is a long tradition of institutions in Britain which have sought both to bring about specific policy changes, as well as to effect "a more general change in the prevailing intellectual climate" (Bradley 1981: 174–5). It can be traced back at least to the Utilitarians, or Philosophic Radicals, who worked under the leadership of Jeremy Bentham and James Mill in the early nineteenth century, and who reached a relatively wide audience of informed opinion through journals such as *The Westminster Review* (Thomas 1979). The tradition continued with the English disciples of Auguste Comte. While these English Positivists were not as influential as their Utilitarian predecessors, they are credited with helping to transform the law relating to trades unions in the mid-nineteenth century (Harrison 1965: 251–342; Wright 1986).

Last in this line of nineteenth-century "philosophical-political ginger groups" – but the first one which can reasonably be described as a think-tank – was the Fabian Society, whose leaders were always aware of their place in this British (or, more exactly, English) tradition (Harrison 1993: 73–4). Not least, as Harrison (1993: 79) has pointed out, there were already "plenty of precedents" for the Fabian tactic of attempting to "permeate" the English political Establishment from within, while (at the same time) bringing to bear upon it pressure from without (see also Mackenzie and Mackenzie 1977: 60–2; there are numerous other works on the Fabians, including Durbin 1985; McBriar 1966; and Pugh 1984: for more sceptical accounts, see Dahrendorf 1995; Hobsbawm 1964; and Thompson 1967).

Immediately after the Second World War 6,000 Fabians and sympathizers filled the Albert Hall for a delayed celebration of the Society's diamond jubilee. Although the limit of its precise influence in the first half of the present century is warmly contested, some of its opponents, at least, were in no doubt about its impact. When in 1947 talks began which led to the formation of the Institute of Economic Affairs, the proposed body was described as an "anti-Fabian Society". Groups set up within the Conservative Party at around this time had the same inspiration; in 1948 Cuthbert Alport, first head of the Conservative Political Centre (and founder of the One Nation group in 1951) wrote of "people known as the intelligentsia . . . who were captured by the Fabian Society and who today dominate the Labour Party"; when the Conservative Bow Group was set up in 1951 its original statement of aims included the intention of "Combating the influence of the Fabian Society" (Cockett 1994: 134; Ramsden 1995: 147–8; Cole 1963: 332). Yet for most of the last 50 years, in John Callaghan's phrase, the Fabian Society's place in the formal institutional arrangements within the Labour Party has been "definitely peripheral", although individual members of the Society contributed greatly to the "revisionist" case within the party (Callaghan 1996: 39, 42). In recent times the Society has grown (claiming around 4,500 members in mid-1996) and returned to favour, but very much as an adjunct to the party (and, at times, simply a convenient venue for speeches from aspiring Labour politicians in search of a cerebral reputation) rather than a source of independent thinking. However, the lasting contribution of the Fabian Society to the history of British think-tanks is beyond dispute; ultimately it, rather than any American organization, has provided the model and inspiration for individuals who wish to influence government policy and public opinion. In the interests of chronology and space (and because of the large number of excellent studies already available) the Fabian Society has not been allotted a separate chapter in the present volume, but evidence of its influence is present throughout.

In Britain today there are think-tanks which cover every conceivable subject of policy interest. With such a wide array of organizations to choose from, any account of British think-tanks is bound to be selective. For thematic coherence, we have concentrated on those groups whose *primary* focus is on questions of political economy. One of the most prestigious British think-tanks is concerned with foreign policy – the Royal Institute of International Affairs (RIIA), based in London at Chatham House. This body was set up in 1920, after the Versailles Peace Conference; it publishes the well-known journal *International Affairs*, and has provided a model for similar bodies in many other countries. In the mid-1990s it had a research staff of 84 and a budget of around £3.5 million (Stone 1996: 248). Apart from its inherent interest, the RIIA illustrates a consistent theme of this book – that think-tanks emerge at times of perceived crisis.

However, a detailed examination of the Institute lies outside the scope of the present volume (for an excellent recent "insider" account, see Wallace 1990; see also Bosco and Navari 1995, and Higgott and Stone 1994).

Summary

We have argued that, for scholars interested in the development of political thinking and public policy in Britain over recent decades, the study of think-tanks is both necessary and difficult. The present volume begins with the assumption that all the problems discussed above are relevant, but that they can be overcome to a sufficient degree provided that care is taken. Many of the individuals who participate in the provision of policy advice – whether inside or outside the institutions of government – have a professional commitment to exaggeration, and showing that their claims are wrong can be as problematic as proving them right. Yet some attempt must be made to gauge the impact of the groups they work within, as well as to explain how each think-tank arose and to describe their activities in the context of political and economic events during the present century. This is the purpose of the following chapters; in our conclusion we offer some general reflections about think-tanks and their place in democratic societies.

The assumption at the outset is that think-tanks are potentially very helpful in ensuring a well-informed electorate; however, this is a view that cannot simply be taken on trust. Another important question for us is whether ideas or events are more important in determining policy. An attempt to provide an authoritative answer to this problem would require a separate volume, but each chapter contains evidence on which the reader may reach broad conclusions.

CHAPTER 1

Political and economic planning

Origins and early days

An important concern of this book is to explore the circumstances in which twentieth-century British think-tanks have emerged. As we shall see, most have done so against a background of perceived economic crisis, political instability and/or social tension. While the relationship between ideas and events is highly complex, the history of British think-tanks lends support to the view that ideas arise from circumstances, rather than vice versa.

This trend can be traced back earlier, to the formation of the Fabian Society – the first British group to satisfy the major requirements of a think-tank – in 1884. The 1880s was a decade of economic depression and social unrest after the "golden age" of Victorian capitalism. The tasks of government were growing more complex after a century of rapid industrial change, and political parties were facing the new challenge of mobilizing consent from an electorate which was enlarged to absorb much of the working class in the year that the Fabian Society started meeting (McBriar 1966: 6–7). The founding Fabians were gifted, dynamic (and quarrelsome) individuals who would probably have made a mark at any time, but the situation fired their ambitions as self-appointed saviours of a society and government apparently in need of radical overhaul. Their perception of a looming crisis was shared by others; in 1889, for example, the Christian Social Union was established with the intention of conducting "careful inquiry and investigation of social problems" (Richter 1964: 127–8).

The fact that Political and Economic Planning (PEP) entered the world when it did, in 1931, is equally significant. Just over a year earlier, the Wall Street crash had led to widespread bankruptcies, mass unemployment and national economic crises in many countries. The "condition of Britain" was deteriorating rapidly, with over two million unemployed and the looming prospect of national bankruptcy. Hopes of a successful post-war revival of Britain had proved short-lived; the "Homes fit for Heroes" promised by the governing coalition led by David Lloyd George in the 1918 general election had never been built. Now Europe was facing both the collapse of the Versailles settlement after the First World War and the alarming rise of Nazism in Germany. Moreover, as Max Nicholson has explained, well-publicized Bolshevik planning initiatives in Soviet Russia, and propaganda from Mussolini's Fascist Italy, were "beginning to exert disturbing pulls on dissatisfied war veterans, young men of the post-war generation, and others" (Nicholson 1981a: 5).

Instead of dubious examples from abroad, enthusiasts could point to Britain's own experience during the war when arguing for the benefits of more directive government. But in early 1931 the Labour administration led by Ramsay MacDonald was disinclined to radical reforms. In October 1930 Sir Oswald Mosley had gained an ovation at the Labour Party conference for his plans to tackle unemployment, but in the vote he was defeated just as he had been when he argued for change within the government. The Liberal Party under Lloyd George was receptive to new ideas, but despite polling over five million votes in the 1929 general election it had returned only 59 MPs and its prospects of forming a future government looked doubtful. Several young Conservatives accepted the need for change, but they were heavily outnumbered within their party. These, then, were the circumstances in which a group of mostly young and committed people felt the need to "face the challenge of the 1930s and, by dint of enthusiastic and searching analysis, influence in some measure the course of affairs in Britain" (Lindsay 1981: 10).

The immediate inspiration for PEP was the supplement to the *Week-end review* of 14 February 1931, entitled *A National Plan for Great Britain*. The document was written by the *Review*'s then

Assistant Editor, Max Nicholson, and argued for a general reorganization of the political, economic and social structure of Britain. This, Nicholson argued, should involve an extensive devolution of power from Westminster and Whitehall and flexible self-government for industry. The machinery of government should be radically changed (as Mosley had urged), and the size of the Cabinet reduced to ten, including Ministers with overall charge of Defence and Economic Affairs. The Post Office and the Ministry of Works should be converted into autonomous public utilities. Priority should be given to building up a satisfactory structure for "pure" and "applied" science and to the creation of a Bureau of Statistics, a Standards and Design Institute and a National Museums and Libraries Trust. The Plan also advocated a National Roads Trust, regionally decentralized; the transfer of education from political and municipal control to a permanent Education Commission; the establishment of a Business University; the provision of satellite towns; the creation of a broad Green Belt for London; the formation of National Parks; a thorough reconstruction of the South Bank of the Thames; a programme for making the country more attractive to foreign visitors and improving the balance of trade through tourism; a Railway Corporation; a National Aviation Board; the organization of agriculture on a commodity basis and much more. Against the background of the domestic and international situation described earlier, this radical document aroused "a lively demand for some continuing body to be formed to carry on independent non-party discussion and study over this whole range of public affairs" (Nicholson 1981a: 8).

Despite the relative inactivity of central government, the idea of forming a permanent research body appealed to a number of people active in British public life at the time. Indeed, the unpromising nature of the domestic political scene for those who wanted reform added to the attractions of an independent group. As Founder Member, Kenneth Lindsay, has recalled: "We all shared a common concern for the declining position of Britain, but had found no focus for our constructive energies" (Lindsay 1981: 11); a new group would provide this outlet. Conversations with a view to forming such a group continued throughout March 1931; eventually the name Political and Economic Planning, suggested by J.C. Pritchard, was adopted.

A brief statement of PEP's purposes, adopted on 29 June, argued that "the failure to formulate a National Plan and in due course prepare the country for its adoption will amount to a major national danger". "For convenience", PEP adopted "as the initial basis for discussion the Draft National Plan of the *Week-end Review*." The business of PEP, the statement continued, would be to institute inquiry into selected aspects of the Plan by means of small study groups, consisting of "not less than 3 and not more than 10 persons". Despite this dispersal of researchers, the new organization would endeavour to prepare an overarching National Plan within three years and to devote its first year to a survey and examination of the respective fields (Lindsay 1981: 13–14).

Latent differences within the Directorate and among members emerged from an early stage. The most important of these was a disagreement over what a National Plan actually involved. As Max Nicholson later recalled: "The regrettable fact was that not only the nation and its leaders but even the main body of PEP members were not really interested in planning as a process and a discipline. The very word eventually became unpalatable to some" (Nicholson 1981b: 35). It was a source of concern from the outset; the name Political and Economic Planning had aroused misgivings when first suggested. Much of this trouble can be traced to imprecision about what the word really meant; in Peter Clarke's phrase, "planning" is an "elastic rubric" (Clarke 1996: 80). Even Barbara Wootton's book *Plan or no plan*, published in 1934, "in spite of its title, leaves the reader with a very hazy notion of what constitutes planning as distinct from government intervention of any kind" (Cairncross 1985: 299 note). This was not the only reason for early tensions; the "Imperialist" tendencies of the first Chairman, Sir Basil Blackett, were opposed by a majority, led by Sir Arthur Salter who worked in the League of Nations until 1931 and wanted PEP to adopt a more internationalist strategy (Nicholson 1981b: 34). These disagreements were an unpromising start; both Blackett and Salter were friends and admirers of J.M. Keynes, and in the divided economic world of the time could have been expected to find enough common ground to work together. However, these and other differences between Blackett and the majority of the Directorate led to Blackett's gradual withdrawal from active participation and on 5 December Israel (later Lord) Sieff was invited to become Chairman (Lindsay 1981: 16–17).

PEP in the 1930s

In the event, PEP failed to meet its objective of producing a systematic National Plan in three years – or indeed within any time scale. Given the majority view in political circles at the time, a more piecemeal approach to policy advice was a logical step for any group wishing to exercise influence on decision-makers. Sieff once summed up the ethos which prevailed for most of the life of PEP by dubbing it "the Ginger Group of Gradualness" (Rothschild 1977: 163). The formation of a National Government in August 1931 could be seen by the new body as an early indication that it had been right to avoid intimate links with any one political party, but rather than providing the basis for a new style of administration the new government was anxious to give the impression that it was "business as usual" in Britain.

Following its piecemeal strategy, between 1933 and 1939, PEP issued reports on several basic industries, including iron and steel, cotton and coal, followed by others on housing, gas and the location of industry (Roskill 1981). These reports and the groups who worked on them brought PEP into contact with key people in industry and the civil service. The purpose of PEP was to influence such people and to rely on the press to carry its message to a wider audience. The latter part of this strategy, at least, appears to have been quite successful in the period 1933–9; it was unusual for the publication of PEP Broadsheets and Reports *not* to be followed by leading articles in the main newspapers. Sales of PEP publications were respectable, if not spectacular; for example, a report on *The British Press* was published in 1938 and sold 500 copies in 10 days (Lindsay 1981: 23, 25–6). Although PEP had no formal relations with the government of the day during these years, members of all political parties, including ministers, attended its functions. Despite its initial caution, the National Government gradually accepted the need for limited state intervention to bring down unemployment. The extent to which PEP's approach tallied with that of the government is illustrated by its work on regional development and the location of industry, which anticipated the Special Areas Reconstruction Act of 1936 and the establishment of the Barlow Commission on the geographical distribution of the industrial population in July 1937 (see also Chapter 2). As early as 1935 the young economist Evan

29

Durbin could write that "it would almost be true to say that 'we are all *Planners* now' " – although Durbin's definition of planning in the economic sphere was no less hazy than Barbara Wootton's attempt of the previous year (Durbin 1949: 41–4).

Two further PEP Reports, *The British Health Services* and *The British Social Services*, were published in June and December 1937. The former was welcomed on publication day by leading articles in 11 national and provincial daily newspapers and given prominent coverage in 40. It received favourable reviews from professional publications such as the *British Medical Journal* and *The Lancet*, and was welcomed in a statement issued by the British Medical Association as representing "an amount of patient inquiry and critical thought which only those who have personally examined the complex problems of health organisation can fully appreciate" (cited by Nicholson 1981b: 45). At the Ministry of Health it became "a sort of Bible", according to the Government's Chief Medical Officer, Sir William Jameson, who, it is claimed, "used it as a basis for designing the National Health Service" (although a non-contributory National Health Service had been official Labour Party policy since 1934) (Lindsay 1981: 27; Morgan 1984: 152). The Report on *The British Social Services* was also favourably received; a leading article in *The Times* was followed by more than two columns of summary on the morning of publication (Nicholson 1981b: 45–6). Each of these Reports sold by the thousand; by 1939, a Pelican edition of the Health Services Report had run into 25,000 copies (Lindsay 1981: 27).

The significance of PEP and other sources of "middle opinion" in Britain during the 1930s has been noted by several historians of the period (Marwick 1964). As Stevenson and Cook have argued, a vital part in the emergence of what has been called a "consensus on social responsibility" in the years leading up to the Second World War was played by inquiries undertaken by PEP and others. Many of the recommendations on social policy underlying the British welfare state after 1945, they argue, "were derived from the investigations and social thought of the 1930s. Articulated through the social literature and given form in reports from professional bodies and groups such as PEP, they were already finding limited acceptance in government circles in the years before the war" (Stevenson and Cook 1977: 29). Another historian of the period has argued that, whereas PEP's influence may have been "limited" in the 1930s, its Broadsheets, Reports and other activities "helped to prepare high-level opinion for the changes of the 1940s" (Addison 1977: 39). The picture is confused (as usual) by similar arguments advanced on behalf of other groups; for example Francis Williams, an early recruit to the socialist XYZ Club founded in 1932 (and in which Evan Durbin was prominent), wrote in his autobiography that this body "has indeed, I think, some claim to have exercised in a quiet sort of way more influence on future government policy than any other group of the time and to have done so in the most private manner without attracting publicity to itself" (quoted in Durbin 1985: 83: note Williams' mixture of rather dramatic claims with heavy qualifications – a very common feature of insider accounts). Whatever the precise role of individual groups at this time, it is clear that collectively they represented a considerable force in informed circles, although in 1944 H.G. Wells characterized one of them as "well meaning (but otherwise meaningless)" (Middlemas 1979: 272). In fact, during the 1940s senior figures in PEP, including Sir Arthur Salter and Nicholson himself, would enjoy the opportunity of influencing "high-level opinion" in a more intimate fashion, because they were obvious recruits for a government anxious to mobilize the country for war. Nicholson also wrote a popular pamphlet in 1940 about the mobilization of Britain's war resources; he argued that even in peacetime orderly national life had depended on some degree of planning and controls (Nicholson 1940).

The Second World War: 1939–45

The Second World War was both a challenge and an opportunity to PEP. Throughout the 1930s, PEP had been calling for national policies to cure unemployment and for a sense of national purpose, backing its arguments with detailed investigation on the subjects of greatest concern. Up to 1939 these demands had been met only in part. Now that the long-expected war had broken out, unemployment disappeared and a grip was taken on the economy; as a senior civil servant later put it, "the war was a prolonged exercise in central planning and control" (Franks 1947: 8). The sense of national purpose for which PEP had been calling since the early 1930s became even more necessary. "Planning" (however loosely defined) was now held to be essential if the British people were to become convinced (as many were not at first) that there was a future worth fighting for; in 1943 one writer even predicted that once peace returned there would be "a world-wide chain of national economic plans" (Bellerby 1943: 38; Young 1981: 82). A few months after Hitler's invasion of Poland, a broadsheet entitled *Reconstruction, 1916–19* was published which expressed the general mood within PEP at this time, and reminded readers that there was no need to rely on overseas experience to prove that planning could work in Britain. Although it was "incontestable" that winning the war must come first, it argued, the "great part which planning for subsequent reconstruction can play even in the immediate task of achieving military victory" should not be overlooked. Nazi leaders, for their part, had "never made the mistake of neglecting to plan ahead or of underrating the force of ideas" and it was "these qualities, rather than any material advantages" that had enabled them to "seize the initiative from military powers controlling a far larger share of the world's human and material resources" (Young 1981: 82–3).

During the early months of 1939, several members of PEP had been enrolled in shadow posts in anticipation of the war and had become "more and more troubled, not least by contact with Ministers, that the government would be caught without any coherent and credible concept of what we would be fighting for, other than to win. The mental and moral confusion which would result, and the effects upon morale and relations among allies, seemed to be totally unrecognised" (Nicholson 1981b: 47–8). In July 1939, several weeks before war was declared, a Post-War Aims Group was created which, while not formally embodied in PEP at the time, drew on its expertise and included some of its members. At least three documents were drafted during the month of August. On 8 September, a week after the outbreak of hostilities, a draft statement on the problems of war aims, peace terms and world order was circulated. Less than a month later, this had developed into a 40-page document entitled *European order and world order: what are we fighting for?*

European order and world order addressed the kind of world that needed to come out of the war and argued that, despite its immense achievements, western civilization now found itself "without a dynamic and simple faith". Although the context was global, the document dealt at great length with Europe and Britain's relations with it. To avoid any repetition of the two world wars which had already begun in Europe, it was argued that nationalism in Europe should be superseded by some form of federalism. A federal Europe must be based on the full participation of Great Britain, on finding Germany a role which would fully absorb her constructive energies and prove permanently acceptable to her people, on giving security to France and all other nations which had felt threatened by German aggression and on recognizing and providing for the interests in Europe of the United States and the Soviet Union. It was thought that the idea of a European federation would appeal especially to France, which had been attacked twice by Germany within a quarter of a century. In order to raise morale in France, *European order and world order* was translated into French and many copies were sent across the English Channel (Young 1981: 83–4).

From the beginning of the war, the future of Europe was *the* great topic for PEP. During the 1930s, the focus of much of its work had been domestic, but the war greatly enhanced the internationalist approach which had always been powerful within PEP. *Britain and Europe*, published in 1941, argued that it was in Europe that the old power-system had most manifestly broken down and where the lessons of "Hitlerism" could be seen most clearly. Hitler had "succeeded in recreating the basis of European unity, although on lines very different from his aims". The issue was no longer whether Europe should remain united, but in what form and by what leadership. Even if Germany lost the war, she might, without a British initiative, emerge once more as the leader of an "impoverished and disunited Europe" – a view supported by the widely-read American writer James Burnham (who also predicted that the post-war world would be dominated by a managerial class responsible for planning) (Burnham 1945). PEP outlined the alternative case for British leadership. Britain's geographical and sea-faring position made the country a "natural bridge" between Europe and the United States and between Europe and the "universal economic commonwealth" of the world as a whole. By giving refuge to the governments or leading representatives of oppressed nations in the fight against Hitlerism, it was argued that, the British people had already accepted "the moral leadership of Europe in war. It would be an act of renunciation amounting almost to betrayal to throw it aside in the peace" (Young 1981: 90–1).

33

Despite its new international preoccupations PEP did not neglect the home front. The submission of evidence to the Beveridge
Committee on social insurance was followed in July 1942 by the
publication of the longest broadsheet PEP had so far produced,
Planning for social security. This proposed a national minimum
income for each family, universal family allowances, a single Ministry of Social Security to take over the administration of all income-
maintenance services and a National Health Service of the kind that
had been foreshadowed in PEP's earlier report on the subject. *Planning for social security* was followed in its main recommendations
by the Beveridge Report itself, with one notable exception. Instead
of making benefits conditional on the payment of flat-rate insurance contributions, as Beveridge proposed, PEP recommended that
the full costs of the new social security system should be borne out
of taxes, involving a "complete overhaul and simplification of taxation machinery and methods". Despite this difference, relations with
Beveridge remained close through most of the war years and PEP
gave evidence to him again for his next report, on full employment
(Young 1981: 42–3).

The first post-war programme: 1945–53

In the immediate post-war period, it appeared that the momentum
established by PEP during the 1930s would, if anything, be aug-
mented. Planning had certainly helped to win the war, and Labour's
victory in 1945 held out the promise that its methods would be
applied in peacetime; the party's manifesto stated that in government
it would "plan from the ground up, giving an appropriate place
to constructive enterprise and private endeavour in the national
plan" (quoted in Dow 1965: 11). Although historical judgements
about this period have tended to lapse into clichés about widespread
idealism, all the evidence, whether derived from the contemporary
Mass-Observation surveys or later research, suggests that between
1939 and 1945 there was a significant shift in British opinion which
reached far beyond Whitehall and the media. There were, of course,
famous rows between the government and the medical profession
over the creation of a National Health Service and some of Labour's

nationalization programme aroused fierce controversy. However, a Conservative Minister, Henry Willink, had proposed a national health system during the war, and in some cases, notably that of coal, the Opposition under Churchill acquiesced in Labour's plans for state ownership. There was general agreement on the need to secure full employment and to ensure decent standards of life for those who lacked work; differences between the two main parties centred mainly on the proper degree of state interference beyond this point. A sign of the basic agreement between the main parties (but equally an indication of how modest PEP's aims had become) is the fact that Angus Maude was a Deputy Director of PEP from 1948 to 1950, and maintained this association for four years after he was elected as a Conservative MP in 1950; the first meetings of the One Nation group of Conservatives which Maude helped to found were held in PEP's offices. Although Friedrich Hayek won an enthusiastic audience for his polemical tract *The road to serfdom* (1944), which argued that state involvement in the economy necessarily leads to totalitarianism, his work was generally regarded as an eloquent exaggeration (see Chapter 3).

From the outset PEP had been striving for what Hayek thought impossible; a combination of at least some central planning with proper democratic accountability. Untroubled by Hayek's prophecies, the executive drew up a programme of work for the immediate post-war period in May 1945. This was completed by October 1948. War and the demands of reconstruction had transformed Britain's economic situation, and produced different problems for policy-makers. Keynes' work on demand-management seemed to have solved the pre-war difficulty of under-use of resources; it was now vital to re-equip industry and provide essential services, while exporting enough goods to finance Britain's overseas debts. The shortage of resources was compounded by the accumulation of large external claims in the form of foreign debt and the sterling balances of Commonwealth countries; there had also been a sharp deterioration in Britain's terms of trade. In June 1947 these problems were addressed in a PEP Report on *Britain and world trade*, which stressed the urgency of an immediate export drive. The report was the first comprehensive post-war treatment of its subject and of international trade generally; it was well received and widely distributed abroad, especially in the United States (Goodman 1981: 101–2).

On the industrial front, work was undertaken on the fuel, power and engineering industries on which the success of post-war reconstruction and the export drive largely depended. A mass of information was assembled, but drawing conclusions for policy from these data proved more difficult. A division of opinion within the Fuel and Power Group and the Executive between those who preferred to "let the facts speak for themselves" and the majority view that the facts needed interpretation was resolved in favour of the latter. A section of conclusions and recommendations was included in the final report, *A long-term fuel policy*, published in 1947 (ironically, the publication of the report was delayed by a fuel crisis in the winter of 1946–7 – an episode which showed how little planning was really undertaken by the Attlee Government) (Goodman 1981: 102–3).

During and immediately after the war, a draft report had been prepared on trade unionism and a collection of studies on certain aspects of the subject was published. With the help of John Edwards, then Parliamentary Secretary to the Board of Trade, and an assistant from Transport House, a volume on *British trade unionism* was put together and published in July 1948; the book ran through two editions, and a revised version was issued in the mid-1950s. Studies on *Manpower stocktaking*, *Mothers in jobs* and the *Employment of women* were undertaken and published between 1946 and 1948; this pathfinding work led to the establishment of a special enquiry by Elizabeth Layton into the difficulties of university-trained women in reconciling the claims of professional and family life, which appeared under the title of *Graduate wives* in 1954. During the late 1940s PEP also undertook studies on population policy and democracy; in 1948 its Press Group reiterated the proposal for a Press Council which PEP had put forward ten years before, and this time the idea was accepted (Goodman 1981: 103–6, 110).

In this period, perhaps inspired by a public desire for escapism in an atmosphere of austerity, there was a surge of activity in the visual and performing arts, prompting the publication of several PEP Reports. The first of these, on *The visual arts*, appeared in 1946; the second, on *The factual film*, in 1947; and a third, on *Music*, in 1949. Each of these attracted attention, especially among journalists. In 1950, the British Film Institute invited PEP to undertake a study of the film industry; this was duly completed some 18 months later and was well-received within the industry. PEP's venture into the world of entertainment during the film industry study inspired younger members of the staff to attempt their own investigations into other leisure industries. In the course of 1951, Broadsheets were issued on *The economics of book publishing* and *The gramophone record: industry and art*. A pair of Broadsheets on *The football industry* (1951) made suggestions for reforming the structure of Association football and the relations between owners, managers and players and was followed by others on *The cricket industry* (1956) and the *Economics of domestic pets* (1957).

Worthy (and at times far-sighted) as these publications were, the economics of domestic pets was a long way from the ambitious ideas set out by Max Nicholson in the *Weekend Review*. The second phase of work in the first post-war decade comprised three studies of more direct economic importance: on the universities, on housing policy and on government and industry. All three had roots in earlier work undertaken by PEP. The 1952 Report on *Government and industry* showed that PEP had not lowered its sights from questions of high national policy, and again the report was well received. But any hopes that the Attlee Government would move closer to Nicholson's preferred approach had proved short-lived. Some commentators have assumed that Churchill's return to Downing Street in 1951 was caused by another change in the climate of opinion – a revulsion against controls and central planning. In fact Labour's percentage support was higher in the October 1951 general election than it had been in July 1945 – a rather strange form for a popular revulsion to take. If there was any public disillusionment, it seems to have originated not because of the existence of controls *per se*, but from the fact that the prolonged regime of rationing imposed such severe restrictions on consumers. Hence a particular form of control which no-one desired as a permanent measure, and which was dictated by Britain's economic plight, could be held to have discredited the idea of planning in general. Harold Wilson, the President of the Board of Trade, indicated that the government had drawn this conclusion when he lit his famous Bonfire of Controls in November 1948; ironically, as a wartime statistician Wilson knew as well as anyone the need for painstaking research and strategic thinking in government. As Sir Alec Cairncross has noted, the *Economic survey for 1947* (heavily influenced by the then Chancellor

Sir Stafford Cripps) was the only official document of these years which even tried "to explain what economic planning entailed" (Cairncross 1985: 304). Although the government had intervened to divert resources from domestic consumption to exports – and even introduced bread rationing *after* the war had ended – it never attempted the kind of partnership with industry advocated by Nicholson (Leruez 1975: 74). Nicholson himself remained within Whitehall after the war, as an adviser to the Lord President of the Council, Herbert Morrison; this posting gave him a privileged insight into the Attlee Government's refusal to plan, even to the extent of co-ordinating policies between the industries which it had national-ized (Morgan 1984: 131, 135–6).

If the Attlee Government had been half-hearted at best in its approach to planning, the return of a Conservative Government in 1951 suggested that the founding ideals of PEP were less likely than ever to be realized. In fact Churchill, through his system of over-lords who were intended to co-ordinate policy between departments, promised to overcome some of the institutional problems which hampered more systematic planning; but the experiment was short-lived. More than 20 years after the end of the war Max Nicholson concluded that without drastic institutional changes it hardly mat-tered which party was in power: "it is idle to speak of economic planning in Britain so long as the Treasury remains with the kind of authority which it insists on exercising" (Nicholson 1967: 298). It is not surprising that after the relative disappointment of the Attlee years PEP's attention turned more towards the international scene.

European studies: 1956–78

The principal departure from PEP's recent activities during the 1950s was the decision to examine the situation in western Europe. As in the early 1930s, PEP could be seen as an outlet for unsatisfied energies, since at this time the established parties shunned serious discussion of European co-operation, regarding this as a tacit admis-sion that Britain could no longer prosper alone. From 1951 to 1959, the office of PEP's Executive Chairman was held by the Labour MP John Edwards, who had been Economic Secretary to the Treasury in the second Attlee administration in 1950–1. Edwards was a member of the Council of Europe, of which he later became President, and of Western European Union (WEU), which facilitated a steady flow of information on European institutions. The first European research programme undertaken by PEP was concerned with European organizations and began in 1956. The study analysed and assessed the work of the eight principal European organizations and attracted a number of politicians, civil servants, businessmen and academics onto its steering group. This group included Derek Ezra (later Chairman of the National Coal Board), Frank Figgures (subsequently Chairman of the National Economic Development Council, NEDC), the economist Eric Roll and Geoffrey Rippon MP, who would help negotiate British entry to the EEC under the Heath Government.

When work on this project began in 1956, the European Economic Community (EEC) was still under discussion; by the time the Report on *European Organisations* appeared in 1959, the Treaty of Rome had been signed, the EEC and Euratom had come into being alongside the European Coal and Steel Community (ECSC), the Organisation for European Economic Co-operation (OEEC) was about to be replaced by the Organisation for Economic Co-operation and Development (OECD) and the British government's failure to recognize the importance of the EEC would soon be signalled by its involvement with the rival European Free Trade Area (EFTA). *European Organisations* (1959) foreshadowed the preference of success ive British governments to move towards European co-operation through intergovernmental action rather than by a federal approach. At the same time, it argued, the need to adjust policies to take account of the emergence of the European Communities, whether Britain was a member or not, clearly created problems for the years ahead. This analysis of the origins and work of European institutions, it has been claimed, helped to establish PEP as "a major contributor to the European debate" (Bailey 1981: 128).

While the *European Organisations* project was still in progress, preparations began for setting up a study of Britain's relationship with the emerging EEC. The idea for this project stemmed from the publication of a broadsheet on *The European coal and steel community*, written in 1956 by Richard Bailey after a visit to the Luxembourg headquarters of the ECSC. Soon afterwards PEP secured a $165,000 grant from the American Ford Foundation to continue its work in this area; this was the largest grant yet received by PEP.

Another study (*Britain and the European Community*) appeared in 1964 (Bailey 1981: 130–1).

PEP was for a time the only British research institution studying the Common Market; in these circumstances, it could scarcely avoid being regarded as "a major contributor to the debate". Its work created a new clientele for PEP publications, including the United States and European Embassies, trade associations and business firms dealing with Europe and others anxious to discover how trade with other parts of the world would be affected by UK membership. PEP staff were invited to speak at conferences overseas, and the new link with the Ford Foundation led to the setting up of a joint committee with three European research organizations. After the first British application for membership of the EEC was vetoed in January 1963, the Common Market study turned to the formation of EFTA and a re-examination of the prospects of extending Commonwealth trade.

In addition to PEP's own research programme of economic and political studies on European issues, joint work was undertaken with the Royal Institute of International Affairs. This marriage between PEP and the RIIA was effectively arranged by Joe Slater of the Ford Foundation. In 1965, Slater visited PEP and indicated that Ford would be unlikely to support two institutes in London on one subject unless they were willing to work together; the result was a new grant for studies of Britain and the European Community, part of it for PEP's own research and part for joint studies with the RIIA. Between 1967 (when Britain unsuccessfully reapplied for membership) and 1976, 27 joint papers were published, on subjects ranging from agriculture to taxation and from regional policy to the European Council; in 1972, a jointly sponsored book entitled *Europe tomorrow: sixteen Europeans look ahead* figured in a national list of best-selling paperbacks. After British entry had been secured in 1971, the European dimension began to feature more prominently in PEP's independent studies of subjects such as unemployment, bureaucracy and parliamentary reform (Pinder 1981: 155–7).

Identifying the influence of PEP's publications on Britain's attitude to Europe is problematic. One insider, John Pinder, claims that there is little doubt that PEP's European studies, beginning with Max Nicholson's wartime advocacy of European union, influenced, to some degree at least, Britain's entry into the EEC. Pinder claims that the scores of PEP publications reserved judgement on the question of joining the EEC, but they "did much to raise British consciousness of Community affairs to the point where membership of the Community became practical politics" (Pinder 1981: 157).

The reasoning behind this view seems to be that PEP established a reputation for its studies of the European Communities, and Britain negotiated entry in 1971. Therefore PEP must have played an active part in this process. However, it is clear that Britain's attitude towards the EEC was dictated primarily by perceptions, among ministers and officials, of the country's economic prospects at various times; others, including Edward Heath, had become convinced of the need for European unity because of wartime experiences. While PEP was busily investigating developments on the continent in the mid-fifties, the British governments of Eden and Macmillan spurned the opportunity of contributing to the movement in the belief that Britain could go it alone. Macmillan's decision to apply in June 1961 arose from a recognition that this had been an over-optimistic assessment and that EFTA was no substitute for the EEC. Statistics for the respective growth rates of Britain and the Six were more influential here than the educative efforts of PEP. UK membership turned out not to be "practical politics" until the successful negotiations of the Heath Government because of two vetoes by General de Gaulle, not because the level of enlightenment in Britain (whose electorate was not consulted on the decision until 1975) was insufficient. People with a connection to PEP, such as Eric Roll and Geoffrey Rippon, are important figures in the story of Britain's attempts to join the EEC, but this only shows that PEP was recognized as a congenial forum for those who were already of a like mind on the subject. One can only conclude that PEP at least helped to inform interested people in Britain, but that UK policy towards the EEC was driven by considerations other than the detailed findings of PEP.

Constitutional and domestic policy studies: 1954–78

Between 1954 and 1964, the type of project most commonly undertaken by PEP was the study designed to attract funding; its identity was now clearly that of a "contract research organization" (see Introduction). In 1953, it was successful in securing support for two studies, on graduates in industry and trade associations in Britain, financed by counterpart funds set up to promote research under Marshall Aid arrangements. Later projects financed by foundation grants were on family needs and the social services, mental health facilities and Trade Unions. By the early 1960s, the usual pattern was for PEP's Council to agree on a number of subjects for study on which applications would be prepared and forwarded to the appropriate foundations; this was quite different from earlier projects, some of which had been financed on a somewhat hand-to-mouth basis. Some of the latter, however, notably *Growth in the British economy* (1960), attracted attention. The study was one of the first attempts to analyse the factors affecting economic growth and its steering group was chaired by Sir Robert Shone, who later became the first Director-General of the National Economic Development Office (NEDO) (Bailey 1981: 125).

The formation of NEDO in 1961 was a sign of renewed interest in planning, fostered by the Prime Minister, Harold Macmillan, who had favoured planning in the 1930s and was increasingly concerned by evidence of Britain's relative economic decline. *Growth in the British economy* had urged new initiatives in this direction; once again PEP was a natural forum for discussions, and in the same year it published a Report on *Economic Planning in France* after a conference on the subject organized by the National Institute of Economic and Social Research (NIESR: see Chapter 2) (Budd 1978: 86).

In 1966 a grant was offered by the Joseph Rowntree Memorial Trust to finance a major survey of racial discrimination in England – an arrangement highly characteristic of a contract research organization (see Introduction). In the late summer of that year, Mark Bonham Carter, the Chairman of the Race Relations Board, asked the Director of PEP, John Pinder, if PEP could measure the extent of racial discrimination in Britain within six months. Bonham Carter and the Home Secretary, Roy Jenkins, believed that discrimination was sufficiently widespread to justify extending the 1965 Race Relations Act through a second Act which would outlaw discrimination in employment, housing and a number of personal services. Indeed, it has been suggested that "the *principle* of extension was uppermost in the new Home Secretary's mind from the *beginning*" of his term of office in December that year (Rose et al. 1969: 515). The Cabinet, however, was unsure and powerful interest groups such as the Confederation of British Industry (CBI) and the Trades Union Congress (TUC) insisted that further legislation was unnecessary. The question put to PEP was simply whether discrimination in these fields was "substantial" or not (Pinder 1981: 140–1). A young researcher, Bill Daniel, responded by devising some innovative tests in which actors of different racial origins applied for the same jobs. Following six months of hectic work, both the surveys and the tests gave similar and hence convincing results; all the findings converged to show that discrimination was indeed "substantial", although not overwhelming (Pinder 1981: 142).

Racial discrimination was published in April 1967. At a PEP dinner later that year, Roy Jenkins, who had recently left the Home Office to become Chancellor of the Exchequer, is reported to have said that the survey had been "decisive" in persuading the Government to proceed with a second Race Relations Act (Pinder 1981: 140). Of equal significance is the fact that the great majority of the Conservative opposition – despite the explosive antics of Enoch Powell – accepted that something had to be done to extend the provisions of the 1965 Act. Quintin Hogg, the then shadow Home Secretary, reported to his colleagues that the PEP report was "a powerful piece of work" which proved that discrimination existed (Leader's Consultative Committee minutes 67: 141). The response of the press to the evidence supplied by PEP was far greater than the sponsors of the Report and its advisory panel had dared to hope. As Rose and his colleagues have argued, "the extensive coverage given to the Report – which easily exceeded that given to even the most prestigious Royal Commission – provided the Home Secretary with the double benefit of the perceived support of public opinion and of convincing evidence to present to Cabinet colleagues" (Rose et al. 1969: 534).

These events, according to one insider, constitute "a classic example of research applied to a policy question which had to be answered by using the tools of empirical social science research. Without the surveys, and indeed without developing the new method of tests in numbers that would produce statistics, the facts required by the policy-makers could not have been obtained". Given the facts, policy-makers could make their decision. PEP's view "was not sought, however, on the implications of these facts for policy. Once the facts had been made clear, the conclusion that substantial

43

discrimination should be countered by a law was accepted by the main political parties and not resisted by the main interest groups" (Pinder 1981: 143). This view seems naïve, if not disingenuous; while it would be wrong to claim that PEP was from the outset driven by a specific ideology, it had remained true to the basic idea shared by its founders that problems can be solved by government action. Against the clear evidence that PEP's innovative researches helped to make the case for legislation, one must also set the fact that the Labour Government needed a face-saving gesture at a time when it had alienated liberal opinion by introducing fresh restrictions on immigration as a panic-response to the expulsion of Asians from Kenya (Layton-Henry 1992: 53, 79).

Whatever the precise influence of PEP on the 1968 Race Relations Act, after the publication of its report its authority in this area was well established. Six years later, the Home Office asked PEP to study the general position of ethnic minorities in British society and to measure the gap between their housing, employment and economic circumstances and those of the white population. As in the previous case, the emphasis was on assembling facts, rather than prescribing particular policies, on the grounds that "confidence in the reliability of the facts, which is a necessary basis for democratic politics, would be undermined if those who obtained them went on and used them to make a case" (Pinder 1981: 143). In the 1970s, a third study on similar lines was prepared and PEP sponsored surveys of the unemployed among ethnic minorities, overseas doctors in Britain, multi-ethnic schools and relations between ethnic minorities and the Metropolitan Police (Pinder 1981: 144).

Other studies completed and published in the late 1960s and early 1970s included work on women and their careers, urban growth and personal mobility. The advisory group for the study on women was chaired by Denis Barnes, then Permanent Secretary of the Department of Employment. Like the work on race relations, this project used a variety of research methods to construct a comprehensive picture of its subject. A further similarity with the work on race relations was that it, too, was followed (albeit, in this case, ten years later) by a new look, on behalf of the Equal Opportunities Commission and the SSRC, at the professions and organizations which had been studied in the late 1960s, to find out what change the Sex Discrimination Act (1975) had actually induced. *Personal mobility and transport policy* (1973), written by Mayer Hillman and Anne Whalley, explored the implications for planning and transport policy of the denial of access to facilities to non-car owners, the elderly and women with young children in different types of locality, in terms of dispersing facilities and controls over the use of the car. Hillman and Whalley also produced reports for the Sports Council and the Transport and Road Research Laboratory, demonstrating the merits of easy access to small and local recreational facilities, and for the British Railways Board, on the social consequences of rail closures. Ironically, the best-publicized bout of such closures, associated with Dr Richard Beeching, had arisen from the Macmillan government's "planning" period. Beeching's plans, which ignored the possibility of a co-ordinated transport policy, provided perhaps the best demonstration that post-war British administrations had lacked the kind of vision demanded by Max Nicholson back in 1931 (Pinder 1981: 145–7).

In January 1967 PEP published Samuel Brittan's *Inquest on planning in Britain* as part of a comparative study of economic planning and policies in Britain, France and Germany which was partly financed by the Ford Foundation. Harold Wilson had continued Macmillan's attempt to revive Britain's fortunes by moving towards continental models of indicative planning. However, the ambitious growth targets set out first by NEDO and then by the National Plan produced by the Department of Economic Affairs (DEA) created by Wilson were sacrificed as the government fought to maintain the value of sterling; the Plan was declared dead in July 1966.

The title of Brittan's pamphlet begged the question – even under Macmillan and Wilson, "planning in Britain" had been at best half-hearted; the setting of targets for future economic growth seemed nothing more than an exercise in wishful thinking when there was so little co-ordination between economic departments and the Treasury's priorities lay elsewhere – notably, at this time, in defending the exchange rate. Brittan, who had served in the DEA for more than a year, noted that chronic balance of payments problems had thwarted the Plan, and recommended floating exchange rates as a means of ensuring that Treasury concern for the strength of sterling would not sabotage any future efforts. Brittan's case was incontestable; whether or not the Plan would have succeeded had the pound been devalued when the government came into office in

45

1964, its chances would clearly have been much better had Harold Wilson not been so anxious to ensure that Labour was not branded as the party of devaluation.

Since almost from the outset PEP had turned away from recommendations on the scale urged by Nicholson, the apparent demise of planning was no obstacle to further work. One of the definitions of planning offered by Durbin back in 1935 – "simply the *intervention of the Government in a particular industry* at a time when the greater part of the economy still remains in private hands" – could still be applied in the absence of a coherent overall strategy; Durbin, indeed, had claimed that "planning does not in the least imply the existence of a[n overall] Plan" (Durbin 1949: 42–3). In the early 1970s, PEP's main contribution to economic policy was through its studies of labour relations, incomes and manpower policy. In 1970, *Beyond the wage-work bargain* was published, in which Bill Daniel showed how productivity bargains, as a means of "collective bargaining for change", could improve relationships at work and increase job interest and satisfaction, as well as pay and productivity. Daniel's work on this led to *The right to manage?* (1972), which demonstrated how relations between managers and employees could be improved, and in enterprising firms were already being improved, by greater worker involvement. Later that year, a research programme was set up to investigate the growing threat from inflation, which in the late 1960s and early 1970s had defied expectations by continuing to rise despite a similar upward trend in unemployment. This "stagflation" (as the Conservative Shadow Chancellor Iain Macleod had dubbed it) represented a threat to the Keynesian approach to economic policy which PEP continued to uphold. The PEP study focused on the way in which attitudes and behaviour could be converted into inflation through the process of collective bargaining; by the end of 1973 a substantial grant had been obtained from the Leverhulme Trust for this work. At about the same time, the OPEC countries quadrupled the price of oil and catapulted Britain's inflation rate into double figures. Inflation continued to rise rapidly through 1974 and the first half of 1975, by which time Bill Daniel had completed surveys which showed that an incomes policy, based on a limited flat-rate increase of around £6 per week, was likely to be widely acceptable. These findings coincided with the policies of successive governments under Heath, Wilson and Callaghan, but with the election of Mrs Thatcher's Conservatives in 1979 incomes policy was dropped, at least in name, and Daniel's subsequent proposals for the future development of such policies made little headway (Pinder 1981: 150–1). PEP had made a constructive attempt to explain the lessons learned from incomes policy in each of its various forms to busy decision-makers, yet this only helped to discredit the idea of state controls because the findings showed how complicated the legislation would have to be if it were to have any hope in succeeding.

Among its projects conducted in the general field of social policy at this time, PEP also examined the other phenomenon which haunted this period – unemployment. The findings of a national survey published in 1974 showed that the costs of unemployment were particularly high for men with families, rather than for the young people on whom the spotlight had previously been turned. In 1976 the Manpower Services Commission (MSC) sponsored a follow-up survey of those who had been interviewed in 1974, which showed how many of them had since experienced a chequered pattern of employment or ceased to be employed at all and on which the MSC based a number of new policy decisions (Pinder 1981: 151). Thinking in favour of the establishment of the MSC had earlier been crystallized by Santosh Mukherjee's comparative study of manpower policy in Britain and Sweden. After the MSC was established by Edward Heath it was confronted by rapidly rising unemployment and Mukherjee was asked to study job creation in Canada; his report, entitled *There's work to be done*, was published in 1974 and became a basis for the MSC's Job Creation Scheme. In 1976, PEP published Mukherjee's *Unemployment costs . . .*, which showed the extent of the burden placed on state budgets in European Community countries by the loss of tax revenue and increased public expenditure due to unemployment. This attracted the attention of (among others) the German federal agency for manpower policy in Nuremberg, which commissioned PEP to undertake a joint study of alternatives to unemployment (Pinder 1981: 149).

The principal theme of PEP's industrial research during the 1970s was innovation. In 1969 Christopher Layton's *European advanced technology* was published, to be followed in 1972 by his *Ten innovations*, based on a report he had produced for the Central Advisory Council for Science and Technology. Other studies during

47

this period included Christopher Harlow's *Innovation and productivity under nationalisation* (1977), and Yao-Su Hu's *National attitudes and the financing of industry* (1976), which compared British financial institutions with continental and Japanese industrial banks which were taken to possess sufficient industrial expertise to be able to judge which investment risks should be backed (Pinder 1981: 152). By the mid-1970s, however, Britain's economic plight was too severe for this sound advice to win a practical response; even when the country became a net exporter of oil in 1980 the emphasis of government policy encouraged short-term gain rather than the kind of far-sighted strategy which had produced such astonishing results in Japan and Germany.

By the mid-1970s the problems of unemployment and inflation had become so severe and political instability so critical that there was talk of Britain becoming "ungovernable'; when the BBC ran a series of programmes on this subject in 1976 two of the five participants, John Mackintosh and Samuel Brittan, had connections with PEP (King 1976). In 1974 PEP had decided to combine its various streams of research into a single report. The result, entitled *Reshaping Britain*, included proposals by Bill Daniel for incomes policy, by Santosh Mukherjee for a stronger MSC, by Yao-Su Hu for a revival of industrial investment and by Mackintosh for a reform to the House of Lords, to accommodate the representatives of trades unions and employers. The Report was received enthusiastically by some politicians and industrialists, as well as by Peter Jay in *The Times*. As the 1970s wore on, however, the idea of systematically combining industrial and manpower policies within a concept of general economic policy was challenged by right-wing commentators (including Jay, who was increasingly attracted by monetarist solutions), and from the left by Stuart Holland and other advocates of import control. The "middle way" which PEP had advocated from the beginning still apparently found favour with a majority of the public, but was increasingly threatened as politicians grasped at less complex solutions.

PEP was a long-standing advocate of constitutional overhaul, and continued to suggest ideas for reform in the 1960s and 1970s, before the question became an important focus of media interest. In 1965, a broadsheet entitled *Reforming the Commons* was published, written by members of the Study of Parliament Group (SPG).

This was followed by more work undertaken with the SPG and financed by the Social Science Research Council (SSRC), which had been established in 1965 with Michael Young, a former Secretary and Executive Member of PEP as its first Chairman (Young became Vice President of PEP in 1966). These studies led to the publication of *The member of parliament and his information*, by Anthony Barker and Michael Rush (1970), John Griffiths' *Parliamentary scrutiny of government bills* in 1974, and other reports on select committees, services and facilities for MPs. All this work appeared in advance of government reform of the Parliamentary Committee system carried through in 1979. Peter Richards, who would later become Chairman of the SPG, also wrote a book for PEP on the Local Government Act of 1972; by the time his study appeared public disquiet about the Act had become widespread, and the problem of the proper size of local authorities, in particular, remained a matter of controversy well into the 1990s (Pinder 1981: 155).

From PEP to PSI: 1976–8

In October 1972, a weekend meeting of members of the Executive Committee and senior staff was held at Dartington Hall in Devon and a discussion took place on the future role of PEP. Although questions about its previous performance were not put in a critical way, there was a clear understanding that PEP must increase its capacity to respond to the problems that beset the country. Eric Roll spoke of the need to develop a centre in Britain on the model of the American Brookings, and the recent establishment of the Centre for Studies in Social Policy (CSSP), which was likely to cover the same fields as PEP, was noted. Prophetic as these thoughts were to prove, PEP tried to expand under its own steam for the time being. It was decided to aim for a research staff of between 25 and 30, which would require twice the current income. New grants were obtained, particularly from industry, as the old ones faded away. Inflation, however, continued to accelerate, with the result that PEP could only offer stability for a staff of fairly constant size. The capacity and reputation of PEP as a social science research institute continued to grow, but "the incoming tide of Britain's problems rose faster, and others took up the cry that a great Brookings-like centre was required" (Pinder 1981: 158–9).

Just as the crisis of the 1930s had created PEP, the problems of the 1970s – different in nature, but apparently equal in severity – fuelled demands for a new impetus. The debate about a "British Brookings" was accompanied, in 1976–7, by two attempts to launch a big new institute, on the part of Derek Robinson at the SSRC, and Ralf Dahrendorf, the Director of the LSE. Dahrendorf issued proposals for a new Centre for Economic and Political Studies in London to help "politicians, businessmen, administrators, professional people and scholars . . . make sense of the economic, social and political predicament of the world in the 1970s and 1980s, and of Britain in it". The LSE, Dahrendorf argued, was, as it had been in the past, a place "uniquely suited to provide a basis and forum for such research". The present predicament was then described: pressure on international economic and political institutions; the Helsinki Final Act and *detente*; the oil crises and limits to growth; new social trends and cultural attitudes and the specifically British problems of low growth, high state involvement, bad industrial relations, a class-ridden society and adversary politics. Too much short-term thinking, Dahrendorf argued, impeded medium-term solutions. "Coming to grips" with such issues required a meeting-place of brains and power (Dahrendorf 1995: 490).

Three options were then described. The first, an "institute of institutes", would bring existing institutions together in a federal or confederal structure. The second, a "centre for the determination of the national interest" would help to "mobilise and stabilise the restless and increasingly disillusioned mass of middle-ground citizens around a focal point which is independent of the existing political parties" (an echo of the early days of PEP's disillusionment with partisan conflict). The final option was for a "socio-politico-economic think tank" which would undertake "dispassionate, but synthetic study of contemporary politics, economy and society with a view to contributing to the clarification of the horizon of decisions which have to be taken in any sector of the community." Such a body would conduct research into the contemporary situation, bring together academics and practitioners and disseminate its findings. The Centre was not to be a purely academic institution; its work should be policy-relevant and should draw on the views and members of all parties and other public organizations. To do its work properly, such a Centre would need £900,000 per year to finance a dozen permanent and two dozen temporary research fellows, as well as the necessary infrastructure (Dahrendorf 1995: 490–1).

In May 1977, a special issue of the *PEP Bulletin* entitled "A British Brookings?" assembled contributions to the debate from various sources. Although the editor of *The Times*, Sir William (later Lord) Rees-Mogg was in favour, the Presidents of the NIESR (see Chapter 3), RIIA and PEP feared a dissipation of research staff; PEP's Director, John Pinder, argued against big research institutes which would endanger the existing pluralism in ideas (Pinder 1981: 159). The project was also opposed by existing social science departments in universities, on the grounds that it would take public policy analysis away from them. As Bernard Donoughue has argued, the prospect of a large injection of funds and stimulus into social research at a time when the traditional financial taps were being turned off "did not influence the British research establishment, which preferred to continue swimming in a shallow pool, rather than allowing big new competition" (Donoughue 1987: 125–6).

The debate about a "British Brookings" subsequently moved to a European plane, but again without much success (Dahrendorf 1995: 493). A series of high-level meetings was held in Europe and by 1977 it was finally agreed to establish a "European Brookings". European Heads of Government were then approached and asked to give their support. The British Prime Minister, James Callaghan, responded with enthusiasm, as did the Head of the Civil Service, Sir Douglas Allen, and the Cabinet Secretary, Sir John Hunt. During a further series of meetings, it was decided to include the European Commission among the sponsors, although the proposed institute was to remain independent of the EEC. Whitehall moved quickly to support the idea of a London location for the institute and produced an impressive list of possible offices. When the German Chancellor, Helmut Schmidt, visited London in May 1979, a minor item on his agenda was to have been to give his support to the idea of a European Brookings, based in London. A week before Schmidt's arrival, however, the British General Election produced a change of government and it was Mrs Thatcher, not Mr Callaghan, who greeted the German Chancellor at 10 Downing Street. Shortly afterwards, Thatcher revealed that she had decided to veto the project on the grounds that it would increase public expenditure (Donoughue 1987: 126–7).

In the summer of 1977, PEP approached the CSSP, which was also considering its future, with the suggestion of a merger between the two institutes. The CSSP was then barely five years old, but had begun to establish itself as a public policy research and discussion institute of some repute, with a Council and staff keen to extend its record of output and influence still further. In the event, however, the Council of the CSSP decided that it would make "more sense in the circumstances for the Centre to build on its five years of development and achievement by joining with PEP to form a broader-based organisation. The two bodies had fairly similar roles and interests, with experience, needs and resources which at that time were as much complementary as overlapping. It could reasonably be hoped that their union would produce even more than the sum of their parts" (Isserlis 1981: 163).

In common with its colleagues in the NIESR, PEP and the RIIA, the CSSP did not favour the idea of a British Brookings. The misgivings of each of these institutes were partly inspired by the threat that a British Brookings might pose to their own future prospects of raising funds and recruiting qualified staff. The proposal, however, also seemed to be based on "an excessive optimism about both the practicality and the utility of setting up a UK body of the kind and scale envisaged. Experience and reflection did not encourage confidence that what was being done or aspired to by the Washington organisation could either successfully or desirably be replicated on this side of the Atlantic" (Isserlis 1981: 163–4). In short, while the Brookings Institution deserved respect for the range and quality of much of its work, it was seen as being far more suited to the American context. Further development of existing institutions, including mergers where appropriate, was assumed to be much better suited to the UK.

Once the talks about merger began, they went ahead very quickly. It was agreed that Eric Roll and Frederic Seebohm would be the Joint Presidents of the merged institute, Sir Monty Finniston Chairman of the Council and Charles Carter Chairman of the Research and Management Committee. Members of the Council would be appointed in equal numbers by each predecessor institute; John Pinder was appointed as the first Director. The staff of both PEP and CSSP could have jobs in the merged institute. The staff at PEP insisted that the new body should be called PEP, but staff at CSSP refused to accept this. The former were shaken when Max Nicholson indicated that the Founding Fathers of PEP knew they had made a bad choice and that he personally had never cared for the name at all; it might have been more pertinent to say that had the founders of PEP been responding to the crisis of the mid-1970s when they set up their organization, instead of the early 1930s when "planning" seemed to hold out so much promise, the old name would never have been considered. The deadlock was only broken by referring the issue to arbitration by the Joint Presidents, who chose a name that both factions eventually agreed on. Soon after this reconciliation, the merger was consummated and the Policy Studies Institute was born on 31 March (*not*, the stage managers were careful to ensure, 1 April) 1978, and established itself at Park Village East near Regent's Park (Pinder 1981: 159–60).

Conclusion: do "facts speak for themselves"?

Judged by the ambitions of Max Nicholson's article in *The Weekend Review*, the history of PEP must be accounted as one of at least relative failure. Britain did not adopt the kind of systematic planning which Nicholson had called for. More seriously, PEP itself never got to the first base of drawing one up. Instead it quickly became occupied with studies which, however rigorous they might have been, at their best merely pointed the way to piecemeal reforms.

The reason for this failure is readily apparent. The same schizophrenic British political culture, at once deferential to the trappings of power and fiercely resistant to the exercise of it, which provoked Nicholson's original outcry, meant that any kind of blueprint – even one which proposed a "middle way" between the available extremes of *laissez-faire* and Bolshevism or Fascism – was ruled out as a practical proposition in the UK. Only when total war came would British politicians look favourably on anything approaching a total solution, and as soon as the war was won the first instinct of even socialist politicians was to restore something akin to normal practice as quickly as possible. PEP, which was set up to change the mentality of British politicians, was left with the alternatives of aping what Nicholson scornfully called "the system" or being ignored; the enthusiasm of its members to do *something*, even if this meant a severe curtailment of its ambitions, coupled with the misgivings of even some founders about the word *planning*, ensured that the first option was taken (Nicholson 1967). Over time it was easy for insiders to judge PEP's record against these revised ambitions; on these grounds they could regard even such basic government assumptions as the need to plan departmental spending for several years ahead as marking a success for their approach. As late as 1976 Lord Rothschild, former head of the government's own think-tank, argued in a lecture commemorating Lord Sieff that planning should not be confused with the emotive word blueprint, and defined it as "the analysis of systems and situations, present and future, and the construction of logical inferences from that attitude" (Rothschild 1977: 166). On this view, rational decision-making of almost any kind could be acclaimed (or, of course, deplored) as an example of "planning".

Since Britain would never adopt systematic planning if left to itself it was natural for PEP to turn towards Europe after the Second World War. When Harold Macmillan applied for membership of the EEC in 1961 this strategy seemed on the verge of paying off for PEP. Macmillan, after all, had once risked his own political prospects by advocating planning in the 1930s and he was convinced that Britain's best interests now lay in a planned strategy of economic growth within the EEC. From this perspective the 1963 veto imposed by General De Gaulle – President of the country which the British advocates of planning took as their model – was a more serious blow against the old ethos of PEP than the later collapse of Wilson's National Plan. Before PEP could respond to Edward Heath's successful application for membership ten years later, the oil crisis arising from the Yom Kippur War ensured that any long-term planning would be swept aside by the imperative of day-to-day survival while policy-makers waited for Britain's own oil to come ashore.

The advent of Margaret Thatcher (who in obedience to her ideological convictions had convinced herself that all Britain's woes were attributable to a full-scale experiment with planning which had never happened) should have set the seal on PEP's demise. Ironically, however, it seems that the merged PSI has survived *because* of PEP's failure to follow the path laid down by Max Nicholson. By concentrating on well-researched publications on specific subjects rather than the kind of overall blueprint envisaged by Nicholson, PEP quickly established a high reputation among those academics, journalists, civil servants and politicians who were not ideologically opposed to government intervention; if it did not set the political agenda at any time, its contributions to the agenda chosen by politicians on a wide range of issues (but especially on subjects like race and gender relations) were always likely to catch attention. PSI, which inherited this mantle, would still be in demand to conduct contract research for government and other bodies when painstaking inquiry rather than ideological advocacy were required – and on occasion even the Thatcher Government recognized that it needed this kind of help.

The survival of PSI under right-wing Conservative regimes apparently suggests that, as insiders claim, this really is a body which allows facts to speak for themselves. In 1989 Bill Daniel argued that PSI had "no basic political position or philosophy underpinning [its] work, other than empiricism and pragmatism" (Daniel 1989: 24). This claim is borne out by the style of PEP/PSI publications, which have rarely exploited rhetoric and, whatever the intentions of the various authors, are suitable reading matter for the policy-making elite rather than for the wider electorate. Yet it is based on a stark distinction between "facts" and "values" which cannot be sustained. Even if facts do "speak for themselves", they will not be heeded unless the right ears are attuned to them (Garnett 1996a: 3–4). What seem to be the promptings of "empiricism and pragmatism" to some appear as dogmatic statements to others even when couched in moderate language. Daniel's remark implies that if the evidence he had produced on race during the 1960s had been used as part of an argument to repatriate immigrants, he would not have complained; in reality, a desire for a successful multicultural society has always been more or less explicit in the work conducted by PEP and PSI in this crucial area.

When the Social Democratic Party was founded in 1981, one of its leaders (Shirley Williams) was a temporary fellow of the PSI, and among its members were the Chairman of PSI (Charles Carter), its Director (John Pinder), and three permanent fellows (Crewe and King 1995: 554). No doubt many members of the SDP thought that their political position was founded on nothing more than "empiricism and pragmatism", but to outside observers it was pretty clear that the party belonged to a distinct ideological tradition – that of progressive or "New" liberalism, which can be traced back to T.H. Green at the end of the nineteenth century. As Max Nicholson himself admitted of PEP's founders, "many would, in an earlier decade, have been Liberals" (Nicholson 1981a: 5). The chance that the SDP would "break the two-party mould" which had existed since the 1930s was too good for some of PSI's members to miss. But although the new party's opinion poll ratings at first topped 50 per cent, its social roots were too shallow for it to survive. Rather than help to build a coalition of solid public support, the rationalistic tone of PSI publications was more likely to reinforce the impression fostered by the SDP's opponents – that it was only capable of enthusing a handful of people within the media and political intelligentsia who hankered after the old post-war consensus at a time when the main political parties were becoming increasingly polarized. The inability of moderates to find a language and a vision which might combat the ideologues of right and left was the main reason why the founders of the SDP had left the Labour Party in the first place.

The Policy Studies Institute has fared better than the short-lived SDP. In 1995 it received over £4 million in grants from a wide variety of organizations, and its operating surplus was almost £100,000. At the time of writing (October 1997) the "New" Labour Government of Tony Blair appears to be far more receptive to the kind of work undertaken by PSI than its predecessor, although of course it is as much a stranger to the kind of programme put forward by Max Nicholson as Margaret Thatcher ever was. Even so, within months of Labour's victory PSI's Director, Pamela Meadows, was reported to be negotiating an intimate link with the neighbouring University of Westminster – a deal which might provide new security for a body which would otherwise continue to suffer the kind of hand-to-mouth insecurity which seems inseparable from contract research organizations, however reputable their research findings might be.

CHAPTER 2

The National Institute of Economic and Social Research

Origins

As in the case of PEP, the economic slump precipitated by the Wall Street Crash of 1929 provided the impetus for the creation of the National Institute of Economic and Social Research (NIESR), although the outlook was much improved when it was finally set up. It was founded in 1938, but the first initiative was launched by Sir Josiah Stamp in the early 1930s. Stamp, a brilliant civil servant who had become a Director of the Bank of England (among many other things), had been connected with a Rockefeller Foundation scheme to provide fellowships in the social sciences and became convinced that a major initiative was needed to address the problem of financing the social sciences in Britain. His objective was to establish a major research institute, with independent funding, with economics as its main interest (Jones 1988: 36).

Stamp discussed his ideas with a group of prominent academics who, like him, were concerned to improve the quality of information available to government. These included William Beveridge, Director of the London School of Economics (LSE), Henry Clay, Economic Adviser to the Bank of England and Hubert Henderson, Stamp's colleague on the government's short-lived Economic Advisory Council (EAC) set up by Ramsay MacDonald in 1930, and former collaborator with John Maynard Keynes. These economists were as well known for their tendency to quarrel as for their dedication to public service; in 1930 Stamp and Henderson had accepted Keynes' view that Tariff Reform was necessary as a remedy for Britain's economic crisis, while Clay and Beveridge furiously dissented (Williamson 1992: 68). From the outset, then, there was a danger that the new body would simply become a new arena for unresolvable disputes between Keynesians and the Free Traders who constituted a majority of the profession at that time. In this context it is particularly noteworthy that the original impetus for the Institute came from Stamp; according to Keynes' biographer, Stamp's role on the economists' committee of the Economic Advisory Council "was to keep the peace" (Skidelsky 1992, 369).

During 1934–5 Stamp, with the help of Noel Hall, then a senior lecturer in the Department of Political Economy at University College London, set out to win financial support from a number of trusts, including Halley Stewart, Leverhulme, Rockefeller and the Pilgrim Trust. The Halley Stewart trustees appointed a small committee to explore the possibility of forming an institute of economic research to study applied problems and provided a grant of £600. The committee, which consisted of Sir Percy Alden (Secretary of the Halley Stewart trustees), Clay, Henderson and Hall, concluded that it was necessary to establish an independent organization which would undertake quantitative economic research. The larger organizing body included Israel Sieff, the Chairman of PEP, Keynes' fierce opponent Lionel Robbins of the LSE and the Trade Union leader Sir Walter Citrine; both Robbins and Citrine had been involved with the EAC.

By mid-1936, a public statement about the need for a national institute of economic research had been agreed. It was proposed that the institute would undertake empirical research into such pressing contemporary problems as the distribution of population, the depressed areas and unemployment. It was also contemplated from the outset that the institute should embark on studies that would require continuous and systematic observation over a period of several years, including changes in the volume and distribution of national income, the relationships between different groups of prices and the results of recent experiments in planning. A further aim of the institute, it was agreed, should be to secure co-ordination of economic research where possible and to organize and finance special studies outside the institute to achieve this. It was also hoped that, as a result of experience in using statistical data, a substantial improvement in both the quantity and quality of statistics could be achieved (Jones 1988: 37).

The formal establishment of the NIESR was delayed by problems concerning the activities of Sir William Beveridge. Beveridge had been seeking permission to give up the directorship of the LSE in order to devote more time to his own research and had proposed a scheme to the Rockefeller Foundation for a "Beveridge Institute". When the Foundation (which had itself been affected by the economic slump) finally turned the proposal down, Beveridge became interested in the Halley Stewart committee's new initiative, of which there was a possibility that he might become the director. At about the same time, an alternative scheme emerged from the LSE for an economic research department to be based at the school, where Stamp was now chairman of the governors. Beveridge himself, however, continued to be actively interested in the proposed new Halley Stewart Institute and even suggested his own amendments to the organizing committee's proposals. In the event, only one of Beveridge's amendments was accepted – namely, the inclusion of the word "Social" in the new institute's name. Although there was clearly a social element in the NIESR's work, however, economic matters have always been its main concern.

There was more delay (and some strain in relationships) while the group canvassed alternatives to the prickly Beveridge for the post of director. It was not until the end of 1937 that the decision was finally taken to set up the Institute. Noel Hall, who had previously been instrumental in the creation of PEP, was appointed director. Sir Josiah Stamp was elected president and Beveridge, who had by this time left the LSE for Oxford, was chosen as the Institute's first Chairman. However, Beveridge attended only one meeting; he was then taken ill and, following a period of convalescence, withdrew from the chairmanship in order to devote himself to his own research. In the following year Stamp was elected chairman and Henry Clay deputy chairman (Jones 1988: 37).

A press statement, issued on 5 January 1938, referred first to the financial arrangements. Support had been promised by the Pilgrim Trust, the trustees of the late Lord Leverhulme and the Halley Stewart trustees. Their contributions would be matched pound for pound by the Rockefeller Foundation, making a total of £10,000 per year for the next seven years. The statement described the motivation behind the new Institute; namely the inadequacy of the research facilities in the social sciences compared with those in the natural sciences and the need for a national institute of independent economic research. The existing university research centres such as the LSE, the Economic Research Section at Manchester, the Institute of Statistics and Nuffield College at Oxford, it was thought, had not met this need. The new Institute was to perform the following functions:

(1) To conduct research, either by its own regular staff, or by other persons temporarily associated with it, into the facts and problems of contemporary human society.
(2) To provide assistance and facilities for research to members of university staffs and others.
(3) To apply for funds in aid of such research, both for use in its own work and for allocation to other bodies and persons conducting approved research in consultation with it.
(4) To collaborate with any similar institutes or organizations in other countries with a view to securing comparative study on similar lines of common problems.
(5) To publish or assist in the publication of the result of researches, subject to adequate safeguards for the impartial and scientific character of these publications (Jones 1988: 37).

As a statement of intent, this was notably anodyne. The proposition that economic policy should be based on research, and that such evidence should be disseminated to the wider public, was uncontroversial by the late 1930s; for example, the government had begun to conduct surveys of domestic economic activity in the previous decade. But any more substantive prospectus for the Institute was ruled out by the divisions among its leading members. As Sir Austin Robinson (chairman of the Council of Management from 1949 to 1962) put it, those outside the top echelons of the Institute in the early days "were frankly puzzled as to what its functions were intended to be"; it is doubtful whether even the guiding spirits were more enlightened (Robinson 1988: 63).

Wartime and early post-war research

Following the delay in formally establishing the Institute, there was a strong sense of urgency about starting a research programme.

The Institute began at once to identify areas for research which were being held back for lack of financial support. Special committees were appointed on national income, unemployment, the location of industry and the distribution of population, economic change in the United Kingdom since 1928 and commercial policy and trade regulations. These questions were already attracting interest from ministers; an official inquiry into the distribution of industry and population had been launched in 1937 under Sir Montague Barlow, and the government had been active from the early 1930s in promoting industrial re-organization, notably through mergers (Hennessy 1992: 209). The special committee on national income studies recommended that the LSE be invited to undertake a study of the national income of the United Kingdom as a whole and of its distribution, although scholars from other universities were involved, including Keynes at Cambridge. Inquiries into credit and money markets, trade regulations and commercial policy were undertaken by staff, in each case as part of an international study. Publications from these early programmes, as well as numerous articles in academic journals, appeared either during or after the war (Jones 1988, 37–8).

When war broke out in September 1939, Institute staff entered government service, which, together with the transfer to war work of associates based in the universities, meant that several projects had to be abandoned or suspended. Despite the problems, work undertaken during the war included population studies, a study of national health insurance, problems of local taxation, the regional and industrial distribution of disease mortality and the effect of the war on money markets and banking. Programmes of research within the Institute were developed along two main lines. Investigations of current importance included the burden of British taxation, a survey of saving and spending, the location and size of plants in particular industries, colonial finance, Soviet economics and the European war economies. The second main line of activity was to promote quantitative investigations into the workings of the economy; major inquiries were into national expenditure, output and income (Richard Stone) and productivity, prices and profits (Laci Rostas). Other wartime activities included the preparation of a weekly diary of economic and social changes and of a register of continuing research in the social sciences.

Towards the end of the war, the broad outlines of the Institute's future research were sketched out and action was taken to secure its financial position for the next few years. It was recognized that some subjects the NIESR had previously studied had been taken over by government departments which could devote much larger resources to them; for example, an Economic Survey of Britain was prepared by civil servants in late 1945 (Cairncross 1985: 320–1). In this sense, ironically, the acceptance by government of the Institute's argument for more professional help from economists had raised questions about the need for such an independent body.

On the other hand, the war had accelerated the extension of statistical studies, many of the wartime recruits left government service as the size of the bureaucracy was run down with the return of peace. Suggestions for new research were also being offered by government departments, academics and businessmen. The Executive Committee decided to concentrate resources on one field with a prospect of achieving definite results and without overlapping too much with university research departments; at the same time it was agreed that work would no longer be commissioned from outside bodies. The chosen field was the structure and productivity of the national economy. Particular attention was devoted to wealth creation and to what could be done to accelerate it (Jones 1988: 40).

During the war, strong links had been established with government departments, as in the case of PEP. The relationship was one of mutual assistance. Statistical investigations on prices, costs, distribution and productivity had been made possible with the help of the Board of Trade at a time when the Attlee Government was at least flirting with the idea of systematic planning; there were Redistribution of Industry Acts in 1945 and 1950, following on from similar legislation in the 1930s (see Chapter 1). Other projects had received support from the Ministries of Health, Labour, Food and Agriculture, the Board of Inland Revenue and the Post Office. These years also saw the strengthening of links with academics both at home and abroad; like PEP, the NIESR was increasingly interested in international trends and comparative studies, and it forged relationships with research institutes in the United States, France, Sweden and the Netherlands. In addition, during the war years the Institute had recruited several talented economists from abroad, notably Thomas Balogh who went on to serve as Economic Advisor to the Cabinet under Harold Wilson (Jones 1988: 40–1; Robinson 1988: 64).

By the late 1940s, most of the research schedule delayed by war conditions had been finished. The work on national income and expenditure (Richard Stone and Deryck Rowe) was by then well advanced and would later appear as six volumes under the joint sponsorship of the NIESR and the Department of Applied Economics at Cambridge (Stone, who when attached to the Economic Section of the War Cabinet Secretariat had devised a new system of national income accounting, acted as general editor, Hennessy 1990: 104). Most of the projects which had begun in 1946 were also nearing completion, notably the inquiries into distribution, the building industry and a study on the lessons of the British war economy. Two new projects began, the first another study on the location of industry (undertaken at the invitation of, and financed by, the Board of Trade in the run up to the second Redistribution of Industry Act) and the second on migration. By this time, however, it was becoming clear to the Executive Committee that the Institute would benefit from the additional impetus of a Director – a post left vacant since the war. In 1949, following Sir Henry Clay's departure as Chairman of the Council, Humphrey Mynors and Austin Robinson were installed as joint Chairmen and set about raising the necessary funds. In 1951, a block grant was awarded by the Rockefeller Foundation for the specific purpose of appointing a Director (an approach to the Treasury having failed because of the need to cut public expenditure in the era of "austerity"). In 1952, Bryan Hopkin took the post on approved employment terms from the civil service – the kind of arrangement that was repeated many times over the coming decades. Over the next few years, the NIESR's research programme covered several new fields and the number of research staff, which had remained static at around ten since 1941, rose to 16 (Jones 1988: 42).

In 1953, the Churchill government made arrangements for the counterpart funds of Marshall Aid to promote increased productivity and stimulate competition. One of these was for the expansion of research into factors affecting economic efficiency. Among the researches financed in this way were several projects undertaken at the NIESR, including a detailed industry-by-industry study of business concentration, a symposium on the structure of British industry, a study measuring the growth of industrial capital and a study of United States' anti-trust legislation. The last of these, written by Alan Neale, went on to become one of the Institute's best-selling publications. Tentative moves were also made in the field of social research, but as in the past, it was proposed to "confine investigations to social problems where the economic aspect, though part only of the relevant considerations, was important" (Jones 1988: 42). An inquiry into the recruitment of industrial and commercial management was developed further, in the hope that this would throw new light on the question of social mobility. A study of costs in the National Health Service (NHS) examined their effect in comparison with alternative health-care systems in other countries.

Since its inception most of the Institute's work had been devoted to the analysis of long-term trends and this emphasis continued after 1953 with new studies on capital and the distribution of industry. In the following year research began on Britain's post-war economic experience. The aim was to study all the factors which had an important bearing on levels of employment, inflation and the balance of payments and (as far as possible) to measure their separate influences. A critical study undertaken by Christopher Dow (on secondment from the Treasury) concluded that government policy had had more success in promoting "full" employment than in accelerating economic growth, but that long-term sustainability of the first policy aim depended on a better record in the second. Dow's subsequent book, *The management of the British economy 1945–60*, published in 1965, was regarded as a standard work in most British universities and sold 13,500 copies (Jones 1988: 43).

The *Economic Review* and other projects: 1955–74

In 1955, the NIESR underwent a major change of direction. Both Dow and Hopkin had worked in the Treasury and had felt that the lack of informed debate about economic policy gave Ministers and civil servants an unhealthy degree of influence on public opinion. The pursuit of full employment policies had led to the development of economic forecasting within government and annual assessments published in the official *Economic Survey* largely set the tone for government policy. Outside government itself, there was no recognised body of expertise, and hence little or no countervailing influence to the government's own; much of the NIESR's work since the war had shadowed research undertaken by civil servants, and it made sense to put this on a more systematic basis. In 1953–4, Dow and Hopkin devised a scheme whereby the NIESR should publish forecasts, report periodically on the state of the economy and seek to underpin such assessments by concentrating resources on research into its behaviour. The proposal received strong support from Sir Robert Hall (later Lord Roberthall), economic adviser to the government, who shared the view that someone outside government should be in a position to challenge the analyses by the Treasury on which policy advice was based. One likely reason for this move was the fact that the Treasury was now beginning to share the NIESR's conviction that Britain's relatively low economic growth needed urgent correction (Lereuz 1975: 87). Hall approached Sir John Woods (the then President of NIESR), and suggested that the Institute might set up a research team on macroeconomic studies and short-term national income forecasting. Hall also promoted the idea that civil servants should work for the Institute on secondment – an idea which promised not only to improve the quality of the NIESR's work, but also to counteract the tendency for economists to become "institutionalized" within the Treasury.

The Executive Committee was, however, anxious that a move into this field of activity should not be at the expense of long-term inquiry. A programme of work was drawn up and a search for financial support began. The Ford Foundation made an award of £100,000 to cover the five-year period from 1957 to 1962, on the understanding that the Institute would seek to increase the income derived from British sources in the meantime and that the programme would be supported entirely by British finance by 1962. By the early 1960s, however, the Institute began to encounter problems with the funding of its regular publication, the *National Institute Economic Review*. It had been decided to price the *Review* at a level sufficient to cover only the costs of printing and distribution in order to achieve maximum circulation (Hall 1969: 4). The Institute had also failed to raise sufficient funds from business sources to replace the Ford grant and the balance needed to meet the costs of the programme. An award of £65,000 from the Rockefeller Foundation to cover the five-year period from 1959 to 1964 was only of limited use; although it included a small sum for work on short-term forecasting and analysis, it was primarily for new projects (Jones 1988: 43).

In 1960, an appeal was made to the Treasury; in the autumn of 1961 it agreed to help. While the Institute and the Treasury agreed that it would be a mistake to use direct government money for the actual work involved in writing the *Review* (because of the doubts this might raise about its independence), in 1961 the Treasury awarded a three-year grant for two research projects, one for a study of long-term growth and expenditure, the other for a study of social expenditure. The relationship between the Treasury and the Institute had become so intimate that the historian of the Macmillan government has called the NIESR only a "semi-autonomous economic forecasting body" – and also dates the Institute's first foundation to 1961 (Lamb 1995: 94 note).

In 1962, Sir Robert Hall succeeded Austin Robinson as chairman of the Institute. In the following year, Hall led a new appeal to business. Covenants and donations from banks, industry and insurance companies which had been falling back since 1959 increased to an annual rate of £34,000. While the new Treasury grants and the extra business money were very helpful, however, they failed to solve the problem of financing the *Review*, which remained a matter of concern in the early 1960s. Indeed, the *Review* could only be produced at all during these early years of publication by drawing on the Institute's own slender resources (Jones 1988: 44).

The first issue of the *Review* had been published in January 1959. Its purpose was to assess current economic developments in Britain and likely trends in the world economy as a whole. The *Review* included an appraisal of events and some indication of the options for policy, rather than the outright recommendation of one particular course of action. In 1961–2, for example, both devaluation (an option which Hall had encouraged the first Attlee Government to take, and had recently been recommending once again in his role of National Economic Adviser) and incomes policy were put forward as measures that might be desirable; according to a prominent financial journalist, the Institute was "howled down" for offering this advice (Brittan 1964: 282). Despite these criticisms of its policy, the Treasury continued to finance the background research programme throughout the 1960s and 1970s, "never appearing to wince at the thought that it might have lent weight to a stick for its own back" – even though on occasion, as in 1964 when it argued that Chancellor Maudling had taken insufficient action to damp down a boom, the Treasury would have had good reason for complaints, because Harold Macmillan had used the Institute's forecasts to press for faster expansion in the previous year's budget (Jones 1988: 44–5; Stewart 1978: 17–18; PREM 11/4202).

In the early 1960s, new projects were launched on the role of innovation and technological development in economic growth in Britain and other European countries, the cost of urban redevelopment, changes in the structure of occupations and the exports of the sterling area. Among other activities, NIESR personnel gave evidence to the Radcliffe Committee on the working of the monetary system. In 1962 its advice to the National Incomes Commission, set up by Harold Macmillan as part of his move towards a more planned economy, led that body to relax its target range for pay increases to 3–3.5 per cent (Jones 1973: 51). The Institute also responded to the new (and short-lived) atmosphere in the Conservative Government by hosting two conferences in 1961 on methods of planning in France, in collaboration with the French planning authorities; the conference was subsequently discussed in a PEP pamphlet (Sandford 1972: 48; see Chapter 1). While the two bodies which had originated in the same decade for very similar reasons remained quite distinct in their functions, this collaboration signified that their approaches to social and economic questions were still complementary 30 years on.

In 1965, Christopher Saunders was succeeded as Director by David Worswick who, unlike his predecessors, had an academic, not a civil service, background. Under his direction from 1965 to 1982, the main emphasis of the Institute's research programme continued to be on the British economy, with occasional projects more broadly related to the world situation as a whole. The size of the full-time research staff fluctuated between 22 and 28 and the number of part-time consultants holding university posts ranged from four and eight. Following a decision by the Executive Committee, the Institute's macroeconomic studies continued to occupy about half of its activity, while its industrial programme was greatly strengthened.

A number of projects outside these two broad programmes were researched. Conferences were held on the themes of an incomes policy for Britain and medium-term forecasting; the Institute's established practice of giving evidence to governmental and parliamentary committees continued (Jones 1988: 46).

At the same time, the Institute was inquiring into ways of improving economic forecasting methods. The need for further improvements in forecasting was obvious, but it is doubtful whether the efforts of the Institute were rewarded in this respect: although one study of 1974 found that the Institute's forecasts for the balance of payments between 1963 and 1971 were actually better than those made in the much better-resourced Treasury, another published in 1970 showed that between 1963 and 1969 these forecasts were still no better than a simple assumption that one year's figures would be replicated in the next (Stewart 1978: 147). As Robert Hall wrily put it, "the hardest thing to forecast is where we are now" (Cairncross 1996a: 36).

The Institute's established practice of discussing the policy implications of its forecasts continued during this period. The perceived need to preserve the UK's competitive advantage after the Labour Government devalued sterling in 1967, and to restrain the growth of incomes thereafter, led to an examination of previous wage and price controls. The Institute was concerned that these seemed to have had at best a temporary effect on inflation. From 1969 to 1972, attention was drawn to the growing gap between output and productive potential and the Institute advocated a series of small injections of purchasing-power to edge the economy back on to the desired path without the risk of overheating. The Institute's views coincided with, and helped to provide arguments for, the growth policy of the Heath Government after 1971 (Cairncross 1996b: 118–19).

In 1970, new work began in the field of industrial structure and competition policy, and was followed by a series of Occasional Papers on the role of mergers and concentration in British industry since 1935. The research projects on social questions undertaken during this period included a study of commonwealth immigration published in 1970, which complemented investigations conducted by PEP in the 1960s (see Chapter 1). This assessed the economic impact of its subject and concluded that no depressing effect on wages and no reduction in output per head could be attributed to immigration; some of the social costs, however, lay in the future and policies to discourage excessive concentrations of the immigrant population would be necessary. In the early 1970s the Institute also conducted studies of poverty and pensions.

In 1971, Frank Blackaby returned to the Institute as Deputy Director and took charge of a study of British economic policy in the 1960s. This continued the work which Christopher Dow's had handled up to 1960 – a time which, from the chastened perspective of 1971, could appear almost as a golden age. The finished study provided a very detailed analysis of the period up to 1974 and covered all aspects of economic policy. An important lesson to be drawn from these years, according to Blackaby's overall (and unsurprising) appraisal, was the damaging effect of frequent policy changes and reversals – a suggestion that Keynes' economic ideas had been corrupted for electoral reasons. A second was the increasing difficulty of combining full employment with a satisfactory balance of payments. Blackaby also discussed the tendency for the British form of collective bargaining to lead to excessive increases in money earnings, and the need to formulate an acceptable incomes policy to deal with this – problems of which the government needed no reminding after the unsuccessful efforts of the Conservative ministry led by Edward Heath. Blackaby concluded that "the problem of devising policies appropriate for a country with a relatively inefficient manufacturing sector and an unreformed pay bargaining system remained unsolved" – of course, this was a difficulty with serious implications for the work of a forecasting organization, as well as for the country as a whole (Blackaby 1978: 652–5; Jones 1988: 49).

Competition, monetarism and decline

The mid-1970s were dominated by the rise in the price of oil – a blow which fell before the lessons of the 1960s could be properly digested. The Institute's programme, particularly the research associated with the *Review*, reflected this crisis, although two separately financed projects were also undertaken. The latter part of the 1970s was associated with the rise of monetarism and with the start of the recession. The *Review*'s dominance gradually declined as other publications, including the London Business School's *Economic Outlook* and the *Cambridge Economic Review*, appeared, supported by different forecasting models or new doctrines. The Institute was now increasingly described as "Keynesian", although by then monetary variables had been introduced into the model. Since the 1960s, it had been recognized that attempts to manage the economy by means of fiscal and credit policies alone had proved inadequate and this had been acknowledged by the *Review*; but the Institute's recognition of the problem could not protect it from the effect of developments which made its profile seem outdated in an utterly changed economic world. Blackaby's book, in particular, could be seen by opponents of "consensus" politics as a cool report on the failure of policies with which the Institute itself was identified. Subscriptions to the *Review*, in common with many other periodicals, began to fall in 1979. The fall occurred among all groups of subscribers, but the greater part of it seems to have been associated with the drive for economy in the public sector; with Britain sliding into its worst recession since the 1930s it may have seemed perverse to allocate even a fraction of departmental budgets to a publication which merely repeated the bad news which staff knew only too well from their daily experiences.

Articles in the *Review* during this period continued to reflect contemporary problems and policies. The oil crisis led to recommendations for a British initiative on an international agreement to recycle the Arab funds and provide aid to the developing countries, but this was a course on which the Heath Government had embarked almost as soon as the first price rise occurred. Warnings were issued about the deflationary consequences of an over-reaction to the rise in the price of oil and the need for action to stop unemployment rising, but the government was more concerned with inflation and introduced drastic expenditure cuts in December 1973. In 1975 Britain saw the deepest recession since the end of the Second World War and the most depressing forecasts since the *Review* began. From 1977, when North Sea oil began to flow, the *Review* was arguing that the exchange rate should be "managed" in order to "preserve non-oil competitiveness if North Sea oil was not to mask a progressive decline in British manufacturing industry". The monetarist-inspired decision by the first Thatcher Government to let the exchange rate rise in order to prevent foreign currency inflows overexpanding the money supply was condemned on the grounds that it would lead to a decline in the competitiveness of exports and greater import penetration (Jones 1988: 53–3). The need for a rule designed to moderate exchange-rate fluctuations was stressed – a question which, arguably, eventually brought about the end of Margaret Thatcher's premiership, then more than six years later the end of the Conservative Government.

In 1976, the Institute launched a series of conferences on important issues of national and international economic policy, an idea derived from the Brookings Panel in Washington and the accompanying Economic Activity Papers. The NIESR series, however, was a more modest operation, partly because it proved impossible to raise a grant large enough to provide the sort of resources involved in the Brookings Papers (Jones 1988: 54). Before 1976 the Institute had only held conferences on an *ad hoc* basis; one-off conferences had included subjects such as incomes policy (1972) and medium-term modelling (1973), both of which led to books. Three titles were now published in a series of Economic Policy Papers, *Deindustrialisation* (edited by Frank Blackaby), *Britain's trade and exchange rate policy* (edited by Robin Major) and *Demand management* (edited by Michael Posner). At about this time, a feeling developed in response to the worsening economic and political situation that there should be more co-operation between research institutes and a decision was taken by the Directors of the NIESR, PEP, and the Royal Institute of International Affairs (RIIA) to intensify their joint activities. This was partly in response to proposals to set up a Centre for Economic and Political Studies in London with the intention of helping "politicians, businessmen, administrators, professional people and scholars . . . make sense of the economic, social and political predicament of the world in the 1970s and 1980s, and of Britain in it" (Dahrendorf 1995: 490). The trouble with such well-intentioned gestures was that at that time the situation was liable to change before specialists could reach a considered opinion – and decision-makers had to act before reflecting.

As inflation fell back from its peak and unemployment rose during the early 1980s, concern about the level of output and the need for some expansion to improve employment prospects continued to be expressed, but the government was set on other courses. The Medium-Term Financial Strategy (MTFS), introduced in Geoffrey

Howe's 1981 budget, came under heavy criticism from the Institute. This was unlikely to endear it to the later Chancellor of the Exchequer and architect of the MTFS, Nigel Lawson, who was also displeased by its forecast of another year of economic standstill in 1983 (Lawson, 1992: 280); it was dangerous territory for the NIESR to tread on when it needed public funding to continue the full range of its activities.

Indeed, further apprehension about finance had already been created when, during the Rothschild enquiry into the SSRC in the early part of 1982, rumours began to circulate that the then Secretary of State for Education, Sir Keith Joseph, wished to abolish the Council. The enquiry's brief was to review the scale and nature of the Council's work in broad terms. Fortunately for economic and social research in general, and the NIESR in particular, its recommendations included one that the SSRC should be neither "dismembered nor liquidated and that its budget should not be reduced in real terms below its 1982–3 level for three years". While the retention of public funds for research in the social sciences was very helpful to the NIESR, however, funds from the private sector failed to match it. The Institute's dependence on public funds had risen and by 1975 was about 80 per cent, divided almost equally between individual government departments and the SSRC. The Institute's total income in real terms was nearly 10 per cent less in 1982 than it had been in 1975–6. While costs had been cut in many areas, however, its research programme had been well maintained (Jones 1988: 52).

As we saw in Chapter 1, existing research institutes based in London were concerned that the proposal for what became known as a "British Brookings" would have diverted both limited research funds and staff away from them. In the event, a much more modest proposal emerged from these discussions in the form of the setting up of the Technical Change Centre (TCC). The latter was wound up in 1987 when the Economic and Social Research Council (ESRC, formerly SSRC) decided not to renew its grant. The Directors of the NIESR, PSI and the RIIA agreed to consider the possibilities for cooperation in research programmes, meetings, conferences and publications. The main outcome was a decision to widen the former's series of economic policy conferences (under the general editorship of Frank Blackaby) to cover major policy issues in which all three institutes would have some degree of interest, even if for one or two of them it was only a minor interest. A grant was raised from the Nuffield Foundation and the series, entitled Joint Studies in Public Policy, was launched in 1979. By the end of 1982, seven conferences had been held and six books published. Topics ranged from slower growth in the western world to the constitution of Northern Ireland; all were on subjects of current policy interest and debate (Jones 1988: 55).

In June 1982, David Worswick retired and was succeeded as director of the Institute by Andrew Britton, formerly of the Treasury. Under Britton's leadership, the main emphasis continued to be on the British economy, but the research programme relating to the world economic situation in general, and the European Community in particular, was also strengthened and, new projects were designed to explain various aspects of recent economic developments. However, the funding problems continued; negotiations concerning the renewal of the ESRC grant in 1983 resulted in a very modest increase in real terms. The 1986 round of discussions with the ESRC resulted in a substantial reduction in the grant for 1987–91, as the Council decided it would no longer finance the domestic economic forecasts published in the *Review*. Even so, the NIESR received the largest grant, awarded in the face of keen competition as most research bodies faced cut-backs.

The NIESR continued to be concerned with the relationship between economic variables such as national output, employment, interest rates and inflation. The Institute's econometric model was also constantly updated in the light of new or revised data. Given the rise in unemployment, a focus on the labour market was again deemed appropriate. Several studies of wage determination were conducted and a variety of different approaches to the modelling of employment investigated. By the mid-1980s, there was renewed interest in the balance of payments and new work was undertaken on both the import and export of manufactured goods, as well as on the determination of the exchange rate. With ESRC support, the Institute embarked on a new approach to world economic forecasting and the analysis of possible policy cooperation between the major countries. Coverage of the world economic situation in the *Review* continued and the Institute participated with other international bodies in discussion of the steps necessary to restore a better balance of trade between the United States and the other major industrial countries (Jones 1988: 55).

The *Review* continued to assess the domestic and world economies and, throughout 1983 and 1984, to search for signs of recovery. Only modest growth was revealed, which was deemed insufficient to reduce unemployment. It concluded that the outlook remained poor, and that unemployment would continue to rise for some time; without active reflation, the rate would stay well above the post-war average. With concern about the need to improve employment prospects in the private sector to absorb the increase in the labour force, the *Review* entered the debate on the relationship between employment and real wages (Jones 1988: 56). Early in 1985, it was noted that the conflict between low inflation and high unemployment appeared more acute than ever and the MTFS was again criticized as too narrow and restrictive. The earlier work on exchange-rate fluctuations led to a study of the European Exchange Rate Mechanism (ERM) as an alternative basis for economic stability to the MTFS – an analysis which Nigel Lawson was beginning to share at just this time. Forecasts for the balance of payments for 1986 revealed a projected deficit for the first time since 1979 and a warning was sounded about Britain's future trade performance and the importance of reversing the decline in manufacturing industry. The need for measures to strengthen the supply side of the economy, particularly through training, retraining and investment, was increasingly emphasized. The fall in unemployment in 1986 was welcomed, but it was argued that this had occurred as much in spite of the monetarism enshrined in the MTFS as because of it – a view often echoed since (Jones 1988: 56; Smith 1987). The problem for the NIESR at that time was that being proved right was not enough under a government which was reluctant to countenance "evidence" which ran counter to its ideological programme.

The Institute's programme on comparative productivity concentrated its research effort on the machinery and skills of the labour force in a number of comparable European countries. The same situation was observed of Britain "lagging behind" her international competitors in training in these industries; the rigours of the market-place might make labour more docile, but it could not conjure skills out of nowhere. This work attracted some public interest (it was featured in a Channel 4 television documentary). The research team also examined the foundations laid by schooling systems to discover which aspects of education might contribute to differences in subsequent vocational qualifications and thereby influence industrial productivity and living standards. In 1986, the Department of Education and Science (DES) became interested in the policy implications of this research and in 1987 Sig Prais and Hilary Steedman were invited to join the Government's working groups on the national curriculum on mathematics and assessment methods respectively. After issuing a note of dissent to the interim report on mathematics, the former resigned as he was not satisfied that the issues were being tackled adequately. Prais was still researching standards of mathematics teaching in Britain for the Institute in the mid-1990s.

Studies in other areas of current concern were also undertaken in the 1980s. Perhaps the most topical were several on youth unemployment and public expenditure. The aim of work on the former was to describe and explain the upward trend in youth unemployment in Britain since 1950 and to compare it with the situation in France and Germany. A special study of retail distribution was undertaken, designed to discover why so many jobs formerly done by girls were now being done by adult women. Malcolm Levitt joined the Institute on secondment from the Treasury to initiate a series of linked studies on public expenditure, including a comparison of its past growth in Britain compared with other OECD countries and detailed studies of the growth, efficiency and productivity of spending on defence, education, health, law and order and social security. Comparisons were also made of systems for managing and measuring productivity in certain government departments and private firms (Jones 1988: 57). In 1983, Christopher Dow returned to the NIESR as a Visiting Fellow to lead a research project on major issues in British macroeconomic policy since 1965, with particular emphasis on the role of monetary policy.

Other projects undertaken during the 1980s included a comparison of international energy policies, a study of macroeconomic policies in the major European countries, one on the British economy in the long term, consideration of the types of protection arrangements afforded by the European Community and a study of import penetration into the British consumer goods market. Work also began on output and productivity changes in the service sector, particularly financial services where growth had been especially rapid. A project on the prospects for employment in Britain, led by David Worswick, examined the link between real wages and employment, the influence of industrial change, regional, occupational and industrial differences and the effects of macroeconomic policy. Two further projects were undertaken which inclined more towards the "social" side of the Institute's work. The first examined trends in employment after the age of 55 and in particular the trend towards earlier retirement. The second project examined the economic aspects of demographic change, including the effects of policy changes on the birth rate and the economic circumstances of one-parent families, as well as consideration of the ways in which society can support them.

Summary and conclusions

When the first steps were taken to establish the NIESR in 1935 and 1936, it was recognized that it was an experiment. One of the original aims was in fact abandoned after the Second World War when the Executive Committee stopped organizing and financing studies outside the Institute. The early programme was an ambitious one, considering that it attempted to cover ground which the far better resourced Whitehall departments were beginning to tackle, and many of the subjects chosen for research were raised to a new importance by the war. Some of the measurement studies were then taken over by government departments, prompting the NIESR to move into other fields of inquiry. The NIESR took advantage of the new fashion for a more professionalized approach to policy-making fostered by the Second World War by extending its own programme and adapting it to post-war problems. The strong links established with government departments during the war engendered a respect for the Institute's work which was retained even when, as later with the *Review*, the NIESR was sometimes critical of government policy. The links forged with industry and the City also helped to strengthen the Institute's work and the majority of firms approached on special inquiries were ready and willing to cooperate. However, the NIESR should be seen as falling within the contract research organization category of think-tank (see Introduction);

it proved highly adept at winning funds for its research, but its agenda was shaped by its knowledge of the sort of project likely to attract funding (hence, for example, the exhaustive efforts to design an economic model which would rival, or preferably surpass, the Treasury's own forecasting methodology).

While many other research institutes and other bodies are now engaged in economic forecasting, the NIESR initially led the way in a number of detailed statistical studies of topics related to economic efficiency. A special feature of much of its work has been the analysis of British economic performance, problems and policies in the light of comparable experience elsewhere and this has arguably helped to encourage the thought – fairly heretical given the political tendency to assert that "British is best" – that lessons could be learned from experiences abroad. The NIESR was the first body to produce and publish economic forecasts and visitors came from other countries to spend time in London and learn about its aims, methods and organization.

Estimating the influence of the NIESR over government policy is subject to the usual qualifications (see Introduction), but some tentative conclusions may be suggested. As in the case of PEP, the impetus for setting up the Institute clearly came from the economic crisis of the early 1930s. After the generally unhappy experience of the EAC, it was natural for some economists to support the foundation of an expert body independent of Whitehall – and the iron grip of the Treasury. From the early 1930s onwards the case for specialist economic advice was increasingly accepted by governments – to the extent that, during the war, it was natural for ministers to look for recruits in the universities and the emerging think-tanks. With the return of peace the old Whitehall culture re-established itself, and the great majority of economists left the civil sevice. There was a difference, however; the importance of economic statistics and forecasting now seemed to have been established beyond dispute. The recruitment of Robert Hall to the NIESR in 1962 is a measure of the Institute's success up to that point – although Hall had been an unorthodox civil service Mandarin in that he consistently regarded growth as more important than a rigid interpretation of sound finance.

In 1964 Samuel Brittan could write of the friendly rivalry which existed between the Treasury and the NIESR, claiming that "the

Treasury economists and the National Institute have more in common with each other than with any other group of laymen or economists in the whole of the country". However, Brittan also classified the NIESR as a representative of the "economic left". While this was rather a cavalier description from someone who later argued that the terms Right and Left were at best irrelevant to serious political debate – in fact, like PEP, NIESR is best described as a progressive liberal body – this perception was bound to cause trouble once a less tolerant right-wing government came into office in 1979 (Brittan 1964: 37, 36; Brittan 1968). A new low-point in relations was reached in the early 1980s, when the NIESR, which generally favoured growth, confronted a government which had committed itself to a policy which deepened an already serious recession.

Although the Institute was founded at a time when Keynes' economic ideas aroused deep controversy, by the end of the Second World War (if not earlier) it reflected the general acceptance of Keynes within the economic profession; its forecasting work was held to be an essential element of the management of demand. As such, it suffered from the problems encountered by all supporters of the Keynesian analysis from the 1960s onwards: the supposed failure of planning, the oil crisis, and the Thatcherite counter-revolution. This history goes to the heart of the question about the Institute's influence. Before the oil shock Michael Stewart proclaimed that "Western governments practise Keynesianism continuously", but he was a highly optimistic disciple (Stewart 1972: 296). Instead of following Keynes, successive governments pursued a form of bastardized or electoral Keynesianism, resulting in the familiar stop–go pattern of economic development. Even the kind of short-term advice which the Institute began to proffer in its *Reviews* after the war was liable to be ignored by governments persuaded, because of the imperative to retain power at general elections, to eschew necessary long-term decisions in favour of the narrowly expedient. As a general rule, only when the advice coincided with the existing intentions of decision-makers was it heeded (cf. Skidelsky 1996). In these circumstances accurate economic forecasting both from within and from outside Whitehall – already, in the nature of human activity, a hazardous undertaking – became an impossibility. The Institute could take account of past mistakes when forecasting the future, but could not build into its calculations a reliable measure of governmental errors to come – or even those which were currently happening. Thus its *Reviews*, rather than fulfilling their intended role as aids to ministerial decision-making, could seem much more like points of contrast between reality and what could have been. At least until the advent of Thatcherite Government these eloquent rebukes were delivered in the Keynesian language understood by Ministers and civil servants. In its forecast for 1983 the Institute gave unpleasant news to a Chancellor who, having discarded his youthful Keynesian views, took special enjoyment from proclamations of his new monetarist faith whether or not it was producing the results he wanted, and it was surely no coincidence that its public funding dropped at about this time. As early as 1981, a distinguished commentator was writing of the NIESR as "a bastion of Keynesian analysis" whose "influence has considerably diminished" (Gamble 1981: 245).

Like PEP/PSI, however, the NIESR has survived. Indeed, it was in a healthy condition by the mid-1990s; over the year 1995–6 its research income rose by 18 per cent (to over £1.1 million), and it yielded an operating surplus of more than £50,000. The Institute's annual report noted that since 1978 the proportion of income derived from public grants had fallen from 71 per cent to 31 per cent – a notable achievement, even if the search for outside funding was originally forced on the NIESR by an unsympathetic government. Since the 1997 election the Institute has returned to an environment where competing voices, rather than the monetarist monotone of the 1980s, can hope for an audience within government, and its views are likely to be heard again – if not acted upon when they conflict with perceived electoral needs. This was starkly illustrated in November 1997, when the Institute warned that the New Labour Government was pursuing a mistaken policy by relying on interest rates, rather than increased taxation, to control inflation. The advice, backed though it was by the findings of other groups and the protests of exporters hit by a high exchange-rate, could hardly make much impact on a government which felt that it had won power largely through its promise to keep tax levels as it had found them – whether or not the responsible ministers might privately agree with the Institute's analysis.

In terms of the wider climate of opinion the NIESR's contribution, like that of PEP/PSI, is more difficult to assess. An insider has estimated that by 1988 the results of its research had appeared in some 80 books and more than 200 articles in the *Review* and other journals (Jones 1988: 58). However, it has to be questioned whether all of this has done much to elevate understanding of economic policy among the wider public. Since the early 1930s the level of economic debate in Britain has probably improved – a cynic would say that at least the sophistication of party distortion has increased – and for this the NIESR must take some of the credit. This success can at least in part be measured by imitation, and for some years the Institute has been only one of many purveyors of economic data and forecasts. Notable among its rivals is the Institute for Fiscal Studies (IFS), which seems rather more media friendly.

Yet this praise must be balanced by recent events from which the Institute itself did not emerge unscathed. During the 1980s, despite its partial reliance on government funding, the NIESR did point out weaknesses in key government policies, including the much-vaunted MTFS. But although the effects of monetarism were unmissable even to those in the more affluent south-east, the first Thatcher Government stuck to its stated course. It would be reasonable to suggest that the kind of criticism levied by the 364 economists who protested against the 1981 budget was not echoed in anything like such a literate form by the general public, and that even opponents who thought that something called "monetarism" was to blame for Britain's economic plight were not very clear about what this entailed (see Chapters 3–6). It may be harsh to blame the Institute (along with other representatives of the Keynesian view) for failing to translate complex economic matters into a language which the average person could readily comprehend – or want to read in the first place – especially when its arguments had to compete with party propaganda and the economy was not the only issue of interest to voters. But the failure still ought to be recorded when discussing an Institute which has always tried to ensure that economic decisions are taken in the light of the best available evidence, and has suffered along with the economy from dramatic policy reversals usually dictated by the need to bribe ill-informed voters (see Blackaby 1978: 652). There are some signs that the NIESR is no longer very interested in reaching wider public opinion; in the Institute's Annual Report for 1996, under the heading of "Dissemination", the Director Martin Weale only mentioned efforts to bring research to the attention of academics, businessmen and policy-makers. Overall, it is safe to conclude that the NIESR has fulfilled the list of functions set out when it was founded, but these stated intentions were modest and presumably the founder-members of the Institute would have hoped for a more significant legacy nearly 60 years later.

CHAPTER 3

The Institute of Economic Affairs

Origins

As we have seen in earlier chapters, the argument for greater state intervention in economic and social affairs gained progressively more ground in Britain in the years before, during and immediately after the Second World War, although this mood was tempered by a deep-rooted resistance to the idea of central planning. In academic circles, the arguments between advocates of economic liberalism and those who favoured a more significant degree of state intervention tilted in favour of the latter, although there were still outposts of dissent, notably at the London School of Economics. Certainly the perception that Keynesian ideas held sway meant that the remaining economic liberals became increasingly disillusioned with the direction of policy; it was natural for them to exaggerate the extent to which collectivist solutions had been continued after the war. Friedrich Hayek, for instance, the most important thinker among members of this group (Gamble 1996), attempted to highlight his own fears for the future in *The road to serfdom*, published in 1944. Hayek argued that Britain had begun to move towards totalitarianism in the early years of the twentieth century; the tendency had been much more gradual than in Germany or Russia, but nevertheless "the history of th[o]se countries in the years before the rise of the totalitarian system showed few features with which we are not familiar". In particular, Hayek identified an increase in government economic intervention from the early part of the century, and argued that talk of freedom without economic liberty was meaningless.

Interestingly, Hayek singled out 1931 as the year in which the British government finally abandoned the road of freedom; as we have seen (in Chapters 1 and 2), almost simultaneously the advocates of planning were thinking of setting up independent groups to press for more state action, because they despaired of the inertia in Whitehall (Hayek 1962: 9). There are few better examples of ideological commitment causing different individuals to view the political scene in wholly contrasting ways.

The road to serfdom had little impact on the result of the British General Election of 1945; as Hayek's admirer Baroness Thatcher noted many years later, his views were "unusual and unpopular" (Thatcher 1995: 51). Winston Churchill, whose notorious attempt to establish a connection between Attlee's mild socialism and the Nazi Gestapo was attributed by some to Hayek's influence, later told the Austrian that his nightmare vision of totalitarianism was not relevant to the British context (Addison 1992: 383). Having played a leading role as a Liberal minister during the period which Hayek identified as the beginning of the end for traditional British liberties, Churchill was always an unlikely admirer of either the book or its author. Nevertheless Hayek's analysis was shared by a small number of economic liberal academics and politicians, who were convinced that freedom was under attack and that there was an urgent need to launch a counterattack on the battlefield of ideas. As one polemical writer (whose work was also read by the young Margaret Thatcher) put it at the time, "the Socialists have taught the people to despise liberty, order and impartial justice" (Brogan 1947: 219). This judgement typifies the strange mixture of disdain and respect with which market liberals viewed their opponents in the post-war years; the ideas of socialism were repugnant, but at the same time they apparently had the power to make free-born Britons sign away their birth-right. Hayek's own apparent confusion on this issue is typified by an article he wrote in 1949; in the space of two pages he first describes intellectuals as mostly "people who understand nothing in particular especially well", then admits that "the typical intellectual is today more likely to be a socialist the more he is guided by good will and intelligence" (Hayek 1967: 182, 184).

Hayek himself thought that "it is no exaggeration to say that once the more active part of the intellectuals [in a given society] have been converted to a set of beliefs, the process by which these become generally accepted is almost automatic and irresistible" (Hayek 1967: 182). This process occurs because "the more active" intellectuals shape what Hayek called the "climate of opinion" – "essentially a set of very general preconceptions by which the intellectual judges the importance of new facts and opinions". Whether or not Hayek's view of intellectuals was wholly consistent, his task as he saw it was clear – to convert as large a number as possible of the more "active" spirits, after which the change in the "climate of opinion" would be "automatic and irresistible". In this view Hayek broadly followed the great legal philosopher A.V. Dicey, who had written in 1905 of the process whereby the ideas of a brilliant individual would be taken up by "preachers of truth" who would, over time, convert the great part of the nation. Ideas on their own would not be enough, however; Dicey went on to suggest that "a change of belief arises, in the main, from the occurrences of circumstances which incline the majority of the world [sic] to hear with favour theories which, at one time, men of common sense derided as absurdities, or distrusted as paradoxes" (Dicey 1905: 23).

Among Hayek's readers and admirers was a young RAF pilot, Antony Fisher, whose "great moment of personal revelation" came when he read a condensed version of *The road to serfdom* in the *Reader's Digest* in 1945. Fisher was born in 1915 and educated at Eton, then Trinity College, Cambridge. During the war, he had become concerned about the perceived intellectual advance and political acceptance of socialism. After reading *The road to serfdom*, he decided to seek out the author himself in order to ascertain what Hayek thought would be the best possible course of action. Hayek advised that entry into politics would prove to be a waste of his time and effort, and suggested to Fisher that he might establish a scholarly research institute, in order to start the process of changing the climate of opinion (Cockett 1994: 123–4).

Although Fisher had insufficient funds to create such an institute at the time of his meeting with Hayek at the LSE in 1947, the idea did not leave him. In 1949, for instance, he heard a speech at a Conservative Political Centre (CPC) weekend conference in Sussex given by Ralph Harris (Cockett 1994: 134). Fisher was impressed and during discussions with Harris the idea of an institute was raised. While Harris went away to teach economics at the University of St Andrews, Fisher continued to work hard at building up his farming business, "began his early political campaigning against the bastions of agricultural subsidies, the British Egg Marketing Board and the Milk Marketing Board, and joined his local Conservative Party association" (Cockett 1994: 124). In 1952, his financial fortunes were transformed, following a visit to the United States to examine the work of the Foundation for Economic Education (FEE). During the trip, he was shown a new farming method at Ithaca, New York. Fisher, impressed by both the revolutionary method of broiler chicken-farming and the work of the FEE was thus "equipped with both the means and the method of establishing a research institute when he returned back to England" (Muller 1996: 91).

For practical advice on establishing such an institute, Fisher sought out Oliver Smedley, an activist for the cause of economic liberalism who was himself running a number of free-trade campaigns at that time. Fisher and Smedley had first met at an organization called (somewhat paradoxically) the Society of Individualists. Unlike Fisher, Smedley belonged to the Liberal Party, but was growing increasingly disillusioned with it. Hence, Smedley was in a highly receptive frame of mind when Fisher approached him with the idea of establishing a research institute to examine the theory and practical application of economic liberalism. Indeed, Smedley was not the only disgruntled Liberal attracted to Fisher's cause. Other former Liberals, including Arthur Seldon and two LSE academics, Jack Wiseman and Alan Peacock, had also become increasingly dispirited with the political course taken by the Party. In 1956, Jo Grimond took over as leader; he was associated with the Radical Reform Group, which was determined that the party should not "retreat from social liberalism but to propose ways in which the institutions and policies of the welfare state and the managed economy could be improved and strengthened" (Gamble 1983: 200). We saw earlier (see Chapter 1) that the Liberal Party of the 1930s was convinced of the need for an interventionist state, although it had little prospect of returning to power. Indeed, given that the Liberal governments of Campbell-Bannerman and Asquith had introduced radical social reforms in the first two decades of the century, the Liberal Party had not been a congenial home for those who opposed extensive state intervention for at least 50 years by the time the IEA was set up; Sir Ernest Benn, the free-market propagandist and co-founder of the Society of Individualists, had given up hope and abandoned

THE INSTITUTE OF ECONOMIC AFFAIRS

the party in 1929, when Lloyd George was campaigning to "conquer unemployment" through government action (Greenleaf 1983: 300). Although Grimond himself would much later embrace the economic liberal views he had opposed in the 1950s, in the short-term his victory was taken as a sign that the party could not be hijacked and turned back into the attractive vehicle for hard-nosed businessmen which it had once been.

The Conservative Party was not much more promising. At the time that the IEA was founded it was in power, and although it had accelerated the retreat from state control which had begun under Labour, it was clearly not about to abandon the economy to the free play of market forces. Any chance of infiltrating the party at this stage was precluded by the fact that the new type of Tory MP bore no relation to relics of the pre-war era like Sir Waldron Smithers and Sir Herbert Williams; rather, the most promising newcomers were people like the members of the "One Nation" group, which included Iain Macleod and Edward Heath. These MPs, first elected in 1950, supported free enterprise but also approved of the welfare state, and although they disagreed with nationalization, their strictures were based on practical considerations, not the kind of ideological fervour cultivated by the IEA. If they read *The road to serfdom* at all, the book would hardly have triggered off in them the sort of personal revelation granted to Antony Fisher. The Institute would have to wait at least until another generation of Tories entered Parliament. Too young to have experienced at first hand pre-war conditions and the success of state action during the war, they would only remember their impatience during the prolonged period of rationing.

With the Labour Party an obvious non-starter, the IEA had independence from partisan commitment thrust on it by circumstances, as in the previous example of PEP (see Chapter 1). Given that in the election of May 1955 the two main parties won more than 96 per cent of the vote between them (Liberal support rose from 0.2 to 2.7 per cent), it was natural for the proponents of economic liberalism to assume that the whole political world was against them, and to lump all their opponents together under the collective title of socialists even though this was an accurate label for only a small minority. The oppositional spirit born out of this situation has remained part of the IEA's ethos ever since. The feeling of upholding a theory when everyone else seems to reject it can be a highly effective bond, even for inveterate individualists. With the recruitment of Oliver Smedley, the economic liberals gained two crucial advantages; he allowed the new institute to make use of the accommodation and facilities of his own organization, Investment and General Management Services (IGMS) Limited, and he suggested the eye-catching name for the new institute (Cockett 1994: 130). Hence, in November 1955, a legal, charitable entity called the Institute of Economic Affairs was formally created.

Early days

The motives and aims of the IEA, then, had been developed over a ten-year gestation period. Smedley and Fisher were drawing on Hayek's advice that effecting a change in the intellectual climate was imperative, but that the process would be long and drawn out. Both saw it as vital to ignore the immediate political situation and to assert the Institute's independence in other ways. In the years that followed, the IEA drew most of its core funding from a large number of corporate and individual donors. By diversifying its sources of financial support in this way, the Institute attempted to "reduce the risk of client backlash over particular research results" (Ricci 1993: 20). Avoiding the accusation of being locked to one particular vested interest through the diversification of support was important for the self-image of the group, and it also enabled the IEA to survive when Fisher ran into financial difficulties in the 1960s (Muller 1996: 92–3).

On 9 November 1955 the three founding trustees of the Institute, Fisher, Smedley and a colleague of Smedley's called J.S. Harding, met to sign the Trust Deed and Rules of the Institute. An Advisory Council was soon established and consisted of the three founding trustees of the Institute, Lord Granchester (formerly Sir Arnold Suenson-Taylor), three LSE economists (George Schwartz, Graham Hutton and Colin Clark), the financial journalist Sir Oscar Hobson and Professor Eric Nash (Cockett 1994: 132).

The reaction of the outside world to the new institute was muted. Only one MP, for instance, appears to have taken an interest in its formation, namely Major Freddie Gough, a neighbour of Fisher's in Sussex (Cockett 1994: 132–3). Public awareness had, however, already begun to grow by July 1955, four months before the IEA's formal creation, with the publication of the first pamphlet commissioned under the Institute's auspices, *The free convertibility of sterling* by George Winder. Fisher had wisely commissioned an academic economist to write about his specialized subject, in order to ensure academic credibility, and had given a copy of the completed pamphlet to a sympathetic journalist, Henry Hazlitt. Hazlitt was a founder-member of the Mont Pelerin Society, an international group formed in 1947 to propagate Hayek's ideas (Hartwell 1995: 40). A favourable review by Hazlitt in *Newsweek*'s Business Tides columns ensured that the pamphlet attracted more attention than would otherwise have been the case; this was an important lesson which the Institute never forgot (Muller 1996: 93).

If the IEA was to survive, however, some permanent staff had to be found and the search began for a Director of the Institute, initially on a part-time basis. Fisher appears to have decided already on the person he wanted and wrote to Ralph Harris to offer him the job of Director. This turned out to be an inspired choice, although at the time it might have seemed that Harris lacked crucial qualities for the job; he had recently written a sympathetic study of R.A. Butler, in which he had expressed the view that compromise "is the hallmark of the civilized and sensitive mind" (Harris 1956: 117). After several reassurances of the seriousness of the offer and the initial success of the IEA, Harris accepted, and was duly appointed on 5 July 1956. Harris' contacts in the academic world, formed during his time at St Andrews, as well as his journalistic experience on the *Glasgow Herald*, were helpful in giving the Institute intellectual credibility and winning financial support. As a partner to Harris, an editorial director was sought who would oversee the Institute's publications programme. Arthur Seldon was recommended for this job by Lord Granchester in 1956 and began to work at the IEA the following year. Seldon had graduated with a First in economics from the LSE, where he was taught by Lionel Robbins, Arnold Plant and, most importantly, by Hayek. Seldon believed that the cause of economic liberalism would be best served by applying economic analysis with academic rigour, but "without creating confusion and incomprehension through needless economic jargon"; for the purposes of the Institute, this was the perfect combination (Muller 1996: 94).

89

The first publication of the IEA under the directorships of Harris and Seldon was *Pensions in a free society* (1957). Written by Seldon, and at a time when the Labour Party, then in opposition, was planning an extension of the state pension scheme, the pamphlet argued for a gradual winding up of that scheme and for its eventual replacement by personal and private savings for retirement. The pamphlet highlighted the strategy of the IEA, at least until the 1970s, of focusing on microeconomic issues rather than dealing with the prevailing macroeconomic consensus as a whole. This strategy enabled specialist economists to pursue particular fields of interest with academic rigour, as well as exposing the economic problems of the day to market analysis and offering solutions (Muller 1996: 94).

By ensuring that its publications, although written by academic economists for the most part, appeared in a style and format that made them accessible to students, as well as academics, journalists and politicians, and by producing pamphlets that were cheap and quite short – about 10 to 15 thousand words, on average – the IEA clearly intended its work to appeal to as wide a market as possible. Apart from Hayek and Friedman, few of the academic economists published by the IEA were natural writers. Indeed, as Cockett has pointed out, it was Seldon who, more often than not, made their work "intelligible to a non-academic readership" (Cockett 1994: 142).

The early publications of the IEA, then, were intended to play a role in debates on current issues of economic policy. For the most part, early pamphlets such as *Pensions in a free society* and *Advertising in a free society* were written in-house, as it was often difficult to find outside authors and contributors. However, after IEA staff had helped to organize the 1959 conference of the Mont Pelerin Society, this problem was alleviated (Desai 1994: 46). In fact, the 1959 conference (held in Oxford) proved how difficult co-operation between principled individualists could be; it helped to provoke a furious row within the Society, which nearly brought it to an end. But the IEA was backed by Hayek, and having found itself on the winning side its profile among international free-marketeers was raised (Hartwell 1995: 107).

Purity of sectarian belief, Desai argues, was important to the IEA and there was "an elaborate selectivity exercised in the choice of authors and topics" (Desai 1994: 46). Desai's account of how this process of "elaborate selectivity" worked in practice represents an important counterweight to the claim rehearsed by insiders (and reiterated by outside observers such as Muller) that "the IEA itself holds no corporate view" (Muller 1996: 89). According to Desai, editorial policy at the IEA

> consisted, first of all, in finding someone who largely, if not entirely, agreed with them on the topic in question. They were then required to submit a summary of the ground to be covered in their paper and the approach. Members of the Council of Advisors read this and offered comments and suggestions about the content and approach, which they sought to have "built into" the paper. This in Seldon's experience always succeeded in moving the paper considerably closer to the IEA view. There were only two occasions Seldon could think of when the difference of opinion remained so great that the work could not be accepted for publication. The preface to each publication also noted the IEA's own differences with the text. Thus what the IEA succeeded in doing was to channel and combine, in a concentrated and identifiable form, what would otherwise have been more disparate interventions from a great diversity of theoretical directions without a readily apparent ideological connection between them (Desai 1994: 46).

Moreover, the IEA's self-conscious focus on microeconomics and apparent disdain for macroeconomics can also be seen as having acted as what Desai describes as "a filter for uncongenial views" (Desai 1994: 46–7). The process of filtration was also assisted by the IEA's preference for clear prose; Seldon's insistence that "economics is really all common sense", and that it may without difficulty be couched in everyday language, meant "not merely good written English, but also that what was not commonsensical from a certain perspective could be ruled out" (Desai 1994: 46–7). While this strategy certainly did not mean that all IEA authors trotted out an identical line – indeed, they scarcely could, since as events in the 1980s proved, even those who agreed on the virtues of the free market found it easy to argue among themselves – there were definite limits to what the IEA regarded as "commonsensical". As one contributor to an IEA volume wryly noted, there was "a dearth of easily identifiable socialist economists among authors" (Culyer 1981: 106).

The 1960s

In 1960, the Institute published its first Hobart Paper, Basil Yamey's *Resale price maintenance and shoppers' choice*, which, it has been claimed, had "a direct and immediate political impact" (Cockett 1994: 145). Yamey, a South-African born Professor at the LSE where he had studied, like Arthur Seldon, under Arnold Plant, argued for the abolition of Resale Price Maintenance (RPM), which, by fixing prices in shops, prevented large retail outlets from undercutting many smaller, so-called corner shops. Yamey argued that a free market in shop prices would save consumers £180 million per year and that prices would fall by 5 per cent. What really caught the headlines, however, was his estimate that the abolition of RPM would save every person in the country £3 10s per year. Yamey's paper was widely reviewed in both the national press and trade magazines. In common with previous IEA publications, the pamphlet was timed to coincide with a period of public debate on the subject to ensure maximum impact (Cockett 1994: 146).

RPM was, in fact, abolished by the Home Government in 1964. Edward Heath, the president of the Board of Trade who had driven through the legislation, at an IEA lunch the same year indicated that the Institute was an important source of inspiration for the policy (Muller 1996: 94). As Cockett has argued, "if Antony Fisher's story of Heath telling him . . . that the troubled passage of the legislation to abolish RPM was all Yamey's fault is to be believed, then Yamey could at least claim some credit for this small step towards a free market" (Cockett 1994: 146). Yet the abolition of RPM had been kicked around Whitehall since Harold Wilson's post-war stint at the Board of Trade – ironically the very time when, according to IEA propaganda, collectivist attitudes were taking over and endangering British freedoms. In the run-up to Heath's legislation (which caused a tremendous row within the Conservative Party and is often blamed for the party's defeat in the 1964 general election), a private member's bill on the subject had been introduced, and Heath's predecessor at Trade, Frederick Erroll, had been slapped down when he had floated the idea of abolition. Heath, who was determined to revive Harold Macmillan's drive for modernization (which had flagged under Macmillan's successor Home), had a clear political incentive to adopt the measure itself, whatever its exact origins (Lamb 1995: 214–6). In his paper to the Cabinet of 9 January 1964, he referred to the arguments of the Consumer Council as a factor in helping him to reach his decision; the Chancellor, Reginald Maudling, mentioned a long-standing Monopolies Commission investigation when voicing his support for Heath. Nowhere in the Cabinet records does the name of the IEA appear (PREM 11/5154; CAB 129/116/1). The story of this episode is so tangled that it would be difficult to trace the legislation back to the IEA with any confidence.

For reasons that have been explored earlier in this book (see Chapter 1), assessments of the influence of think-tanks on political thinking and the policy process are inherently problematic. Indeed, in the case of the IEA, it has been argued that the task of evaluating the extent of its impact on government, its thinking and its decision-making is especially difficult, given that the Institute "engaged less in offering practical solutions and means of implementation to government and rather sought to change the climate in which government thinking was taking place" (Muller 1996: 95). The Institute's main audience was (and continues to be) not so much people with day-to-day policy-making responsibilities as those who help to frame the context in which policy-making takes place, namely "those who teach and are taught and those whose opinions 'count' – the politically-aware intelligentsia" (Culyer 1981: 117). At the same time, however, recent research does provide some insight into both the response of government officials to the work undertaken by the IEA in the early 1960s and the alleged weaknesses which were present, at least in the early part of the Institute's history, in many of the publications produced (Muller 1996: 96).

From the outset, the IEA had commissioned a number of re-search reports, based on empirical research and economic analysis and leading to recommendations for policy. In 1959, for instance, a survey of large companies was undertaken by Harris and a new recruit to the IEA, Michael Solly. A more interesting and, in many ways, more important such report, however, was *Choice in Welfare*, published in 1963. The findings of market research, the report argued, demonstrated that "a majority of the adult male population favoured a switch of public welfare towards a concentration of benefits for those who need them and a development of private alternatives for those who wish them" (Muller 1996: 95). The report, it seems, was read in August 1963 by the senior civil servant Richard "Otto" Clarke, who, together with John Boyd-Carpenter, the financial secretary to the Treasury, established an inquiry to discuss its findings. While the latter advised a meeting held on 24 October 1963 that he was not keen on the report's conclusions, Clarke was sympathetic to the idea that people could and should pay for the use of public services. The reaction of several *departments*, however, was hostile. The Department of Health, for instance (which the economic liberal and friend of the IEA Enoch Powell left in October 1963) did not even bother to provide a written response to the report, while the Education Department dismissed it as running counter to "half a century of history" (cited by Muller 1996: 96).

It was, however, the Treasury itself, usually the most keen of all government departments to reduce expenditure, which produced the most devastating critique of the report, suggesting that, in general, the universal benefit system was electorally popular, fair and efficient. The report, it argued, also failed to take account of the danger of "free riders" in that, if individuals were allowed to opt out of the national insurance scheme, some would probably be unable to contribute anything, and would continue to rely on the state scheme. The Treasury also argued that a system of vouchers and private insurance for health services would be unable to provide a guarantee of care for the chronically sick. The idea of a voucher system for education was viewed more favourably by the Treasury. At the same time, however, it was noted that the introduction of such a system would, in effect, offer a "subsidy" (in the form of tax relief) to those parents whose children already attended private schools, thereby adding a deadweight cost to current expenditure. It was agreed that the IEA had highlighted some important considerations concerning public ignorance about a "free" welfare system. At the same time, it was argued, much of the report condemned itself because the research on which its findings were based had not been conducted sufficiently broadly or with sufficient academic rigour. In short, the evidence produced by the IEA "was not deemed of sufficient calibre to provoke any change, and certainly not strong enough to counter the enormous political backlash which

would have occurred should a policy of selective benefits be proposed" (Muller 1996: 96). While for a body like PEP these findings
would have been hurtful, to the IEA they could only confirm that the
Treasury, no less than other government departments, was infected
with "a set of very general preoccupations" unfavourable to economic liberalism. The struggle to change this climate of opinion
had to go on.

The British General Election of 1964 resulted in defeat for the
Conservative Government and provided an opportunity for both
former members of the government and new Conservative MPs to
reconsider their ideas and policies. While the influence of the IEA
on the Conservative Party at this time remained limited, a number
of younger MPs, notably Geoffrey Howe and Sir Keith Joseph, "beat
a path for the IEA door. Dismayed by electoral defeat, they came in
search of economic education" (Cockett 1994: 167). By this time,
the IEA had published extensively, including 28 Hobart papers which
sought to offer market solutions to long-standing economic problems which, it was believed, were rarely examined in universities.
However, while Howe, Joseph and (during this period at least)
Enoch Powell were seen as rising stars of the Conservative Party,
the party leadership continued to view the economic liberalism
advocated by the IEA as irrelevant and out-of-date. Indeed, both
the new party leader, Edward Heath, and his Shadow Chancellor,
Iain Macleod, were old members of the "One Nation" group who
continued to approach economics from a problem-solving rather
than an evangelical viewpoint.

While the Conservative opposition showed little sign of adopt-
ing the economic liberalism advocated by the IEA, however, the
Conservative-inclined press did begin to move slowly in its direction.
The new editor of the *Daily Telegraph*, Maurice Green, for instance,
described by one of those who worked under him, John O'Sullivan,
as a "very firm economic liberal", took a keen interest in the ideas
and analyses of the IEA (Cockett 1994: 183). Green not only recruited
a new generation of economic liberal journalists to the paper, but
also allowed the staff of the IEA generous access to its centre pages.
Arthur Seldon alone wrote over 60 leader-page articles for the paper
during the 1960s (Cockett 1994: 184). The Institute also benefited
from more informal contacts, since its offices were located near Westminster, a convenient place for Parliamentary sympathizers to drop

in for lunches. The potential benefits of this strategy far outweighed any costs; having eaten well in congenial company, the MPs who visited the IEA were likely to act as enthusiastic recruiting-agents for the Institute on their return to the Commons.

In 1964 the Institute published a collection of essays by journalists, scholars and politicians entitled *Rebirth of Britain*. This was a conscious counter-thrust against a series of books recently published by Penguin, which pointed out the shortcomings of many British institutions. Powell was prominent among the contributors to *Rebirth of Britain*. The title and contents of the volume both suggested that the IEA was a source of hope among so many doom-mongers. As the Labour Government led by Harold Wilson began to develop further the experiment with planning begun under Macmillan, the Institute could be seen as the standard-bearer of an attractive alternative approach; the fact that its ideological colours were mostly derived from the writings of previous centuries, or from very different political and cultural contexts could be overlooked. Some right-wing Conservatives, notably Angus Maude whom Heath would sack as Shadow Colonial Secretary in 1966, began to call for a rethink of the party's philosophy; only the IEA seemed ready with radical ideas. Events were finally beginning to move its way. In 1965, for instance, the Institute published a preliminary assessment of the Labour Government's National Plan. The paper, by John Brunner, was described by *The Economist* as a "corrosive examination of the ponderous portmanteau questionnaire that the Department of Economic Affairs sent out to businessmen to help it prepare its plan" (cited by Muller 1996: 98). Brunner's attack brought a response from Austin Albu, a junior minister in the Department of Economic Affairs; this kind of intervention is always more likely to bring prestige to a think-tank rather than succour to a government. As we have seen (Chapter 1), the Plan was launched in very unpromising circumstances, and was quickly wound up. Whatever the precise reasons for this failure, the IEA attack appeared to have been a sound prophecy when the Conservative Party (which lost another election) was in sore need of good news. In 1965 the Institute drew attention to (among other things) the kind of problems which the NIESR had experienced in predicting the future (see Chapter 2) in the pamphlet *Lessons from central forecasting*; it returned to the attack on the intellectual foundations of planning in 1969, when it published Vera Lutz's *Central planning for the market economy.* The arguments of IEA authors on this theme were all highly cogent, even if British forecasters were hampered by the stop–go problems which could not be blamed on their methodology; more seriously, to the extent that the value of the whole economics profession depends on the accuracy of assumptions about future human behaviour, it could be argued that there was a danger of the pamphlets proving too subversive for comfort. *Lessons from central forecasting* also showed that the IEA's contributors were not afraid of criticizing their political allies; it contained a sharp attack (by J.R. Seale) on Enoch Powell's record at the Ministry of Health.

Monetarism and the IEA

As inflation and unemployment began to rise in tandem during the late 1960s the Keynesian analysis seemed in need of serious re-examination, and far-reaching alternatives could at least hope for a more patient hearing than ever before in the post-war period. As early as 1960, the IEA had issued the first in a long line of publications linking the supply of money to the rate of inflation. The pamphlet, entitled *Not unanimous,* was a critique of the report published by a committee chaired by Lord Radcliffe in 1959 (see Chapter 2).

As the 1960s progressed, a number of papers published by the IEA, including Professor E. Victor Morgan's *Monetary policy for stable growth* (1964), further explored the link between the supply of money and inflation. After 1967 Milton Friedman argued that inflation was invariably a monetary phenomenon and that government should seek to restrain the rate of growth in the money supply in order to reduce inflation. As interest in Friedman's theories began to grow in the academic world, the IEA invited Alan Walters, a professor of economics at the LSE who would became Margaret Thatcher's personal economic adviser in the 1980s, to write a paper with the object of bringing monetary theory to the attention of a wider audience. Press comment on this paper, entitled *Money in boom and slump* (1969), was considerable, but mixed (Muller 1996: 98).

The interest generated by the IEA's publications on monetary theory and policy during the late 1960s and early 1970s was mainly due to the economic problems which both Labour and Conservative administrations continued to suffer. In December 1970, after Edward Heath had been elected as Conservative Prime Minister, the IEA published Friedman's Wincott lecture of that year as an occasional paper, entitled *The counter-revolution in monetary theory*. The lecture itself had been attended by several prominent academics and politicians; however, a meeting between Friedman and Heath soon after the 1970 general election had merely revealed the great gulf which remained between the respective positions of the IEA and senior policy-makers. Early expectations that Heath would drastically revise the post-war settlement – the product of wishful thinking on the right, and scare-mongering on the left, rather than a careful assessment of the government's intentions – were quickly dashed as unemployment rose further and the government moved to revitalize the economy.

Naturally this experience did not deter the IEA; instead it added to the existing oppositional ethos of the Institute a story of "betrayal" which whetted the cutting edge of its message. Events continued to favour it when the war of Yom Kippur triggered a more than fourfold rise in the price of oil just before Britain's own reserves came onstream. During the 1970s, the IEA continued to examine the macroeconomic issue of inflation as part of its publications programme, to which Friedman was a regular contributor. In addition to several revised editions of *The counter-revolution in monetary theory* the IEA published Friedman's *Monetary correction* (1974), *Unemployment versus inflation* (1975) and *Inflation and unemployment* (1976). The IEA also continued to publish work by Professor Alan Walters. Examples here included the latter's contribution to *Crisis '75* (1975) and his *Economists and the British economy* (1978). Prominent journalists, whether or not they agreed with the IEA began to treat its publications more seriously. Perhaps the best-known contribution of this kind came from the respected *Times* commentator Ronald Butt, who in January 1976 wrote that although the IEA had been "regarded as a bit of a joke by most economic writers" ten years previously, its message had now "taken on a new relevance" (Cockett 1994: 196). During this period the IEA's political economy was enriched by the incorporation of the public choice theory developed by the American "Virginia School". In 1976 it published Gordon Tullock's *The vote motive*, which enabled economic liberals to attack believers in consensus from an unexpected angle. While Hayek had portrayed his opponents as well-meaning but misguided, public choice theory enabled economic liberals to claim that socialists were no better than anyone else. Far from being actuated by a desire to serve the public, bureaucrats associated with the welfare state could now be presented as empire-builders, using big government as a means to enhance their own powers and prestige. In time-honoured IEA fashion, the argument was deployed without any acknowledgement of factors which might make it tenuous in the British context; it was implied that bureaucrats are the same everywhere, regardless of whether they entered public service through competitive examination or through a system of political patronage as in the United States. Blessed as it is with the allure of extreme simplicity, the theory has had a lasting impact on university teaching.

Trade unions, the professions and restrictive practices

A key objective of many economic liberals – though not of Milton Friedman, who thought the question of secondary importance – was to reduce the power of trade unions. Hayek, in particular, was concerned about the unions' increasing capacity, as he saw it, to disrupt the workings of the market economy by distorting the price mechanism. The IEA's first foray in this field was *Trade unions in a free society*, published in 1959, when the Conservative Government of Harold Macmillan was keen to conciliate the unions. In an attempt to offer friendly advice to the National Union of Railwaymen (NUR) and to increase the impact of the paper, the IEA commissioned an author who was himself sympathetic to the trade union movement and had benefited from it, Ben Roberts. However, the IEA's was not the first voice raised on this subject; a group of Conservative lawyers had already advanced a strong case for union reform in the pamphlet *A giant's strength* (1958). In addition to attacking the unions for their restrictive practices in the building industry and elsewhere, the IEA also sought to expose the distortions of the market found within the legal and accounting professions. An early example of this was a research monograph by Dennis Lees entitled *The economic consequences of the professions* (1966). While the reviews of publications such as *Restrictive practices in the building industry* (1966) were, for the most part, unfavourable – and often highly critical – growing public concern about the power and influence of trade unions during the 1970s provided the IEA with an opportunity to publish papers on the union issue that won a more sympathetic reception, particularly after the failure of the Heath Government's Industrial Relations Act (1971) and the coal miners' strike which helped to bring down that administration. Hayek himself made several contributions to this debate, notably through his pamphlets *A tiger by the tail* (1972) and *Economic freedom and representative government* (1973). While the idea of a Labour Government introducing legislation to curb union powers really would have been unthinkable in 1959, by 1969 even Harold Wilson and other senior Labour ministers had accepted that action needed to be taken (although the White Paper *In place of strife* remained a dead letter because of resistance in the unions and the party).

Permeation and persuasion: the 1970s

The influence of the IEA increased steadily during the late 1960s and early 1970s among both politicians and political commentators. The perceived failures of the Heath Government of 1970–4 created a far more determined group of Conservative politicians eager to explore an alternative economic strategy, of the kind that had been set out over many years by the IEA. The accession of Margaret Thatcher to the leadership of the party in 1975 gave the IEA indirect access to the policy-making machinery of the Conservative Party which, while not directly sought by the Institute itself, had previously been unthinkable. Mrs Thatcher had known Harris and Seldon from the early 1960s, and in a speech to the Conservative Political Centre at the 1968 Conservative Party conference had given the first clear indication of her free-market leanings (Cockett 1994: 171–2). While most Conservative politicians remained unconvinced by the market analysis provided by the IEA, men such as Sir Keith Joseph and Sir Geoffrey Howe were placed by Mrs Thatcher after she had

ousted Heath as Conservative leader in vital economic policy positions and it was their convictions, many of which had been articulated by the academic economists published by the IEA, that now
began to influence the policy thinking and overall economic strategy of the party. As one of Mrs Thatcher's senior colleagues put
it later, the party's ideas originated "in heavy tomes, then they get
popularised and put in more digestible form by an IEA pamphlet,
and then a *Daily Telegraph* article, chat, etc. And it permeates in that
way" (Whitehead 1985: 334). This was almost exactly the method
which Hayek had laid down after the war.

At the same time, however, many at the IEA continued to
entertain suspicions about politicians in general and Conservative
politicians in particular, given that even the sympathetic Joseph and
Thatcher had boasted about their generosity with public money
during the Heath Government. To emphasize the Institute's view
of itself as a lonely voice of virtue, its twentieth anniversary publication, *Not from benevolence* (co-written by Harris and Seldon),
included a lengthy list of occasions when the IEA's advice might
have been taken, and coyly left it to readers to judge whether
governments had been right to turn a blind eye (Harris and Seldon
1977: x). By this time the Labour Government led by James Callaghan
had reluctantly adopted monetarist policies in return for an IMF
rescue package, but the IEA knew that the government's conversion was skin deep.

Despite these suspicions, and the legal requirement to remain
independent of any political party, the IEA was still keen to seek
out opportunities for interested and sympathetic politicians to meet
with free-market academics and thinkers. The Institute therefore
established a series of lunches and dinners, the purpose of which
was to enable the potential policy-makers to meet the policy thinkers.
The importance of this strategy lay in the fact that it kept key
figures, and Mrs Thatcher in particular, briefed on the latest developments in free-market economic analysis (Muller 1996: 101).

It was also during the 1970s that the IEA's influence among
students on several university campuses, notably perhaps the
London School of Economics (LSE) and St Andrews, began to be
felt. Although the mood on the university campuses during the
1960s is usually seen as an expression of left-wing idealism, in important respects it represented an opportunity for the IEA, those

self-conscious rebels against a disapproving establishment. It was no accident that during the 1970s several people who had achieved public prominence as spokesmen for the student revolt accepted the IEA's case that economic liberalism was the only viable alternative to what they had always regarded as the fragile compromise of a mixed economy.

In the meantime, the perceived intellectual "consensus" in favour of collectivism which the IEA had contested for so long in the debate about economic policy, had been identified in other academic disciplines such as sociology and social policy. Seldon, in particular, realized that many of the economic arguments deployed by the IEA were being attacked not only by Keynesian economists but also by sociologists. During the 1960s and, more especially, the 1970s, much academic sociology had become dominated, it seemed to many at the IEA, by Marxist thinking, thus providing another opponent in its crusade for economic liberalism. Following discussions with an academic from Nottingham University, Digby Anderson, the IEA therefore established the Social Affairs Unit (SAU) in December 1980, under Anderson's direction. Within a few years, the SAU, which had initially operated, like the IEA, from 2 Lord North Street, became independent from the IEA and acquired its own premises. The SAU was created to provide an alternative academic perspective to collectivism in areas such as education, health and law and order. It at least tried to foster an uneasy marriage between traditional social values and economic liberalism; ironically this project had little chance of succeeding, because so many of the iconoclastic believers in liberal economics had been exposed to (and enjoyed) the social freedoms of the 1960s. The difficulty facing the SAU was neatly illustrated after the Conservatives had fallen from power when in November 1997 it published a well-publicized pamphlet on women's magazines. Predictably enough, the SAU found that the content of most magazines was highly trivial, with something like an obsession with sex. However, the publishers of the magazines could simply reply that this subject won readers, and in a free market it only made sense to cater for the biggest possible audience. An article in *The Times* compared reading the pamphlet with "being buttonholed by a London cabbie: you are overwhelmed by the crudity of the polemic". Older readers of the report could reflect that the trend deplored by the authors had accelerated since 1979. Arguably the governments of Margaret Thatcher and John Major had suffered a greater loss of public esteem through numerous sex scandals than their distinctly patchy economic records. This could be explained by reference to a media fixation with sex which had grown throughout the period; ironically, the public's interest in the subject had been fostered above all by newspapers owned by Margaret Thatcher's warm supporter, Rupert Murdoch (see Chapter 4 for further discussion on this issue).

Thatcherism and the IEA

The disillusionment felt by Sir Keith Joseph with the performance of the Conservative Government of 1970–74 led him not only to reappraise his own economic and political views but also to consider the need for the Conservative Party to establish a policy centre, modelled to some extent on the IEA. Unlike the IEA, however, which had sought to publicize economic liberal thinking on a range of policy issues to a wide public audience, the new organization would be linked directly to a political audience, with the purpose of influencing the next Conservative manifesto. The motivation of the Centre for Policy Studies (CPS) was directly concerned to map out policy for the Conservative Party in preparation for the next General Election (see Chapter 4). Hence the IEA, in contrast to the CPS, was able to continue to analyse markets with the unique advantage of being removed from immediate political pressures.

After her party had won the 1979 general election, Margaret Thatcher wrote to thank Fisher for his contribution: "You created the atmosphere which made our victory possible" (Blundell 1990: 6). Certainly the IEA had bolstered her confidence in the free market message; a book on Mrs Thatcher's first year in office argued that the IEA's pamphlet *Over-ruled on welfare* (1978), which brought together the findings of surveys conducted over 15 years, "gave support to Mrs Thatcher's political instincts and strengthened her view that she was . . . in touch with the feelings of ordinary people" in the run up to the 1979 general election (Stephenson 1980: 20–1). Thus the advent of the 1979 Conservative Government placed the IEA in an entirely new position, in that, at least to the extent that many of the new economic ministers were believers in the beneficial effects of markets and in the necessity of monetarism, much of its economic thinking and analysis was accepted by the new government. An early and spectacular success came with the abolition of exchange control; for this measure, Geoffrey Howe paid explicit tribute to "a splendid IEA pamphlet from John Wood and Robert Miller . . . that helped to break the intellectual ice-pack" (Howe 1994: 141). Inevitably perhaps, this new situation caused a certain amount of confusion among both admirers and opponents of the IEA, even though it was political circumstances that had changed and not the Institute, which could never be accused of compromising its beliefs to win friends at Westminster. The journalistic appellation "Thatcherite" was routinely attached to the IEA, a development which some at the IEA, particularly Arthur Seldon, viewed with some irritation. When Ralph Harris was nominated as a life peer in Mrs Thatcher's first Honours List this was an understandable reflection of his connection with the Prime Minister, but Harris chose to sit as a cross-bencher even though he was in far closer agreement with the economic policies of the government than many who took the Conservative whip in either House.

In the early years of the Thatcher Government, the IEA continued to provide principled support for the economic policies of the government and its publications tended to agree with the general direction (if not always the practical implementation) of economic policy. At the same time, however, the Institute's publications programme maintained the established policy of extending market analysis to every conceivable subject. Recognizing the minority position in which the Prime Minister found herself for much of the time, both inside government and outside of it, Harris and Seldon extended several invitations to Mrs Thatcher to visit the IEA in order to reassure her that, in doing so, she would be "amongst friends" (Muller 1996: 103). Ironically, though, when tensions between Geoffrey Howe, Nigel Lawson and Thatcher were reaching snapping point in October 1989 an IEA dinner held to mark the tenth anniversary of the abolition of exchange control provided an opportunity for the disillusioned ministers to compare notes (Howe 1994: 603–4).

At crucial moments in the development of economic policy before these "friends" fell out, the IEA was able to provide the government with intellectual ammunition to counter the academic and political backlash its policies were encountering. The clearest example of this was in the aftermath of the 1981 Budget, when 364 economists (including some IEA authors) signed a letter published in *The Times* urging a retreat from monetarist policies and declaring that there was no justification in either logic or economic history for the government's (then) economic direction. To counter these arguments, Harris and Seldon encouraged Patrick Minford to publish a response. The ease with which the IEA could obtain academic authors by this time also provided the opportunity for the Institute to establish another medium through which market thinking and analysis could be pursued and, in 1980, *Economic Affairs* was launched as the official journal of the Institute. Edited by Seldon, the journal enabled the IEA to publish short articles by a large number of academics on a more frequent and topical basis (Muller 1996: 104).

A central plank in the economic policy programme of the Thatcher administrations during the 1980s was privatization. While this policy was not pursued in earnest until after the 1983 General Election, the IEA was broadly, if not entirely, supportive of it. The IEA had, after all, published a number of pamphlets examining the shortcomings of political and governmental control over electricity, coal, telecommunications and other services and industries. As the 1989 volume *Privatisation and competition* complained, in some cases privatization merely led to the substitution of private for public monopoly (Veljanovski 1989). The IEA journal *Economic Affairs* carried a series of articles making similar points; the issue of June 1993 was given over to a generally hostile treatment of the Conservative record (Stone 1996: 183).

Again, while the policies of economic liberalization and trade union reform undertaken by the Thatcher Government met with broad approval from the IEA, for many of the Institute's supporters even the radical nature of Conservative Party policies during the 1980s was insufficiently bracing, and disillusionment was common (Denham and Garnett 1996: 53). Even on the overall conduct of economic policy the IEA was an awkward ally; its published verdict on the first Thatcher Government's record was *Could do better*, a title which must have caused deep irritation among ministers who had pushed their attachment to economic liberalism well beyond what had previously been thought politically sustainable. It must have been particularly irksome to encounter these thrusts when Keynesian economists were still insisting that the government's departure from "consensus" politics meant that on a range of issues its performance could not have been worse. Ironically Jo Grimond – whose emergence as Liberal leader in the 1950s had done so much to help in the formation of the IEA – was among the contributors, in his new economic liberal guise. In other fields tension grew through the 1980s. Muller, for instance, has recently argued that

> in the public services of education and healthcare, the Thatcher administrations proved to be no less timid than previous governments. As the market began to be more [widely] accepted in economic policy, the welfare state was still considered by politicians to be beyond the [IEA's] market analysis. A new political consensus was beginning to be forged, one which continued to deny the use of markets in areas such as health, education and welfare. In response to this and learning from the success of specialization in its early endeavours . . . the IEA created the Health and Welfare Unit to concentrate on [the] politically sensitive aspects of welfare. The Unit's authors took the view that the Government's Health Service reforms were a betrayal of the very philosophy which the IEA had done so much to inculcate (Muller 1996: 104–5).

In a pamphlet entitled *The NHS reforms: whatever happened to consumer choice?* published in 1990, David Green, Head of the Institute's Health and Welfare Unit, argued that the government ought to have ended the "paternalism of providing services in kind, paid for by taxes" and predicted that the reforms would neither prevent demands for more funding for the NHS nor provide the government with more votes. The government, he argued, had apparently forgotten that Thatcherism at its best had been about reducing the state's power and increasing that of individuals and families. Education was another source of serious contention. Arthur Seldon, with his wife Marjorie, had strongly advocated a system of vouchers, but not even Sir Keith Joseph could win this battle, and by 1984 he had abandoned the idea (Seldon 1986; Denham 1996). His retirement from the government in 1986 was a far less serious blow to the IEA than might have been expected.

By 1987, Ralph Harris had resigned from the post of general director and had become chairman of the Institute, a position he held until 1989. Arthur Seldon had originally retired as editorial director in 1981, but stayed on as a consultant until 1988. In 1987, a new director, Graham Mather, was appointed. Mather had previously worked at the Institute of Directors (IoD) and welcomed the opportunity of assuming overall responsibility for a research institute, expressing the view that at the IEA he would have a better chance of influencing policy than on the back benches. However, harmony within the Institute was short-lived; Harris and Seldon soon grew alarmed at what they saw as Mather's excessive interest in current political debate. In turn, Mather believed that the former directors had not relinquished complete control of the IEA to him as he had expected; they remained much more than "back-seat drivers" (Muller 1996: 105).

While these tensions were developing, the IEA under Graham Mather continued to pursue an intellectual agenda of issues pertaining to law and the economy, the future of regulation, the application of public choice analysis to public bureaucracies and the challenge of constitutional reform to support an ever-increasing role for market institutions. The IEA also commissioned a number of surveys, one of which involved circulating a questionnaire to economics departments in British universities designed to establish the extent to which the IEA had been successful in effecting a change in the intellectual climate within academic (and other) circles over the previous 30 years (Ricketts and Shoesmith 1990).

In the early 1970s, a survey of British economic opinion found that "well over 75 per cent of the economists who took part" subscribed to a distinct policy outlook which the survey coordinator, Samuel Brittan, termed the "liberal economic orthodoxy". This embodied a belief in competitive markets and pricing, but also in income redistribution and in the effectiveness of the Keynesian techniques of demand management and fiscal policy which the New Right groups vigorously opposed (Brittan 1973: 20–2). We have noted above that the prevalence of intellectual opposition to monetarism was publicly attested by 364 university economists in 1981. Disappointingly for the IEA, the results of its survey published in 1990 merely confirmed that the established trend of intellectual opposition to economic liberalism in general and monetarism in particular has continued, at least among academic economists. Indeed, the results showed that, by international standards, British economists were "more redistributive than those of any other country for which survey data are available" and also more Keynesian in the sense of accepting at least a short-run trade-off between unemployment and inflation (Ricketts and Shoesmith 1990). In short, far from "converting" the British economic establishment to "economic liberalism", this evidence suggests that the IEA and its free-market allies have been forced to "by-pass" it (Denham and Garnett 1996: 51).

Economic liberalism after Thatcher: the 1990s

The dispute within the IEA between the two styles of leadership continued, leading to much acrimony on both sides and often considerable press coverage. The battle for the leadership of the Conservative Party, which culminated in the eventual fall of Margaret Thatcher in November 1990, also created tensions within the Institute. Eventually, Graham Mather resigned to set up a new think-tank, the European Policy Forum (EPF), in 1992 (see Chapter 6). After the resignation of Mather, the IEA appointed a new general director, John Blundell, in January 1993. Blundell had studied economics at the LSE and had absorbed most of his economic ideas from the IEA and from working in US think-tanks. Blundell had shown that he would be an excellent choice in a 1989 lecture, when he warned an audience at the US Heritage Foundation against being "duped into believing . . . that the battle is won" (Blundell 1990: 9). A new editorial director, Professor Colin Robinson, was already in place. Robinson was professor of economics at the University of Surrey, an established IEA author and a long-standing member of its Academic Advisory Board.

During the 1990s, the IEA has commissioned studies examining the notion of regulation in all its manifestations. This new interest has meant that, after years of relative neglect, the Institute has begun to cover European issues, notably those concerned with regulation and the environment, which since 1993 have been covered by an Environmental Unit. The IEA has also begun to identify the thinkers of the future by targeting students with an effective Student Outreach

Programme, taking note of the fact that many of today's thinkers and politicians were themselves influenced by the publications of the IEA as undergraduates. Publications, however, continue to be the core activity of the IEA, which remains as committed to the free market cause as it has ever been after four decades of energetic activity on its behalf.

Conclusion

Given the circumstances prevailing at the time of its foundation, the IEA looks at first sight to have been a remarkable success. Due to the efforts of Fisher and his colleagues, associated bodies have been established in many other countries. Unlike other organizations studied here, the IEA did not arise in response to a particular crisis – at least, not one perceived by more than a small number of people. Events certainly favoured its message from the mid-1960s onwards, but the perseverence of its personnel and supporters in the face of a broadly hostile "climate of opinion" must be acknowledged. While the occurrence of circumstances in the mid-1970s provoked soul-searching and major developments among other British think-tanks, the IEA was in a position to respond with grim satisfaction. Its ideas were not original, but they were promulgated in a fashion which caught attention when the situation had become more favourable; to apply Dicey's phrase in a later context, events had apparently inclined "the majority of the world to hear with favour theories which, at one time, men of common sense derided as absurdities, or distrusted as paradoxes" (Dicey 1905: 23).

After the Conservative victory in the 1979 general election, the economic ministries were filled with people who had either first been exposed to economic liberalism at the IEA, or had been confirmed in their personal instincts by that body. Although the Institute's traditional suspicion of politicians was apparently as strong as ever, by the time that it came to celebrate its first 25 years in 1981 its history could be portrayed as a heroic saga, and the original members were hailed as Founding Fathers (Seldon 1981: xiii). But while the influence of the IEA on economic policy during this period can hardly be denied, its record was not one of unqualified success. Richard Cockett wrote in 1994 that economic liberalism "never captured the hearts, let alone the minds, of more than a small minority of Conservative MPs", and surveys by political scientists have backed up this claim (Cockett 1994: 325; Norton 1993). Precision on this matter is complicated by the fact that even MPs who disagreed with Thatcherism had a strong incentive to act in the 1980s as if they did, but most accounts agree that during the Prime Minister's last years in office she had to appoint ministers who were clearly not fellow-believers, for want of talented alternatives. An even more significant failure than this, perhaps, relates to the fact that Britain's role in Europe (the issue which eventually brought down Margaret Thatcher) was rarely discussed by IEA authors during the 1970s and 1980s. Whether or not busy politicians and officials can be excused for not taking proper account of the likely impact of European developments on domestic policy, bodies like the IEA are in a far better position to provide early warnings of long-term problems. As Cockett has noted:

> One searches in vain for any pamphlet or publication on the whole range of European issues – from the EMS to the Single European Market – produced by the IEA or the CPS until the late 1980s when the subject was no longer avoidable . . . It is ironic that, at the very moment when Geoffrey Howe was finally breaking free from Britain's fixed exchange rate regime in 1979, Britain's European partners were embarking on the creation of the European Exchange Rate System, thereafter a slow fuse under the Thatcher Governments of the 1980s, eventually detonating in 1990. Nothing that the economic liberal intellectuals and propagandists wrote or said in the 1950s, 1960s or 1970s prepared the Conservative Governments for the complexities of dealing with the European issue in the 1980s. This was their failure. They might have had the "big idea" – the free market – of the 1970s, but as far as the art of government was concerned this proved to be of increasingly marginal relevance as the 1980s progressed (Cockett 1994: 327–8).

The IEA's relative neglect of European questions indicates that its primary interest lay in domestic policy issues, which it felt far more confident of affecting. In an increasingly inter-dependent global economy, this can only be judged a serious- and most instructive-failing. Elsewhere, Cockett argues that far from having "marginal relevance", economic liberalism as applied in Britain in the 1980s "effectively wiped out a large part of Britain's manufacturing industry and, at the end of a decade of economic experiment and dislocation, left as many people unemployed as there were in the 1930s" (Cockett 1994: 328). Even for the sympathetic Cockett, the "intellectual triumph" of economic liberalism in the 1980s demonstrates both the importance and the danger inherent in strong ideas. Even if the connection between the IEA's views and specific policy decisions has been overstated in Cockett's account, he implies that at the very least the Institute is open to criticism for having helped to convince ministers that there was no alternative to economic liberalism.

Muller has argued that the IEA was notably more successful in the first Thatcher years and earlier, when it advocated the abolition (or repeal) of legislation, as in the case of exchange controls, than in the later part of its career, when IEA authors began to advocate specific policies in areas, such as health and education, where it was inevitably much more difficult to build a consensus around specific reforms. This points to the conclusion suggested earlier – namely that the IEA was more successful as a source of spiritual opposition than of constructive policy ideas. Once the Institute's suggestions had entered the realm of the politically thinkable, they became bogged down in the usual departmental squabbles and compromises. This was an uncongenial arena for the ideologues of Lord North Street – after all, a collection of Ralph Harris' articles would later be published under the characteristic title *No, prime minister!* (Harris 1994). It is instructive that tensions within an organization which had flourished before 1979 began to surface as the Thatcher revolution proceeded. After the government's re-election in 1983 it seemed that all the enemies against whom the IEA had defined itself were scattered – and that Falklands-inspired victory was won more in spite of the Conservatives' economic record than because of it. The New Right – like most ideological sects – needed at least the impression that there were "unifying enemies" to fight against (Denham and Garnett 1994). By the time that John Blundell, who repeatedly warned against complacency, had replaced Graham Mather as general director of the IEA, it was apparently too late for him to reinvigorate a New Right which thought that economic liberalism had triumphed the world over.

Ironically, then, the IEA's record as an influence on the direction of policy should be judged as being successful from the time when circumstances began to favour it in the 1970s up to the point when the economic liberalism it upheld came into power, after which its performance, when compared with its opportunities, was disappointing. The Institute may have spawned similar bodies across the world, but this only illustrates the well-known fact that its creed had attractions to people of a certain disposition – in itself, it cannot be taken as proof of policy influence. As the later Conservative minister (previously a member of the CPRS) William Waldegrave correctly noted before the 1979 victory, "Economic Liberalism is a splendid philosophy for opposition"; but not suitable for office (Waldegrave 1978: 71–2). It could be argued, however, that it is unfair to conclude that the IEA's ideas were unsuitable for government; after all, the Institute was avowedly more interested in ideas than in the detail of policy, and whatever the record of the Conservative Governments after 1979 in practice the underlying philosophy of economic liberalism has continued unchanged. Although there is something in this point, the IEA certainly published policy suggestions in advance (notably on RPM in the early 1960s), and chided governments for straying from its preferred line on specific matters. While the Institute should be treated differently from other think-tanks of the New Right (see Chapters 4 and 5), the distinctions should not be taken too far. Thus the IEA's strictures on government performance after 1979 can only be taken at least in part as (unconscious) criticisms of itself.

In 1987 Dennis Kavanagh confidently asserted that "the IEA has undoubtedly played an important role in changing the climate of opinion from the mid-1970s onwards" (Kavanagh 1987: 83). This is a prime example of the confusion which can arise in connection with the phrase "climate of opinion"; while the IEA saw its ideas reach a dominant position within government, the opinions of the intellectuals and more general public assumptions, which Hayek saw as the key to lasting success, were much more resistant. In a 1986 contribution to an IEA collection of essays in honour of Arthur Seldon, Milton Friedman provided a curious updating of Hayek's much earlier attack on socialist intellectuals. The average advocate of free-market ideas, he suggested, was now declining in quality because the climate of opinion had moved so strongly against socialism that it was no longer necessary for liberals to think carefully before expressing their views (Friedman 1986: 136–7). However, Friedman's fascinating reflections – which strongly imply that economic liberalism only thrives in adversity – must have been grounded on his experiences in the United States, because free-market intellectuals in Britain have never enjoyed the apparent dominance won by their political counterparts. Equally, Friedman's suggestion that market liberals had honed their skills during a period when they suffered discrimination is interesting as an insight into the oppositional psychology of the IEA and its allies rather than as a picture of reality at any time during the post-war years.

We have already noted the negative response of the academic economic profession, where Keynesian ideas remained strong; to that extent, if by discrimination Friedman really means being outnumbered in argument, free marketeers continued to suffer discrimination throughout the 1980s within academia. Here the slogans about freedom and choice which went down so well with some politicians were far less effective, presumably because academics were aware of the real complexities of the post-war British experience. The very simplicity of presentation which attracted politicians in search of easy answers tended to damn IEA publications in most university common rooms. The general antipathy of intellectuals to free-market ideas was symbolized by Oxford University's refusal to award Margaret Thatcher an honorary degree; in the 1987 general election a higher percentage of the unemployed than of academics voted Conservative (Willetts 1992: 21). A survey of "heavy-weight" newspaper columnists during the period after 1975 would probably reveal very strong support for economic liberalism, but it is notorious that the British press was biased towards the Conservative Party during this period, and evidence of surveys hardly proves that these pundits won widespread assent – or even attention – from readers. With the general public the record was no better; as Ivor Crewe has shown, while opinion polls revealed that tax cuts and better public services were equally desired in 1979, only a few months of exposure to economic liberalism in government produced a 22 per cent majority for improved services, and by 1987 this had stretched to 55 per cent (Crewe 1989: 244–6). The Conservatives achieved four consecutive election victories between 1979 and 1992, but received a lower share of the popular vote at each contest. Since so

113

many of the government's departures from the letter of economic liberal teachings were inspired by electoral considerations (including a lapse into the bad old ways of "Bastard" Keynesianism before the 1987 election), it would be perverse to argue that it would have been more popular had it clung more tenaciously to the ideas of the IEA. Perhaps the most accurate measurement of the IEA's failure to change the wider climate of opinion was offered by David Green, who in an interview as late as 1993 admitted that "over the past decade something of an assumption has grown up that free market ideas are associated with greed, and that misconception has to be countered" (Richards 1993). In fact, this was a misconception that the IEA and other New Right bodies had been trying to counter from the start; insofar as their voices were heard at all by the general public, they only appear to have made matters worse by a tendency to protest too much.

In the run up to the 1997 general election the IEA began to experience retribution for its perceived success since 1979. It was seen as a body which had run out of ideas. This was an unreasonable view, because its supporters believed as strongly as ever in economic liberalism, and could claim that despite a change in rhetoric the Labour Party under Tony Blair seemed to be as firmly committed to their creed as Margaret Thatcher had ever been. But in spite of its consistent attempts to avoid identification with a single political party (and its trenchant criticisms of government policy since 1979) the Institute was now seen as being so closely tied to the fortunes of the Conservatives that it shared in the fatal decline of the Major Government's appeal. At the same time, the media preoccupation with splits in the New Right led in 1993 to questions about the IEA's absence from John Major's strategy meetings – events which, as Blundell pointed out, the Institute had never attended in the first place (Richards 1993). The IEA had slender grounds for complaint about this confusion by media pundits of appearance with reality; after all, it had won its reputation largely by exploiting the failure of its supporters to distinguish simplistic myths from complex economic history, and the false identification of Conservatism with free-market thinking was no further from the mark than the IEA's confusion of Keynesian views with socialism. Although the IEA was less guilty than other groups on this score, or of indulging in triumphalism, the tone of some of its publications during the

1980s had been provocatively smug. For 18 years the Institute won increased public exposure from its supposed connection with one governing party which was out of step with majority opinion, and it is unlikely that this will be repeated under New Labour, despite early signs of collaboration with a government which talked loudly of thinking the unthinkable (Foot, 1998). To the extent that Tony Blair and his colleagues embraced economic liberalism, they did so in defiance of a continuing barrage of evidence that the public had never accepted it, and that if New Labour ever ran into electoral trouble it would be because it had given too much credence to the notion that the electorate had been Thatcherized; one easy way of assuaging public hostility will be a cutting of lingering ties with groups like the IEA.

On this view, Hayek's insistence that the IEA should reach out beyond decision-makers and convince the widest possible audience has proved to be perfectly justified, and the Institute's failure to follow his prescription despite its unprecedented opportunities to spread the word during the 1980s can only be explained by reference to the unappealing nature of the ideas it professed. The story of the IEA has been marked by so many peculiar twists that predictions for the future are unusually hazardous, but it seems likely that its full vigour could only be restored by the election of a government committed in principle to Keynesian economics; like Mrs Thatcher herself, it cannot thrive without feeling itself to be in combat with a powerful enemy. Tony Blair's evident sympathy with the market means that he is unlikely to provide the economic liberals with such a feeling; even if this sympathy brings about his downfall, he is unlikely to be replaced by anyone who can be tainted by the broad brush of socialism. Thus, despite the new Director's concerns about complacency, the false idea that the IEA and its allies really have triumphed in the battle of ideas is likely to have precipitated a long-term decline in the Institute's fortunes.

CHAPTER 4

The Centre for Policy Studies

Origins

Sir Keith Joseph explained the decision to set up the CPS in an interview with Anthony Seldon, published in 1987:

> [The idea] was mine and Alfred Sherman's . . . I did it to try to persuade myself and then . . . the Party and the country, that the German social market philosophy was the right one for the Conservatives to adopt. I set it up – with Ted Heath's understandably slightly grudging approval – to research, and then to market, social market philosophy (Joseph 1987: 29).

As the Centre's former Director of Studies, David Willetts, recalled in 1991, Joseph and Margaret Thatcher had become disillusioned with the direction Conservative Party policy had taken towards the end of the Heath Government's period in office and "wanted instead to take conservatism back to what they saw as its true roots" (Interview, April 1991). The CPS was created as a limited company on 20 June 1974, with Thatcher, Joseph and the businessman Nigel Vinson as its directors. In July, the Centre moved into a "rather small, cramped building" at 8 Wilfred Street, London SW1, with Joseph as Chairman, Thatcher its Vice-Chairman and Alfred Sherman (later Sir) its first director of studies (Todd 1991: 12).

Edward Heath called a general election in February 1974 against the background of the second miners' strike to arise under his government. At the time, the election was widely perceived as a contest to decide "who governed" Britain, although Heath, as a "one nation" Conservative, was understandably reluctant to call a poll on such a divisive issue. This led to delays which undoubtedly affected the outcome; had the election been fought in January, when the party was ahead in the opinion polls, the Conservatives would probably have won. In the event, the government was defeated and the Conservative party was returned to opposition. The "failure" (as he saw it) of the 1970–74 Conservative Government led Joseph, in particular, into a period of deep reflection to try to assess where the government had gone wrong. This was potentially a dangerous exercise for Joseph, who despite his earlier exposure to the ideas of the IEA had proved a free-spending minister at Social Services – as had Margaret Thatcher at Education. Nevertheless, after the defeat of February 1974 he returned once more to the IEA, to reacquaint himself with the intellectual case for economic liberalism. He became convinced that he had been too engrossed in the business of his own department to notice what was going on in the broader governmental picture – an excuse so lame that it would appear wholly self-serving if rehearsed by a person less complicated than Joseph.

A further influence upon Joseph after February 1974 was Alfred Sherman. Joseph had first met Sherman in 1962 when he was Minister for Housing and Sherman, a former Communist, covered local government matters for *The Daily Telegraph*. Sherman helped Joseph by editing his speeches, in the first instance, and later writing them, when the Conservative Party was in opposition during 1969 and 1970. After the Conservative victory in the 1970 general election, however, contact became less frequent and the two eventually lost touch. When Joseph's party returned to opposition Sherman discussed with him the reasons for the Heath Government's perceived failure, and suggested that its troubled career was mainly attributable to its attachment to Keynesian ideas. These talks led to the idea that an institution might be set up to examine these issues in more detail; the IEA's history of stubborn independence made it an unsuitable body for concentrating its efforts on the Conservative Party.

Shortly after the February 1974 defeat, Joseph was offered a Shadow Cabinet post. It was at this point that Joseph mentioned to Heath the idea of setting up an institution. Joseph asked Heath if he could have a Shadow Cabinet position without a specific portfolio and went on to explain that he wanted "to research the relevance to this country of the West German social market economy and . . . to set up an institution" (quoted in Todd 1991: 10). Given Heath's interest in European developments, the stress on West Germany in this application was a clever move.

During the spring of 1974, Joseph introduced Sherman to Margaret Thatcher and Sherman began to write speeches and articles for her, as well as for Joseph. As James Prior has recalled, this was a period when Thatcher and Joseph "began to work together and became, as it were, more and more isolated from the main trend of what the Conservative Government had tried to do between 1970–74. They came much more under the influence of Hayek" (although Thatcher had first read *The road to serfdom* much earlier) (quoted in Young and Sloman 1986: 29). At a Shadow Cabinet meeting during the summer an inquest into the Heath Government's economic record was held, despite the leader's understandable reluctance to open large philosophical questions with a new election looming. According to John Ranelagh, when Heath refused to accept that the strategy had been wrong "Sir Keith Joseph's eyebrows shot up . . . Sir Geoffrey Howe looked astonished, and Margaret Thatcher sat without expression with her back to the wall" (Ranelagh 1992: 235–6). Thatcher and Joseph had boasted about their expensive spending plans before the government fell, while Howe had played a central role in the operation of the Government's prices and incomes policy. John Ranelagh's account is obviously coloured by hindsight, but it suggests that what had been a remarkably united team in government had, within months, become irrevocably divided on ideological and strategic grounds. Given the intimate connection of the dissident ministers with the IEA, it is hardly surprising that Heath should be highly suspicious of any proposal for a new think-tank at this time. Whatever the real story of Heath's discussions with Joseph about the CPS, the ex-Prime Minister soon believed that he had been tricked into authorizing a body which diverted funds from the central institutions of the party into an organization which was dedicated to transforming Conservative policy.

Early days

The CPS, according to an early statement of its objectives, was founded "to secure fuller understanding of the methods available to

119

improve the standard of living, the quality of life and the freedom of choice of the British people, with particular attention to social market policies". The Centre, it was argued, would state the case for a social market economy, or "a free market economy operating within a humane system of laws and institutions". This case would be presented "in moral as well as economic terms, emphasizing the links between freedom, the standard of living and the profit discipline". The Centre's work, it was further argued, would at all times be (or seek to be) "intellectually respectable". The Centre would have several tasks, including those of formulating the questions on which government must have policies in order to achieve an effective social market; studying the answers to such questions, including those adopted by some countries abroad; appraising policies for the United Kingdom; presenting such appraisals privately to the Shadow Cabinet (and, when suitable, publicly) and arranging to help people, including Members of Parliament, in London and elsewhere "to understand the arguments for and against the social market economy, private enterprise and the profit discipline" (CPS 1974). In some respects this prospectus resembled the role played by the Central Policy Review Staff (CPRS) which had been set up by Heath in 1970 to advise the Cabinet; the obvious difference was that while the CPRS had no clear ideological identity, the new Centre was founded with the clear aim of driving the Shadow Cabinet in a particular direction.

In parallel with such work, the statement continued, speeches would be made presenting the case for a social market economy and opportunities sought to debate the case on television and in the universities. Since the task of "sustaining and adapting to current need" the social market economy concept would be a continuing one, it was argued, the Centre should "exist for the foreseeable future. Certainly it should exist during periods of Conservative Government". The Centre's activities, it was argued, would not be "party-political", in the sense that many of its studies would be published and so be of use to politicians in, and members of, all political parties. At the same time, however, because much of the Centre's output would be used as a basis for Conservative Party discussion and preparation for government, financial donations to the CPS should "properly be declared as [Conservative] *Party* contributions" (CPS 1974). As Michael Harris has recently explained,

At its [the CPS's] launch it was emphasized [that] it was an independent body (financed by voluntary contributions and not
part of the official organisation) but with close informal links to
the [Conservative] Party. Charitable status was impossible due
to its self-proclaimed political role, the unavoidable Achilles'
heel of its fund-raising (Harris 1996: 52).

The Centre's founders sought, above all, to "change the climate of
opinion to make possible policies not now feasible". In a statement
issued in 1975, for example, it was asserted that:

> The Centre will help to redress a distortion which has come
> to affect British intellectual and political life during our lifetime
> . . . Socialist assumptions in economics, social policy and edu-
> cation have generated general bipartisan acceptance with only
> minor modifications. As a result, the workings of the market
> have been hampered. These induced failures have been used as
> excuses for even more damaging intervention, until economy and
> society alike have become increasingly beset by contradictions.
> We believe, therefore, that the time is ripe for re-examining the
> new conventional wisdom pragmatically in the light of a quarter
> century's experience in Britain and other industrialized coun-
> tries (CPS 1975a: 3–4).

Thus the Centre had given itself a similar task to that of the IEA,
and its interpretation of post-war British history was almost identical. The main difference was that while the IEA had been battling
against the perceived climate of opinion for the best part of two
decades, the CPS was conscious that the circumstances at the time
of its foundation were far more helpful than they had been in the
1950s – "the time is ripe". In short, the post-war priorities of economic growth and full employment now seemed open to serious
question, largely because of the oil shock of late 1973. Like the IEA,
the CPS deployed rhetoric which begged important questions, but
with less excuse given that the hard-edged phrases of the IEA had
first been used at a time when events were seemingly going against
economic liberalism. Existing sympathizers would hardly pause
over the bald statement that "Socialist assumptions" had "generated
general bipartisan acceptance", but this would provoke a violent

121

reaction from anyone – like the bulk of the existing Conservative Party – who believed that their outlook represented a genuine Middle Way between market and socialist solutions, and that their views could be challenged because of catastrophic developments in the world economy rather than any integral flaws in their thinking. It was more likely that people whose disillusionment with social- ism had already triggered off an extreme reaction – people like Alfred Sherman himself – would approve of the CPS's approach, rather than long-standing members of the party which it had been set up to help.

There was understandable consternation within the Conser- vative party in general, and the Conservative Research Department (CRD) in particular, about the creation of the CPS. While the CPS initially saw itself as performing a quite different function from that of the CRD, others saw it as being, at least to some extent, in com- petition with it. As a result, there was much ill-feeling towards the Centre and its founders from some of Edward Heath's supporters during its early days. According to one (unnamed) source:

> It was a fraud. Keith Joseph went to Ted and asked his permis- sion to set up a fund to see how private enterprise worked in other countries. He then went round the City saying that he had Heath's permission to raise money. Then it became the Joseph/Thatcher power-base for attacking everything Ted stood for (Keegan 1984: 47).

Writing about this period in June 1979, Sherman recalled that one member of the CRD had coined the term "mad monk" for Keith Joseph and "began to tell his familiars in press and Party that we were a dangerous band of right-wing fanatics out to overthrow Heath, undermine the CRD and turn the Party into a small southern minority" (quoted in Todd 1991: 13). The CPS was similarly attacked by key Conservative front- and back-benchers. As Joseph himself remarked in 1991, the CRD strongly disapproved of the CPS: "After all, we were singing new tunes. They were still intent on putting as good a face as possible on the old tunes" (Interview, May 1991). As we shall see later, the (often intense) rivalry between the CRD and the CPS for the intellectual "soul" of the Conservative Party (Halcrow 1989; Young 1989) is important, not least in relation to Margaret

Thatcher's attitude towards the CRD and her use of the CPS as an alternative source of advice in the period after she became Leader of the Conservative Party in February 1975. The feeling of some Conservatives that the CPS should have been strangled at birth meant that it was bound to share some of the oppositional ethos which has always characterized the IEA, yet the psychology of the Centre was also likely to be more confused, because other circumstances were working in favour of its message even before it was devised, and before long its founders were to enjoy a new prominence which they may have hoped for but hardly expected in June 1974.

The ideological conflict within the Conservative Party soon spilled out into the public arena. In the same month that the CPS was founded Joseph embarked on a series of speeches which, while including apparently contrite statements about his own actions in the recent past, subtly insinuated a distance between himself and the party leadership. A speech at Upminster in June 1974 about the problems caused by government intervention was followed, in August, by one at Leith which had as its subject-matter the problem of inflation and its destructive effects upon British industry. It was, however, Joseph's speech at Preston, delivered on 5 September 1974, that was to cause the greatest furore before the October 1974 election, both inside and outside the Conservative Party.

The Preston speech was written for Joseph by Sherman, although others such as Alan Walters, Peter Jay and Samuel Brittan were also consulted about its content and asked for their comments. On hearing that the speech was to be made, and knowing its broad subject matter and Joseph's intention to criticize the policies pursued by the Conservative Government of 1970–74, Heath's supporters attempted to dissuade Joseph from delivering it. To this end, James Prior, one of Heath's closest advisers at that time, and someone who had witnessed the behaviour of the economic liberals while they were in government, was sent to see Margaret Thatcher. As Prior later recalled:

> I was asked to see Margaret to see whether she could bring any influence to bear on Keith Joseph to stop him making [the speech] and Margaret said, "Oh, I don't know. I think Alfred . . ."
> – and that, I thought, was significant, because it wasn't even Sherman, it was Alfred – "I think Alfred has written it for Keith,

123

and I think you'll find that Keith is most determined to make it, and I don't think I can influence him" (Young 1989: 88).

As Young has argued, Prior's account of this episode "brings the intimacy of the little cabal [between Sherman, Joseph and Thatcher] vividly to life" (Young 1989: 88).

Joseph's Preston speech, entitled "Inflation is caused by governments", argued that if government spends too much, the result is inflation which, in turn, "destroys jobs [and] prices us out of international markets". In the speech, Joseph prepared his ground by criticizing himself for his part in the collective actions and decisions of the Heath Government. He emphasized the "self-inflicted wound" of inflation, the "folly" of incomes policies, the "imaginary" evil of unemployment, the "failure" of Keynesian demand management and the problems caused by "excessive injections of money" into the economy. "Monetarist" solutions, he argued, should be implemented to bring inflation under control. At the same time "monetarism" *per se* was not enough to solve Britain's problems, a theme which he would later repeat in other speeches and papers. Todd has argued that Edward Heath "was not to forgive Joseph for the way in which he felt he had been attacked in this speech. He took it as a personal attack, which was not what Joseph had intended" (Todd 1991: 16). This assessment shows how successful the economic liberals have been in discrediting their chief opponents. Since Labour had formed a minority government, a new election could not be long delayed; whatever Joseph might have thought, the leadership of his party was certain to regard the speech as an invitation to the electorate to withhold its support. The idea of a thin-skinned leader sulking because of a personal attack in these circumstances is to miss the essential point, that whatever the personal feelings involved, the divisions within the Conservative Party were based on principle; however, from the outset the economic liberals used the "sulking" interpretation to deflect attention from the significant battles of principle which were going on within the Shadow Cabinet.

The timing of the Preston speech led many Conservatives, as well as political commentators, to question Joseph's political judgement. *The Times*, for example, while praising, on the one hand, the content of the speech, also argued, on the other, that Joseph had "handed a political blunderbuss loaded with duck shot to Mr Wilson and invited him to blow the Conservative Party's head off". Todd has offered a defence of Joseph's behaviour, which again is rather an odd picture of an experienced politician:

> Joseph had tried to convert Heath, and the rest of the Shadow Cabinet, to his cause by the strength of his arguments, but had largely failed. So, he brought the subject into the open. Although Joseph sought much advice about the Preston speech, it may well be that he did not appreciate how some would receive it; it was widely regarded as both a personal attack on Heath and a launching-pad for his challenge for the Party leadership. Certainly the Preston speech brought into the public arena the "monetarist" elements within the Conservative Party and opened up discussion of monetarist solutions (Todd 1991: 16–17).

In fact, Joseph seems to have concluded that the Conservatives were bound to lose the next election. The eventual result in October 1974 was almost another hung parliament. For much of its time in office, Labour would be dependent on minority party support; had it won a bigger majority it would not have needed to resort to the desperate deals and constitutional short-cuts which, added to Britain's economic plight, helped to produce the feeling among economic liberals that the post-war approach had collapsed in ignominy. Ironically, the Labour Government would eventually be forced by the International Monetary Fund to adopt monetarism itself, so the election in 1979 of a Conservative Government wedded to the same policy represented anything but a new departure. Although Joseph's outburst probably did not by itself win the October 1974 general election for Labour – just as Enoch Powell's injunction to his admirers to vote Labour in February could not have brought the Heath Government down on its own – the impression of disunity cannot have helped his party's cause. With just a handful of extra seats for the Conservatives, another new election would have been almost certain and Heath's position as leader significantly strengthened.

At the time of Joseph's speech, no-one, it seems, had even considered Margaret Thatcher as a possible contender for the leadership and she remained in the background, even within the CPS. Although Mrs Thatcher was the only member of the Shadow Cabinet, apart from Joseph, to publicly associate herself with the CPS and had supported him in his arguments with the Heathites in the Shadow Cabinet, she would certainly not have stood against her friend.

Once the October 1974 General Election had been lost, it was made clear to Heath, at a meeting of the Conservative 1922 Committee, that he would have to surrender the leadership of the Party with immediate effect or seek re-election. Heath agreed to seek re-election and, once new procedures had been worked out, it was decided that the date of the first ballot be set for 4 February 1975. Shortly before Christmas 1974, after a month's careful deliberation on the subject, Joseph ruled himself out of contention for the leadership, partly for personal reasons and partly because of the doubts regarding his political judgement which his recent activities had raised. While Joseph's economic views had won widespread coverage the greatest outcry had arisen from a speech in Birmingham soon after the October election. In this speech Joseph suggested that the poor were having too many children; the fact that Joseph's final calamity concerned social policy (he had been Social Services Secretary in the Heath Government) is fitting in view of the CPS's later history. It is equally appropriate that he told Mrs Thatcher of his decision not to stand at a CPS gathering; her reported response was "Well, if you won't stand, I will" (Ranelagh 1992: 140).

The leadership election itself has been well documented elsewhere (Keegan 1984; Young 1989) and the details need not detain us here. On 10 February 1975, Margaret Thatcher became the first woman to lead a British political party. Significantly, the announcement of the establishment of the CPS was made on 14 January 1975, during the campaign for the Party leadership, even though the Centre had been in existence legally since June 1974 and had started work several months earlier.

At the outset, five major areas were identified for detailed study – inflation, industrial policy, housing, ownership and wealth. The Centre's policy studies, it was argued, would "look at the motives that spurred people on to try to establish individual independence" (Todd 1991: 19). In a speech to the Economic Research Council the following day, Joseph stated that:

> Our Centre is a new venture. Our name, Policy Studies, indicates that we shall work towards influencing policy, rather than just producing research briefs (with no disrespect to the latter).

We shall work to shape the climate of opinion – or, to be more exact, the various micro-climates of opinion . . . Much of our work will be comparative. We shall see in greater detail what people are doing in other lands. We shall look at the success stories and ask why they succeeded. But the main thing is that we shall argue. In the first instance, we shall argue the case for the social market economy (Joseph 1975: 63).

The reference to "various micro-climates of opinion" indicates that Joseph carried into the CPS a relatively sophisticated view of the task which confronted economic liberals. It recalls Dicey's view that at any given time there are bound to be "cross-currents" of opinion, rather than Hayek's assumption that an overwhelming majority will follow once a few active intellectuals have been captured (see Introduction). The overriding impression, however, is one of great confidence in the power of ideas. In some fields, years of research and education would be necessary before new ideas could be expected to "impinge effectively upon opinion and policy", but in others the timescale would be much less, "months, weeks or even days". The Centre, Joseph continued, already had in hand studies that would "challenge many received ideas".

"Britain needs a social market economy"

From the beginning, then, the task of the CPS was "to build, and take to the country, policies of conviction based on the justice of giving people as much freedom as possible, and the necessity of reviving a culture of enterprise" (CPS 1989a). The Centre, in other words, has sought, since its inception, to "make market economics acceptable in a society that had previously taken a measure of socialism, or at least of state intervention in the economy, for granted" (Halcrow 1989: 67). As Halcrow has pointed out, however:

There was much discussion in the early days whether it might be too daring to talk overmuch about "the market economy". One school of thought was that it would be better to talk of the "social market economy". This was the literal translation of *Soziale Marktwirtschaft*, the system that had been so effective in [West] Germany – roughly speaking, the philosophy that market economics, allowed to operate freely, provides the goods and services that people want, and does so more democratically than any system of central planning can do (Halcrow 1989: 67).

The phrase "social market economy" had two important advantages over "market economy" for the Centre's founders in the early days of the CPS:

One was that the word "social" conveyed the idea that market economics was not in conflict with social idealism; indeed, that social idealism was unrealistic without market economics. The other advantage came from the connection with West Germany: it gave credence to the reputation they wanted to maintain *vis-à-vis* Tory Central Office that [the CPS] existed simply to study the workings of business economics internationally (Halcrow 1989: 67).

At a time when West Germany was recognized as having enjoyed the kind of economic miracle which had eluded Britain, this reference was particularly well judged. However, it once again begged a serious question; the evidence suggested that an important factor in the success of West Germany had been the kind of corporatist measures deplored by the CPS and its allies (see Marquand 1997: 179–85). If it were argued that West Germany could prosper *in spite* of this corporatist culture, at best this raised the question of why West Germany was so different – and, more seriously, whether the past efforts of groups like the NIESR to study other countries for policy-relevant answers had now turned into an unquestioning assumption that ideas are applicable regardless of context. At worst, it could lead the curious to speculate whether Britain's plight was due to its *excessive* individualism, as manifested by trade unionists who put self-interest above national considerations, and industrialists who preferred to invest abroad in search of maximum profits. Doubtless answers to these queries could be found without discarding economic liberalism, but once again the unargued assumptions of the CPS reveal that it was exploiting the sense of certainty which comes from preaching to the converted. Despite the Centre's obvious concern with academic debate, its use of the slogan "social market economy", reveals that its main hope was that readers would be carried away by enthusiasm, rather than being convinced by detailed, self-critical analysis. At this time the IEA was showing increasing signs of self-congratulation; given the close cousinhood between the organizations, it is hardly surprising that the CPS should fall into the same trap from the outset.

In 1975, the CPS issued a pamphlet entitled *Why Britain needs a social market economy*, written by Nigel Vinson and Martin Wassall and with a Foreword by Keith Joseph (CPS 1975b). Britain, the paper argued, needed a "social market economy", for a number of reasons, but chiefly because:

> Experience has taught us that the only real alternative to a market economy is a command economy, in which narrow short-term expedients reflecting conflicting party-political considerations dominate government economic behaviour. We are also learning – or re-learning – that a command economy means a command society; that the state, in order to secure its uncontested domination over economic life, must increasingly dominate people's livelihoods, and limit their freedom of choice in education, health, housing, jobs, careers, savings, their access to the media of expression and later their access to information. In short, a command economy means increasing dependence for the citizen. Hence our reiterated conviction that a market economy with freedom to own property and engage in [the] production of goods and services is an essential precondition for all other freedoms (CPS 1975b: 3–4).

A market economy "within a humane framework of laws and social services", the paper argued, gives "freest scope for material, social and cultural development and the quest for happiness" (CPS 1975b: 4). Indeed, the scope and quality of social services

> depend crucially on the health and efficiency of industry. Industry alone creates the wealth which pays for social welfare. The more industry is left free – and indeed encouraged – to get on with its vital job of creating wealth, the greater will be the money that can be devoted to social purposes. Conversely, when

129

industry is vilified and squeezed, the result is lower profits, lower wages, less employment and thus a reduced capacity to pay the taxes which alleviate distress and advance education. In short, a profitable, efficient and thriving industry is the pre-condition of a humane, compassionate and civilised society (CPS 1975b: 4).

In declaring their support for the free market, the authors denied that this necessarily implied advocacy of *laissez-faire*, in the sense of wishing to exclude government from economic and social affairs. The market system, they argued, was not, after all, without "imperfections" of its own:

> The market's shortcomings are well-known: it does not in itself ensure that the occasional divergence of private and social costs/benefits is reflected in prices; it often fails to provide for those who, through misfortune, cannot provide for themselves; it may bring about a distribution of income, wealth and economic power which many people find unacceptable (CPS 1975b: 8–9).

These imperfections and shortcomings, the authors argued, implied a "clear need" to "complement" the market system with various social policies to assist the elderly, the sick, the disabled and the unemployed. Poverty and deprivation should not be tolerated where, in the absence of any form of intervention, they would otherwise occur (CPS 1975b: 9). In short, there was a need for *some* government intervention in the economy. At first sight this runs counter to the CPS's allegation that there could be no middle way between total economic freedom and complete state control, but such details did not worry the free-market enthusiasts in their desire to piece together a philosophy of capitalism with a human face. Government intervention, they argued, should take a form which would limit the resulting market distortions:

> Government involvement is necessary to create and regularly refurbish a framework of law in which private enterprise can be truly competitive and responsive to consumer demands. Government has a clear responsibility to curtail restrictive practices

and the abuse of monopoly power, whether perpetrated by companies, trade unions or professional associations. Government must be there, both as a forum for establishing the rules and to appoint an umpire to interpret and enforce them (CPS 1975b: 9).

Social market philosophy was not, however, an egalitarian creed, based as it was on the recognition of the "fundamental conflict" between equality and personal liberty. Beyond a certain degree, the authors argued, equality could only be enforced at the cost of sacrificing individual freedom:

> It is certainly possible to modify by government action the dis tribution of income and wealth without destroying the market economy – but this process can be carried only so far. Despite the achievements of competitive capitalism in breaking down class barriers and official hierarchies, a viable market economy does entail some private individuals with wealth and incomes considerably higher than the average citizen enjoys (CPS 1975b: 13).

Britain, the paper concluded, must seek to nourish "a free enterprise society in which, over all but a limited area of their lives, adult individuals are left free to make their own decisions and enjoy the dignity and self-respect which comes through so doing" (CPS 1975b: 16). It is, after all, "only through the operation – as unfettered as possible – of the free market that the life of each citizen will be enhanced" (CPS 1989b).

A moral issue?

The CPS has not, of course, been alone in arguing that the opera tion, "as unfettered as possible", of the free market is a necessary condition for enhancing the lives of individual citizens. As discussed elsewhere in this book, this neo-liberal conviction is common to other New Right groups such as the IEA and the ASI (Chapters 3 and 5). In arguing the case for a social market economy, however, the CPS has also been concerned with the question of the moral values which, it is claimed, are essential to underpin, and ultimately to sustain, market institutions. As we saw earlier, the founders of the CPS sought to present the case for "a free market economy, operating within a humane system of laws and institutions . . . in *moral* as well as economic terms". The cultural problem in the early days of the CPS was said to be "statism". Too many people were alleged to be dependent on state provision; too few were deemed sufficiently independent and self-reliant. This diagnosis seems to clash with the notion that state support for the poor was necessary for a healthy market economy, but for the economic liberals the contradiction was more apparent than real. Hence, there was early interest among the founders of the CPS in reviving the so-called Victorian values of hard work, thrift and self-sufficiency; the focus shifted from the contemporary experience of West Germany to Britain's (now very distant) past. Indeed, Victorian values has been a recurrent theme (in the political rhetoric at least) of Thatcherite conservatism since the mid-1970s.

In January 1975, for instance, Joseph argued that "*the* political objective of our lifetime" should be to encourage *embourgeoisement*. An important element in bourgeois values, according to Joseph, was "a further time-horizon, a willingness to defer gratification, to work hard for years, study, save, look after the family future". Historically, he continued, bourgeois values had always rested on "personal economic independence". Anticipating the Conservative Party's return to office, Joseph added that an important task to be undertaken by a future Conservative Government should be to "re-create the conditions under which the values we cherish can form the cement of our society. Our job is to re-create the conditions which will again permit the forward march of *embourgeoisement*, which went so far in Victorian times" (Joseph 1975: 56).

In July 1976, Victorian values also made an appearance in Margaret Thatcher's address to the Greater London Young Conservatives. On that occasion, Thatcher insisted that:

Choice in a free society implies responsibility. There is no hard and fast line between economic and other forms of responsibility to self, family, firm, community, nation, God. Morality lies in choosing between feasible alternatives. A moral being is one who exercises his own judgement in choice on matters great and small, bearing in mind their moral dimension, i.e. right and wrong. Insofar as his right and duty to choose is taken away by the State, the party or the union, his moral faculties – his capacity for choice – atrophy, and he becomes a moral cripple. A man is now enabled to choose between earning his living and depending on the bounty of the State (Russel 1978: 104–5).

In spelling out her personal moral vision, Thatcher left her audience in no doubt as to its origin and inspiration:

The Victorian age, which saw the burgeoning of free enterprise, also saw the greatest expansions of voluntary philanthropic activity of all kinds: the new hospitals, new schools, technical colleges, universities, new foundations for orphans, non-profit-making housing trusts, missionary societies. The Victorian age has been very badly treated in socialist propaganda. It was an age of constant and constructive endeavour, in which the desire to improve the lot of the ordinary person was a powerful factor. We who are largely living off the Victorians' moral and physical capital can hardly afford to denigrate them (Russel 1978: 105).

Clearly Mrs Thatcher believed that Conservative critics of Victorian abuses, such as Lord Shaftesbury and Benjamin Disraeli, ought to be numbered among the "socialist propagandists" whom she deplored.

For Thatcher, Victorian values "were the values when our country became great" (Jenkins 1989: 67). The implication was that the departure from such values had something to do with Britain's economic decline – decline which Mrs Thatcher was pledged to arrest and reverse. As with other versions of this thesis, there was no attempt to explain how the process of decline started; the work of Martin Wiener, for example, would suggest that the age of philanthropy was also the period when successful Victorians were sending their offspring to public schools, where they learned to look askance at entrepreneurial values (Wiener 1985). Even so, Mrs Thatcher was quite certain that economic and moral regeneration would proceed in tandem; this assumption was reflected in the activities of the Centre which she and Joseph had founded.

133

Interviewed on LBC radio in April 1983, Mrs Thatcher returned once again to the theme of Victorian values and suggested that a recovery of such values might be a prerequisite for economic regeneration.

I was brought up by a Victorian grandmother. We were taught to work jolly hard. We were taught to prove yourself; we were taught self-reliance; we were taught to live within our income. You were taught that cleanliness is next to godliness. You were taught self-respect. You were taught always to give a hand to your neighbour; you were taught tremendous pride in your country. All of these are Victorian values. They are also perennial values. You don't hear so much about these things these days, but they were good values and they *led to tremendous improvements in the standard of living* (Crewe 1989: 239).

Those close to Thatcher personally, and in particular authors published by the CPS, have frequently sought to address economic problems in terms of values; they have been keen to stress that for all the claims of socialists, capitalism is a morally superior system (see, *inter alia*, Griffiths 1985; Harris 1986). In the context of economic decline and regeneration, there has been much editorial interest at the CPS in the rediscovery of traditional – or Victorian – values.

In a Summer Address to an invited audience at the CPS in 1987, for instance, Gertrude Himmelfarb took as her theme "Victorian values – and twentieth-century condescension". Some historians, she argued, have interpreted the idea of respectability and the values connected with it as a technique or device of social control used by the ruling (or middle) class to dominate the subordinate (or working) class. This social control thesis, Himmelfarb argued, is seriously flawed and fails to explain the "inconvenient fact" that a great many working-class individuals and their families – not merely the "labour aristocracy", but also lesser skilled and even unskilled workers – appear to have embraced these values as their own. In short, Himmelfarb argued, values such as hard work, sobriety, frugality and foresight were not, and are not, exclusively middle-class or bourgeois values, but mundane virtues within everyone's reach. There was, she claimed, nothing particularly exalted or heroic about them and attaining them required no special breeding, status, talent or money. In this sense at least, Victorian values can also be seen as democratic values, or common virtues well within the reach of ordinary people (Himmelfarb 1987). The problem missed by Himmelfarb, as by Mrs Thatcher, was that of recreating a Victorian framework, so dependent on Christian mores, in an increasingly secular society. Even Himmelfarb – an acknowledged expert on the period – could not provide a satisfactory analysis of why Victorian sensibilities were lost. If the answer was given that increasing state intervention destroyed virtue, the further question of why the sensible Victorians allowed themselves to be drawn into such socialistic practices would have to be raised. Understandably, for the economic liberals, the subject of "how we got here" was best addressed in broad brushstokes rather than exhaustive historical research. Like "social market economy", Victorian Values can only be regarded as a slogan which raised more questions than it answered; as a body with a keen interest in social questions, the CPS must take at least part of the responsibility for encouraging the repetition of these phrases as if that was a satisfactory alternative to fleshing them out.

A further example of the interest the CPS has shown in moral and cultural issues, particularly since the mid-1980s, concerns the work of leading American "dependency" theorists such as Lawrence Mead and Charles Murray. Despite their differences on the design and implementation of appropriate policies to deal with the problem of welfare dependency, what unites these theorists is the claim that the problem of poverty in modern society is not simply a question of economics (or lack of resources among the poor), but partly also a question of the cultural attitudes and dispositions of many poor people. Under the welfare state, they allege, the poor have grown increasingly dependent on the state and have lost their sense of initiative, the work ethic has weakened and at least some of the poor have lost their sense of obligation to their families and indeed to society as a whole. In March 1987, the CPS organized a one-day conference in association with the Manhattan Institute (which originally commissioned Murray's book on American social policy, *Losing ground*, published in 1984), the purpose of which was to bring such issues to the attention of British academics, journalists and policy-makers (CPS 1987). As in the case of public choice theory (see Chapter 3), American analysis of social problems tended to be accepted by the economic liberals without sufficient attention to the impact of different cultural settings, but the important point for the CPS and its allies was that such theorizing seemed to fit with their pre-existing economic creed (for further discussion, see Hoover & Plant 1989; Denham 1996).

Central Office and the CRD

Initially at least, when Mrs Thatcher became Leader of the Conservative Party in February 1975, she was unable to make many changes to the existing structure and organization of the party or to the composition of the Shadow Cabinet which she had inherited from Edward Heath. She did, however, appoint Angus Maude chairman of the CRD in place of Sir Ian Gilmour, and Keith Joseph chairman of the Party's Advisory Committee on Policy (ACP). Significantly, Joseph was also given overall responsibility for the formulation of party policy (Ramsden 1980). In effect, as Todd has argued, this gave Joseph "a foot in both the CRD and CPS camps and was no doubt intended to reassure those within the Party who had become concerned with what they saw as Joseph's preoccupation with the CPS" (Todd 1991: 19–20). Joseph's appointment to these two key positions was, no doubt, also intended to help reduce (even if it could not ultimately eliminate) the tensions and conflicts between the CPS and the CRD.

After she became Party Leader, Thatcher was, to say the least, suspicious of Conservative Central Office (CCO) and the CRD. Many of the staff employed at CCO and the CRD at that time had, after all, been appointed by Heath, and had therefore failed to support the new party leader in her campaign to succeed him. A second, and arguably more important, factor at work in shaping Thatcher's attitude towards CCO and the CRD, however, was the extent to which many CCO and CRD staff also thought differently from Thatcher and her supporters within the party. The CRD in particular, which was directed at that time by Chris Patten, seemed to Thatcher and her supporters to have remained loyal, in too many respects, to the philosophical and policy outlook of previous party leaders – up to and including Heath. In the event, the new ascendancy within the party hierarchy enjoyed by Mrs Thatcher, and Sir Keith Joseph meant, as the Centre's former director of studies, David Willetts, recalled in 1991, that much of the work done by the Conservative Party in preparation for the 1979 general election, both at the policy level and at the philosophical level, was carried out at the CPS under its then director of studies, Alfred Sherman (Interview, April 1991). The CPS, as Lord Joseph emphasized, "was at that stage a very significant and positive contributor to the re-education of the country and of the Conservatives" (Interview, May 1991). Patrick Cosgrave (Thatcher's special adviser from 1975–79) has related that although he "spent much time" with the CPS, he "never once consulted" the Conservative Research Department (Cosgrave 1985: 33).

Methods of operation

Since its inception in 1974, the CPS has operated by, for example, sponsoring the publication of speeches by Conservative politicians (notably Thatcher and Joseph), presenting evidence to parliamentary and select committees and establishing study groups to examine particular policy measures. The Centre's principal aim has been the "translation of belief in individual freedom, economic enterprise and social responsibility into [the] recommendation of policies which governments can, in practice, carry out" (CPS 1989a). It has published numerous policy studies which "are despatched to Cabinet Ministers and Departments of State, to the media and to a wide circle of those engaged in the political life of Britain" (CPS 1989a). In 1991, the Centre's director of studies, David Willetts, identified three functions that he saw the CPS as carrying out. The first, he argued, had to do with the underlying philosophy of contemporary British Conservatism, namely "to remind people, from time to time, what we think Conservatism stands for". A second function of the CPS, Willetts argued, was to produce pamphlets and hold discussions on particular aspects of policy in areas such as education, health, social security and privatization. The Centre's third function, according to Willetts, at least after the Conservative Party returned to office in May 1979, had been to make itself available to Conservative ministers and to offer a kind of private resource for ministers (and members of the Downing Street Policy Unit) wanting to try out new ideas

(Interview, April 1991). In pursuit of these objectives, the Centre's work has tended to proceed in the following way:

> Study groups or working parties are set up of men and women eminent in education, law, commerce, local government, defence and other areas. Meetings are regularly held in Wilfred Street to discuss the problems of today and formulate the policies of tomorrow. Sometimes this – voluntary – work issues in Policy Studies, sometimes in written submissions to Ministers and Departments [and] sometimes in conferences and papers called in response to government proposals (CPS 1989a).

According to the Centre's former Chairman, Lord (Hugh) Thomas of Swynnerton, writing in 1989, its *modus operandi* is as follows:

> We scent a problem, or an interlocking series of problems; perhaps from conversations with our directors or donors; perhaps from visits to the corridors of Westminster or Whitehall. We then find an author, or set up a working party, to consider the matter. We put that author in touch with others working on the same theme, either in academic life, in business or in the Government. We draw the undertaking to the attention of Ministers who, we think, are sympathetic to our approach. We act as outriders, scouts, as a vanguard – who can . . . if necessary, be disavowed (CPS 1989b: 6).

Despite the similarities in terms of its ideology, the CPS has always viewed itself and its role as being, at least to some extent, different from that of other think-tanks such as the Institute of Economic Affairs (see Chapter 3). "It saw these other groups as being two steps away from the politicians and aiming at a more academic audience, whilst the CPS saw itself as being only one step away from the important decision makers" (Todd 1991: 20–1). It will be noted that neither Willetts nor Thomas name original research among the Centre's main functions – a verdict backed up more explicitly in the account of another former Director of Studies, Jeremy Shearmur (Shearmur 1995: 3).

As the above account suggests, the CPS has employed a variety of methods to influence public policy in Britain since 1974. At a very early stage in the Centre's life, for instance, and indeed prior to the formal announcement of its existence, Sir Keith Joseph stated that the CPS would put up suitable speakers whenever media outlets in general, and television and radio broadcasters in particular, were "looking for protagonists on economic arguments" (quoted in Todd 1991: 22). This strategy, it was felt, would enable the views of CPS personnel to reach a much wider audience than, for example, those of groups such as the IEA whose publications were addressed primarily at an academic readership.

Initially at least, the Centre's work, and that of Sherman in particular, was channelled mainly into the writing (and subsequent publication) of speeches delivered by Thatcher, Joseph and other Conservative politicians. The CPS, and again Sherman in particular, also provided briefings to Shadow Ministers and other Conservative MPs, arranged meetings between them and academic monetarists such as Professor Alan Walters and held regular off the record lunches with "opinion-forming" journalists in order to influence the direction of political debate. Particular broad policy areas were discussed, chiefly in the form of study groups comprising CPS staff, politicians, academics and business representatives. Following the Conservative victory in the 1979 general election, the Centre continued to brief ministers as well as presenting evidence to parliamentary select committees. As one internal CPS document, drafted by Sherman shortly after the 1979 general election, put it, the Centre would continue to provide services, speech-writing, briefings and expertise directly to Margaret Thatcher, Keith Joseph and "other Ministers or Party Officers who might require them". The CPS, Sherman argued, would also work closely with Number Ten, the Downing Street Policy Unit, the Prime Minister's Private Office and the CRD (Sherman 1979). The perceived relationship between the CPS and Mrs Thatcher became so close that in 1985, when Jeremy Shearmur was appointed Director of Studies, he was told by a member of the Board that it was vital not to do anything which might embarrass the government (Shearmur 1995: 2). Seen from this perspective, it is difficult to take seriously the claim of the CPS in its 1989 statement of *Aims and objectives* that the Centre was "Jealous of its independence" (CPS 1989a).

A further form of CPS activity has been the publication of pamphlets known as *Policy Studies* and the issue of press releases which summarize the content of each study in an abbreviated form. The Centre's publications list has grown substantially over the years – in its first decade it produced more than 80 pamphlets (Kavanagh 1987: 90). The Centre also organizes conferences and holds discussions on particular policy areas, as a different means of generating publicity for the CPS and of disseminating the ideas of its personnel. These meetings would often be addressed by government ministers, eager to exploit the CPS's reputation as a forum for the kind of radical thinking which appealed to the Prime Minister.

In addition, there have been important personal links between members of the CPS and the Conservative leadership. The businessman Sir John Hoskyns, for example, was introduced by Alfred Sherman to Sir Keith Joseph, in the first instance, and then to Margaret Thatcher. Hoskyns began to work at the CPS in the late 1970s, when the Conservative Party was still in opposition, and wrote a series of policy papers for the Shadow Cabinet at Mrs Thatcher's request. These papers, as Sherman later recalled, began as "an exercise in coaching Shadow Front Benchers in policy presentation. But it soon became apparent that policy formation and its harmonization with political assessment and presentation were a prior necessity" (Sherman 1988). The papers, collectively entitled *Stepping Stones*, suggested how the Conservative Party should deal with specific problems, such as industrial relations, as soon as it got back into power, utilizing a step by step approach.

In 1979, Hoskyns became the first head of Mrs Thatcher's Policy Unit in 10 Downing Street, and was accompanied there by Norman Strauss, who had also been introduced to Joseph and Thatcher by Sherman via the CPS. Informal and personal links between the Downing Street Policy Unit, on the one hand, and the CPS, on the other, appear to have been a consistent feature of Mrs Thatcher's premiership after 1979. Significantly, perhaps, all four Heads of the Downing Street Policy Unit under Thatcher – Hoskyns, Ferdinand Mount, John Redwood and Brian Griffiths – had some connection with the CPS, whether as an author of policy papers (Hoskyns, Redwood) or as a member of the Board of Directors (Mount, Griffiths). Two further examples are those of Professor Alan Walters and David Willetts, a former member of the Policy Unit and later a Conservative MP:

[Walters] was originally introduced to Mrs Thatcher by Sir Alfred Sherman. He has written for the CPS and has addressed at least one of the CPS fringe meetings which are held during the Conservative Party conference. Interestingly this address, which was on the economic adviser's role, was only given after Mrs Thatcher's approval had been obtained. One final and [more] recent example of the . . . close relationship between the CPS and the Conservative Party leadership is that of . . . David Willetts [who] was seconded to Conservative Central Office during the 1987 General Election campaign [and] took charge of briefing Mrs Thatcher each morning for the press conferences at Smith Square (Todd 1991: 27).

These informal links between the CPS, the Downing Street Policy Unit and the Conservative Party leadership were supplemented by contacts with other MPs, often those who either became ministers or who already held junior rank. An internal memo written by Sherman named Patrick Jenkin, Kenneth Baker, Dr Rhodes Boyson, Tom King, Cecil Parkinson, David Howell, Norman Fowler and others (Todd 1991: 27). Significantly, several of these were seen as pragmatic figures rather than ideologues; Baker, Howell and Jenkin had been associated with the Heath regime. Their co-operation with the CPS is a decisive indication of the importance attached by ambitious Conservative politicians to being seen in the correct ideological company, even if their own approval of economic liberal ideas was little more than skin deep. By contrast, the more enthusiastic Parkinson and Boyson had both at one time been socialists.

A Thatcherite Party

Staff at the CPS in its early days "were already committed to the new economics of the market and monetarism. Their task was to change other people's minds" (Cockett 1994: 239). Specifically, Joseph's aim in founding the CPS was to convert the Conservative Party to economic liberalism and, as Nigel (now Lord) Vinson explained in an interview in 1991, to "articulate in political terms what the IEA had been thinking". Cockett argues that

The perception of Joseph and his co-founders was that many of the problems that Heath's Government had encountered during its supposedly "free-market" phase in 1970–1 were essentially "political" problems. The actual economic thinking had been right, but the political application of that thinking to the real economy had not been thought through. It was a job that the IEA could not do; but one which the CPS should. For a future Conservative Government led by Joseph and Mrs Thatcher to put the ideas of the IEA into practice, they had to have a Party more effectively convinced of the need for economic liberalism, which it clearly was not in 1974 (Cockett 1994: 237).

The task of the CPS between 1974 and 1979 was to translate the broad principles of economic liberalism into practical policy proposals and "to win acceptance for those policies within the Conservative Party, much of which was still wedded to the old consensus politics" (a statement which contrasts with Cockett's own earlier judgement that the Heath Government's "actual economic thinking had been right") (Cockett 1994: 244). Yet while Joseph and the CPS sought to link the reinvigorated market economics of the 1970s with an older tradition of "liberal-Conservatism" and, in doing so, to argue that economic liberalism lay within the "mainstream" of Conservative thinking, free-market ideas "never captured the hearts, let alone the minds, of more than a small minority of Conservative MPs, even during the heyday of Thatcherism in the mid-1980s" (Cockett 1994, 325). Given the style of CPS publications, which generally dismissed all thinking outside economic liberalism as symptomatic at least of "socialism", it is hardly surprising that the record was so patchy.

Survey evidence supporting this contention continues to mount, despite the problems experienced by John Major at the hands of "Thatcherite" MPs and former ministers such as John Redwood. Philip Norton, for instance, has calculated that at most only 72 Conservative MPs (or 20 per cent of the parliamentary Conservative Party) could be classed as convinced ideological allies of Margaret Thatcher (Norton 1993). Moreover, the findings of a more recent survey of Party members suggest that "grass-roots" Conservatives are much more "progressive" than conventional wisdom might lead one to expect – even if affection for Margaret Thatcher remains strong.

There is still, it would appear, significant support at constituency level for incomes policy, strong regulation of markets and social welfare spending – all of which are "anathema to dyed-in-the-wool Thatcherites" (Whiteley et al. 1994: 202). These findings are open to question like all attitudinal surveys, but overall, they support the conclusion that the Conservative Party as a whole has not been converted to economic liberalism, despite the election victories of the 1980s and 1990s. Instead, the impression remains of an ideological *coup d'état* in the higher echelons of the party, the success of which should be explained by the course of events combined with the traditional Conservative deference to a leader, much more than the persuasiveness of economic liberal thinking. Given its original objectives, this must be a disheartening outcome for the CPS.

Recruitment and Ideological Fellowship

Perhaps, as Cockett has argued, it would be more true to say that the primary contribution of New Right think-tanks in general, and the CPS in particular, to Thatcherism was the extent to which economic liberals, at the CPS and elsewhere,

> succeeded in convincing a section of the leadership of the [Conservative] Party in the mid-1970s that they should embrace economic liberalism as an alternative to a failed status quo; and then provided not only practical policy proposals but also, just as importantly, the personnel to implement a political programme of economic liberalism (Cockett 1994: 325).

This programme, of course, could be carried through provided that the minority of economic liberals were in the key positions. As Sherman noted in an article in *The Times* in 1984, this was a fundamental shift in the nature of the Conservative Party – and one which continues to affect it in the 1990s. The Centre's work in the realm of political and economic ideas, Sherman argued, may have been less important than its part in "generating in the Conservative Party a sense of intellectual excitement which had hitherto been largely a monopoly of the left. No one calls the Conservatives the stupid party any longer; at worst, they accuse it of indulging in ideology" (quoted in Harris 1996: 58). Ironically, these words were written when Sherman's own "sense of intellectual excitement" had been replaced by disillusionment at what he regarded as the excessive spirit of compromise in the first Thatcher Government; by 1985 he had left the CPS to found a new organization, Policy Search.

Certainly the CPS acted as a useful source of recruitment for the Conservative Party. Perhaps more important – in the early days, especially – was its ability to provide ideological fellowship for economic liberals already within the party. It must have been a great relief for senior party members to leave tense meetings of the Shadow Cabinet and join gatherings at the CPS where no doubts were harboured about the course which Mrs Thatcher wanted to pursue once she had won power. In time, of course, this feeling of "us and them" had unfortunate results for the party leadership, but in the opposition period the CPS clearly played an important role in sustaining the morale of the New Right within the Conservative Party.

Policy

Michael Harris believes that the influence of New Right think-tanks in general, and the CPS in particular, on contemporary British politics has been profound. At the same time, he argues, such influence is difficult to isolate precisely, given the complexity of the policy-making process, conflicting accounts and the often long time-lag from ideas to practice. But given the intimate contact between the CPS and the leading actors in the Thatcherite revolution, claims to influence over government policy (as opposed to the wider "climate of opinion") are difficult to contradict (Harris 1996: 58).

In the early post-1979 period, Harris argues, the Centre's main influence concerned the early budgets (especially 1981), monetarism and the trade union issue, on which it was crucial. Hoskyns and Sherman, along with Leonard Neal, chair of the Trade Union Reform Study Group (TURC), played an important part in keeping up the pressure to translate ideas on trade union reform into law, even if the subsequent legislation did not (always) follow their particular prescriptions. Thus, as Cockett has pointed out, the Employment Bill which became law in July 1980 went "only some way towards the full reform of trade unions that the CPS wanted to see; outlawing secondary picketing, for instance, but failing to abolish the [so-called] Closed Shop". Moreover, while Hoskyns, Neal and the TURC apparently succeeded in persuading Mrs Thatcher that trade union reform should not stop with the 1980 Bill, the legislation introduced by the new Secretary of State for Employment, Norman Tebbit, "owed little to the suggestions of TURC or any other outside body" (Cockett 1994: 301). Ironically the gradualist approach to union reform was established by James Prior, one of the most determined opponents of economic liberalism in the Cabinet, who had been dismayed by the alternative course laid down by *Stepping stones*. Nonetheless, Cockett argues, other CPS study groups did have isolated successes through their involvement in the work of several government departments:

> One of the more successful groups was the "Personal Capital Formation Group" chaired by Nigel Vinson. This group came up with three proposals which later became Government policy – Personal Pensions, Personal Equity Plans (originally called "Personal Savings Pool") and the Enterprise Allowance Scheme. The latter scheme was Vinson's . . . and he put the scheme personally to [James] Prior while he was Minister for Employment. In March 1983, when the Government finally introduced the . . . scheme, Prior sent Vinson a letter of congratulations: "It has taken a long while to persuade the Treasury to make the enterprise allowance a national scheme – the wheels of Government grind slowly. It was an idea that you hatched in my office and I am delighted that it has come to something" (Cockett 1994: 301–2).

The CPS pamphlet *Personal and portable pensions for all* (1981), Cockett notes, was used by Norman Fowler when he was Minister of Health and Social Security, and Personal Equity Plans (PEPs) "were eventually introduced by Nigel Lawson in 1987, although, again, it is impossible to ascribe the introduction of PEPs solely to the work of the CPS" (Cockett 1994: 302). As it turned out, this policy turned out to be one of the most serious failures of the Thatcher years, since thousands of workers were persuaded to contract out of secure occupational pensions. Other instances of CPS work with apparently happier results included John Redwood's advocacy of privatization (in the Nationalized Industries Study Group), which led to his appointment as head of the Number 10 Policy Unit in 1983, specifically to develop the government's privatization programme. A further study group which appears to have exerted at least some influence on policy during the 1980s was the Education Study Group (CPSESG), chaired by Caroline (later Baroness) Cox. As Cockett has pointed out, the CPSESG

> included several [people] who had been involved in [the work of other] "New Right" groups, such as Dr John Marks (co-author with Cox of the celebrated pamphlet *Rape of reason*), Dr Digby Anderson, Professor R.V. Jones, Patricia Morgan, Marjorie and Arthur Seldon, Oliver Letwin, son of William and Shirley Letwin, and Professor Arthur Pollard. The Education Study Group put forward several proposals on such themes as accountability, parent choice and school standards, many of which found their way into government legislation – eventually – in the late 1980s. A "ginger-group" of the Education Study Group, the Hillgate Group, consisting of Cox, Marks, Roger Scruton and Jessica Douglas-Home, produced an important report which was received sympathetically by the Prime Minister, and much of the document found its way into the 1987 Conservative Party election manifesto (Cockett 1994: 303–4).

One recent study has attacked the Hillgate Group's *Whose schools?* on the grounds that it included several notes and appendices, most of which on inspection turned out to refer to other New Right publications. Thus what "to the inexperienced eye" might look like a well-researched publication was, in the authors' view, merely a piece of ideological advocacy (Carr and Hartnett 1996: 145). Even so, ideas arising from groups like this are held to have affected government education policy, especially in the later 1980s; it became a regular complaint that instead of listening to people within the profession, successive Secretaries of State paid undue attention to the think-tanks (Lawton 1994: 80–1). Indeed, education policy has been a more recent area of influence for the CPS in the 1990s:

> [F]ollowing [John] Major's promise of a pre-school place for every four-year-old, the CPS has organised a number of con-

ferences on th[is] issue, at which government figures have been present (Eric Forth, then Education Minister, and Jonathan Aitken, then Chief Secretary to the Treasury). This has been one of the CPS's more rapid achievements (discounting that the idea of vouchers in education has been around since the 1960s) and education remains one of the CPS's key concerns (Harris 1996: 60).

Yet, despite all the CPS's efforts, Tony Blair's insistence before the 1997 general election that his three main priorities for government would be "education, education and education" showed that this subject, among many other possible policy areas, was the one on which New Labour sensed that the Conservative Party was weakest even after 18 years in power. Important changes in the education system continue to occur on a regular basis, as politicians and officials pore over national test results and weigh the arguments of rival theorists. It could be claimed that the effect of think-tank intervention in the national debate on education has been to spark off something approaching a state of permanent revolution; certainly not until the current upheavals are over will it be possible to draw firm conclusions about the lasting impact of the CPS and its allies.

For a crusading think-tank like the CPS, getting policies implemented can only be half the battle at best; more important for them is the fate of such policies when they come into operation. Indeed if they are perceived to have failed in practice, the outcome can be worse than if they were never tried in the first place. As supporters of Keynesian ideas discovered after the mid-1970s, even problems arising from developments outside the control of policy-makers can lead to the "failed" approach to government being spurned for many years. The story of the CPS neatly illustrates the tensions that can arise while an ideological programme is being subjected to the test of practice; by 1983 Thomas and Sherman (both converts from the left) "were scarcely on speaking terms" (Cockett 1994: 318). Economic liberalism was an effective ideological glue for such characters during the opposition years; once Mrs Thatcher was in power and her supporters turned to the question of how their "victory" in the Battle of Ideas should be exploited, relations often turned sour. Whether or not the CPS was to assert its independence from the Conservative Party or to act as a support-group suddenly became a crucial question once the Conservatives had taken office and were in a position to act as well as talk.

This problem of the CPS's status helped to cause the rift between Thomas and Sherman, but if anything became more acute over the years, as the Centre's authors reflected on the period of Conservative rule. During his period as director David Willetts expressed the view that "If we criticize the government, then we do so from the point of view of supporting what the government's trying to do, of having fundamental sympathy with it" (Interview, April 1991). However, as the controversies deepened and even ideological soul-mates of the Prime Minister saw fit to resign, this approach proved easier to state than to carry out in practice without ruffling feathers. In 1989, for example, the Centre published Tim Congdon's *Monetarism lost*, which contained some trenchant criticisms of Nigel Lawson's performance at the Treasury; this followed a similar volume of December 1985, to which Congdon had also contributed (Congdon 1989; CPS 1985). The difficulty for the CPS was that whatever the views of its permanent staff, in a loyalty contest between party and principle many of their best-regarded authors could be expected to plump for the purity of their ideas. Yet the role of "keeper of the conscience" was more suitable for the independent IEA than for the CPS, which the Prime Minister had helped to set up. It is little wonder that when Jeremy Shearmur arrived at the Centre in 1985 he was "unclear what its functions were" (Shearmur 1995: 2). Funding was apparently not a problem even in the mid-1990s, but despite the vigorous efforts of David Willetts and his successors as research director, Gerald Frost and Tessa Keswick (from October 1995), the CPS has never fully recovered from the departure of Sherman and the issues which underlay the quarrels of the previous decade. With the Conservative Party now back in opposition, the Centre is an obvious venue for leadership speeches (and even for Labour's "radical" kite-flying exercises), but despite its evident desire to distance itself from the Thatcherite past the future for the CPS looks deeply uncertain.

Conclusion

Michael Harris argues that the Centre has always trodden the thin line between intellectual integrity, on the one hand, and access to the Conservative Party and (since 1979) successive Conservative Governments, on the other:

> It was formed to speak over the heads of the Party to create a public debate, yet relied on the Party as the vehicle to implement its ideas. Perhaps the central paradox of the CPS has been its closeness to power and yet its apparent marginalisation. The CPS has continued with its Thatcherite agenda, fully conscious that there are areas in which more can be done (further privatisations) and where governmment policy in the 1980s has been self-destructive (the "traditional" family) (Harris 1996: 60).

In speaking over the heads of the Party to the wider public, the fate of the CPS has been similar to that of the IEA (see Conclusion to Chapter 3). The economic arguments swayed some people before 1979, but there was nothing like the kind of seismic shift in the climate of opinion hoped for by the founders of these institutions. As Harris's remarks suggest, social questions (particularly those concerning the family) preoccupied the CPS far more than the IEA. Here, if anything, the record is even more at variance from the triumphalism reflected by authors such as Richard Cockett. Despite repeated efforts, including a pamphlet written by David Willetts in 1991, a coherent policy on the family remained elusive. The extent to which the implementation of economic liberalism undermined social stability was a serious blow for which the CPS seems to have been unprepared; the response was more to wish the problem out of existence rather than address it at its roots. Willetts, for example, produced figures which showed a connection between social deprivation and family breakdown, which merely drew attention to the fact that under Conservative Governments since 1979 the gap between rich and poor had increased (Willetts 1991: 12). Although the motive force behind John Major's ill-starred Back to Basics campaign of 1994 came from the Downing Street Policy Unit, the fiasco merely reflected the failure of the government and its advisers in the CPS to overcome the discrepancy between economic freedom and social authoritarianism – a division symbolized by Jeremy Shearmur's account of the members of the education study group in the mid-1980s, who saw "themselves as engaged in a crusade to save education from the depredations of the loony left", and thus seemed "politically rather different from the rest of the Centre" (Shearmur 1995: 2).

It would be a mistake to assume that ideas will always fail to take proper root in a political society if they are incoherent, but the outburst of ridicule which accompanied Back to Basics strongly implies that the tensions within the New Right project could only be held in check while ministers could still talk of a West German-style economic miracle with some hope of convincing the public that their policies had helped to bring widespread prosperity. Once that illusion had disappeared in the second recession, which brought economic insecurity to those who remained cushioned and complacent during the first one, the Conservative Party might still have retained power if it had made the public believe, not in the clarity of its thinking, but in its good intentions. While the economic liberals within the Cabinet continued up to the end to argue that the message was right but communication poor, the evidence does not support this. By 1997 the government had enjoyed 18 years in which to convince the public that it stood for a mixture of economic efficiency and social compassion – the kind of stance promised by the phrase "social market economy" – and yet the majority of voters saw the Conservatives as uncaring and impotent.

Whatever the real views of the New Labour leadership, the crushing defeat of the Conservative Party in May 1997 must at least in part be attributed to the failure of the CPS to develop a coherent philosophy for government (especially in its special field of social affairs). The Centre made the fatal mistake of believing its own propaganda, encouraged in this error by successive election victories which the Conservative Party achieved despite a steady drop in its share of the popular vote. Leaving aside the vexed question of the CPS's status, its self-proclaimed position one step away from policy-making could have granted it the extra perspective which busy ministers might be excused for lacking. The Centre's failure to make proper use of its opportunities overshadows any short-term successes it might have had in helping to shape the radical changes of the 1980s.

CHAPTER 5

The Adam Smith Institute

Origins

The Adam Smith Institute (ASI) was conceived in 1976 by three graduates of St Andrews University in Scotland, Madsen Pirie and the brothers Eamonn and Stuart Butler. Following a year-long period of preparation, the Institute was formally established on 31 August 1977 when it moved into offices in Great George Street, WC1, close to the Treasury and the Palace of Westminster. The principal figures in the ASI are its president, Madsen Pirie, and director, Eamonn Butler. Together, Butler and Pirie "run the Institute as a team. The functions both men play appear to overlap, but the general impression is that Butler is involved more with the day-to-day running of the organization, while Pirie is the ideas man" (Heffernan 1996: 73). Stuart Butler, the third founder member, went on to work as a policy analyst at the Heritage Foundation, a Washington-based think-tank (see Chapter 1) which enjoys friendly relations with the ASI, in 1981 and is now its vice-president for domestic policy studies (Cockett 1994: 282). As Hames and Feasey (1994: 223) have pointed out, the ASI resembles the Heritage Foundation, albeit on a much smaller scale than that wealthy organization. Like Heritage it "specialises in relatively short and issue-oriented publications", and some of its best-publicized activities have apparently been copied from American conservative bodies.

Described as the "youngest, most aggressively ideological, and self-confessed *enfant terrible*" among British New Right think-tanks (Hames and Feasey 1994: 223), the ASI resembles the IEA insofar as it exists to promote free-market ideology (see Chapter 3). Hames and Feasey suggest an important difference between the two organizations:

> . . . the Adam Smith Institute . . . tends to offer more practical free market solutions to political problems, rather than engaging in the rather dry and didactic style of [the IEA]. The ASI [also] aimed to be different from the CPS, with fewer institutional ties to the Conservative Party organization. However, as the ASI's enthusiasm for the Thatcher regime blossomed, maintaining such strict independence became more challenging (Hames and Feasey 1994: 223).

In fact, as we have seen, the style of the IEA is anything but "dry and didactic"; it would be more accurate to say that the ASI has adopted all the populist techniques of the older Institute, but has applied this more directly to policy work.

The origins of the ASI lie in St Andrews University in Scotland. Adam Smith himself was born within 50 miles of the University campus at St Andrews; the bicentenary of his death fell in 1976, the year that discussions about the new Institute began in earnest. The university has produced several high profile members of the New Right, including the later Secretary of State for Scotland, Michael Forsyth. In naming the Institute after Adam Smith, the founders of the ASI intended to affirm both their faith in market liberalism and their own Scottish origins. Whether the founders of the ASI were entirely justified in claiming Smith as "one of us" remains controversial; Smith's *Theory of moral sentiments* (1759) is anything but an individualistic tract, and in its eighteenth-century context his more familiar *Wealth of nations* (1776) might have been read as an appeal for more government intervention in the domestic economy; its main thrust was against the mercantilism which protected the home market against foreign traders. Certainly Smith, a careful scholar whose life-work was left incomplete, would not have felt at home amidst the rather frantic activity of the Institute which bears his name.

The ASI is nominally run by a six member management board, chaired by Sir Austin Bide and comprising (in addition to Eamonn Butler and Madsen Pirie) Sir Ralph Bateman, Sir Robert Clark and Sir John Greenborough. While the four lay members of the board have long experience in industry and in public service, Pirie and Butler remain the driving forces behind the organization. In addition to the Institute proper, two new divisions, a Conference Division and an International Division, were added in 1992. Each division is run on a separate basis from the others. Each has its own board (under the overall supervision of the board of management) and the finances of each division are ring-fenced. Butler and Pirie are the only individuals on the board of all three divisions (Heffernan 1996: 75).

The new International Division was given separate premises from the mainstream ASI and is charged with the task of overseeing the overseas work of the Institute. It marks an attempt by the ASI to capitalize on the growing international trend towards economic liberalization and marketization. The International Division claims to have conducted projects in over 30 countries worldwide (ASI publicity claims that its members have "briefed government leaders in over fifty countries") and its literature carries endorsements from both past and serving ministers in Moldavia, Poland, Mongolia, Equador, Lithuania and Trinidad and Tobago. Through the work of its International Division, the ASI has sought to establish itself as a global policy consultant, prepared to offer advice and instruction in the general field of economic liberalization. Heffernan has argued that the establishment of the Conference and International Divisions appears to mark something of a new departure for the ASI, "perhaps signalling a shift toward[s] policy consultancy which may eventually boost the income and turnover of the organization" (Heffernan 1996: 75); indeed, in 1996 Adam Smith International reported a profit of nearly £300,000 on a turnover of £1.5 million, making it in financial terms easily the most significant of the ASI's activities (*Labour Research* 1997: 11). A more cynical view would be that with the collapse of the post-war international order, foreign customers (especially those in former Communist countries) might be able to implement radical policy changes without experiencing the resistance which arose in the longer-established western democracies. Indeed the first full-scale monetarist experiment took place in General Pinochet's Chile.

As far as its domestic operations are concerned, the ASI employs only three or four full-time members of staff, supported by a number of young interns and students on short-term contracts. From the outset, the ASI was a "low cost, low budget operation" and for the first ten years neither Pirie nor Butler drew salaries from the Institute (Cockett 1994: 284–5). Like the IEA, the ASI basically depends on corporate and individual support for its funding. Unlike the IEA, however, the ASI is not a charitable organization. In 1993–94, it received donations of almost £100,000 – miniscule by the standards of its American counterparts (Heffernan 1996: 76).

The founders of the ASI had long track records of political activity on the political right. Pirie and the Butler brothers were all familiar with the publications of the IEA and were long established enthusiasts for the cause of economic liberalism. Eamonn Butler, in particular, was a very active consumer of IEA literature, while Pirie expressed his admiration for its work in a letter he wrote to its founder, Antony Fisher, from the United States in 1975.

> The point which I always try to make about the Institute of Economic Affairs is that it has its most far-reaching effect on the up-coming generation in the universities and colleges. I, as thousands of others must have done, first encountered the work of the Institute when I was at university and was just in the process of developing my own ideas. The fact that the IEA has such academic prestige, and publishes research [on] such a wide range of topics, acts as a considerable reinforcement to those who are groping their own way towards a commitment to free-market and liberal ideas . . .
>
> Since the IEA has concentrated much of its work on empirical studies, they have forced into the academic study of economics an emphasis on the practical effect of policy. It has become impossible for abstract reasoners to speculate about "ideal" economic systems without having the IEA's evidence from the real world thrust under their noses. I think that this, more than any other factor, has brought about its academic triumph. IEA views do not dominate everywhere, but they do dominate in more than a few institutions, and, more importantly, they are represented everywhere. When you reflect what the influence of the IEA [has been] on my ideas, and remember that I am a philosopher, you can gather how much more dramatic its effect has been on economists. One generation of students is the next generation of teachers; which is why the

IEA is so well represented among the younger economists now working their way through university departments . . .

The IEA not only alters the background intellectual climate of the debate; it puts arguments directly into the mouths of interested parties. You must take great satisfaction in seeing how many times it is that IEA work finds its way immediately into debate in the House of Commons, as well as in the media. Such are my views on the IEA as an outsider, a non-economist (in Cockett 1994: 190–1).

In the light of later events, it is ironic that Pirie should have referred to the IEA's alleged concern for "the practical effect of policy"; it was certainly odd that he should congratulate the IEA on this achievement, when the NIESR had been focusing on policy outcomes more consistently and for much longer.

In 1971, the St Andrews University Conservative Association delegation to the Conservative Party Conference included all three founder members of the ASI. As a protest against what they saw as the Heath Government's U-turn (then in its infancy – if such a thing ever happened at all), the St Andrews delegates produced a spoof front page of the *Daily Telegraph* for June 1981, predicting the triumph of various free-market ideas. The mock-up front page reported on the floating pound, a rise in shares for "Telecom" which had replaced the GPO and the sale of the last council house to its tenants. At least this showed that the St Andrews contingent were blessed with political imagination unusual among students at any time. As Cockett has recalled:

They not only got the price of the paper exactly right after inflation (15p), but also reported on the forthcoming serialization of a book about the success of "one-time film star" Ronald Reagan in the previous November's Presidential Election. There was a temptation not to take these young free-market radicals too seriously, but even in 1971 they showed that they were already thinking "the unthinkable" (Cockett 1994: 281).

Later, in 1987, Pirie would say of the ASI that it "propose[s] things which people regard as on the edge of lunacy. The next thing you know they are on the edge of policy" (cited by Heffernan 1996: 74). From the position of determined out-riders, the founders of the ASI claim they are now part of the process of government. Indeed, in an interview published in the *Guardian* in November 1994, Pirie asserted that think-tanks such as the ASI are now "part of the constitution" (Denham and Garnett 1996: 58).

The distinctive features of the ASI's work are its close concern with policy implementation, support of the free market and the wide range of its proposals (Kavanagh 1990: 87). Specifically, it has produced a number of studies on quangos; it provided an extensive listing of such bodies and monitored the Conservative Government's (mixed) record in abolishing them. It has also been particularly active in promoting policies of privatization, deregulation and the contracting-out of services from local government. Privatization, Pirie argues, derives from a recognition that the weaknesses of public sector supply are inherent. Since there is no way of achieving effect-ive control over public sector output, services and activities cur-rently performed in the public sector should be transferred, wholly or at least in part, to the private sector, a transfer which will take away their status as political entities and transform them instead into economic ones. According to Pirie, only the private sector can impose the economic disciplines and create the incentives required to ensure that the output (or supply) of goods and services is both sensitive and responsive to the choices (or demands) of individual consumers (Pirie 1988b: 52–3).

The Omega project

In the period from 1982 to 1985, the ASI's energies were mainly devoted to the so-called Omega project, a series of reports which built up into a fairly systematic governmental programme. As Levitas has argued, the project represents "the most ambitious attempt to date to spell out the implications of neo-liberalism for social policy and . . . is the main articulation of the liberal New Right's utopia" (Levitas 1986: 82). The Omega project was conceived to fill a sig-nificant gap in the field of public policy research. As the editors of the ASI's *Omega file* (Butler et al. 1985), published in 1985, argued in their introduction to the project's published findings:

Administrations entering office in democratic societies are often aware of the problems . . . they face, but lack a well-developed range of policy options . . . The Omega project represents the most complete review of the activity of government ever undertaken in Britain. It presents the most comprehensive range of policy initiative which has ever been researched under one programme (Butler et al 1985: 1).

Kavanagh (1990: 88) has recalled that:

Teams consisting of people from business, the media, public affairs and the universities were assigned to examine the work of each government department. The remit of each group was to suggest [which] activities could be transferred from the public to the private sector and where opportunities for choice and enterprise could be opened up (Kavanagh 1990: 88).

The Omega reports (published individually in 1983–84, then as a collection in 1985, Butler et al. 1985) proposed a massive programme of privatization of local and central government activities, services and industries, and advocated greater parental choice in education, contracting-out, the reorganization of the National Health Service and the encouragement of private insurance, among other things.

The ASI's *Omega file* is not, however, simply a collection of ideas. After each policy proposal, there follows a section written in legislative language, explaining exactly how the proposal is to be implemented. According to Pirie, interviewed in 1983, the reason for this was that it seemed to take "a long time to gear civil servants up to getting things done" (cited by Wade and Picardie 1983: 8). The Omega Project, Pirie explained, was designed with the specific intention of "short-circuiting" this problem by offering politicians a comprehensive range of policy objectives as well as the means to achieve them.

The major themes which recur throughout the Omega reports are those of deregulation and privatization. The assumption throughout is that greater accountability can and should be achieved by limiting the role of government and increasing the role of the market. The Omega report on Local Government, Planning and Housing, for instance, asserts that "independent" providers are necessarily more in tune with public demand than local authorities can ever be, because "their perpetual search for profitability . . . stimulates them to discover and produce what the consumer wants". In this sense, the report argues, the market is "more genuinely democratic than the public sector, involving the decisions of far more individuals and at much more frequent intervals" (cited by Levitas 1986: 83).

The first hundred . . . ?

The ASI claims a long list of "battle honours", in the sense of having had its ideas adopted as government policy in Britain during the 1980s and 1990s (Adam Smith Institute 1990; Oakley 1989). These include the Thatcher Government's early (and short-lived) assaults on quangos, the breaking-up of the Department of Health and Social Security (DHSS) into a Department of Health and a Department of Social Security and the use of the private sector in infrastructure projects such as the Dartford Bridge. In local government, the ASI urged the privatization of council services such as refuse collection as long ago as 1980. The Institute also put forward recommendations for "competitive tendering" in local government services, the abolition of the Greater London Council (GLC), the creation of Urban Development Corporations (UDCs) and the introduction of the community charge (or poll-tax) and uniform business rate. All of the above were adopted as policy by the Thatcher Government in Britain during the 1980s – although they might not all prove lasting.

On housing, the Institute called in 1983 for the ending of rent controls on new leases, the phasing out of stamp duty, the sale of council estates to developers and the termination of the solicitors' monopoly in conveyancing. In education, the ASI urged (from 1984 onwards) various measures which, it claims, found their way into the Education Reform Act of 1988, including greater say for parents, the capacity for schools to opt out of Local Education Authority (LEA) control and the creation of "centres of excellence", introduced in the form of City Technology Colleges (CTCs). On transport, the Institute urged (from 1983 onwards) the deregulation of rural bus services, the privatization of the National Bus Company, the introduction of mini-buses for urban transport and the privatization of airports. In 1984, it called for the privatization of gas, electricity and water, the privatization of Rolls-Royce, the splitting-up of British Leyland, the transfer of warship yards to the private sector and the phasing out of regional development grants (Adam Smith Institute 1990: 5–6). The Institute also argued for the phasing out of the State Earnings Related Pension Scheme (SERPS) and the introduction of portable pensions. A further recommendation to come on to the government's political agenda in 1990 was the termination of the compulsory division between barristers and solicitors (Oakley 1989).

In a report published in 1990, the ASI claimed that "more than one hundred of the innovative ideas researched and published by the ASI have now made their way into public policy" (Adam Smith Institute 1990: 1). The report went on to claim that:

> Some of these proposals have been implemented already; some are firmly on the agenda; others are stimulating a lively public debate. Sometimes that process of debate has led to improvements or amendments to the original initiative; on other occasions, its form has remained firmly intact. In some cases, [the] ASI was clearly the prime source of an idea, while in others it was only one voice in a chorus.

Part of the task which the ASI sets itself, according to the report, is the "research of innovative ideas so that they can be presented to decision-makers as realistic and practical options". Potential objections to the Institute's proposals are anticipated and, where possible, further measures designed to deal with such objections are incorporated into the proposals *before* they are subjected to public scrutiny and debate (Adam Smith Institute 1990: 1).

The ASI claims that it achieved "remarkable success" during the 1980s in Britain. It also claims that many of the strategies it has "pioneered" are now being taken up by "a host of other countries, suitably tailored to fit their own special circumstances". At the same time, while congratulating itself on the perceived impact of its work, the ASI was also prepared to concede that a large part of the credit for its success was due to those who had seen merit in its proposals and who had "worked to put them on the public agenda and take them through the other stages of the policy-making process". Nevertheless, the report credited the ASI with an "outstanding record of achievement" (Adam Smith Institute 1990: 1). While some would dismiss the ASI's claim to have reached its *first hundred* as wildly overstated (see later), "few would deny [its] ability to put subjects onto the political agenda" (Oakley 1989). From an early stage it had demonstrated its presentational flair; in particular, it made full use of its slender resources by targeting decision-makers at the appropriate level and mailing information packs to them (Kavanagh 1987: 88).

Ideas are not enough

After graduating from St Andrews, Pirie and the Butlers, Stuart and Eamonn, worked in the United States for several years and became increasingly interested in the work of the school of "public choice" developed by James Buchanan and Gordon Tullock at the University of Virginia in Charlottesville, which sought to apply the principles and techniques of market economics to the analysis of political behaviour. Public choice theory is concerned to design political institutions in such a way as to "maximize individual freedom for libertarian reasons. Most importantly, these institutions must impose constraints on the scope for spending allocation (and hence taxation needs) by politicians, and minimize the monopoly of the public sector" (King 1987: 12). Tullock's work had first been exposed to a British audience in an IEA publication of 1976 (see Chapter 3), but Pirie had absorbed the theory earlier. As Cockett has recalled:

> The Heritage Foundation developed its own application of this philosophy, by making relatively specific policy proposals which would be applicable in practice to a given set of political and institutional circumstances. It was this strategy . . . that the founders of [the] ASI imported back into Britain when they returned from the United States in the mid-1970s (Cockett 1994: 282).

Interestingly, while the IEA could regard public choice theory as a good reason to remain aloof from the sordid world of practical politics, the ASI tended to regard it as a promising opening through which they could push their ideas on institutional reforms. Arising from their experiences in the United States, Eamonn Butler and Pirie saw the ASI as a vehicle through which they could become "scholar activists" by suggesting specific policies to put their ideas into practice. Only through detailed policy proposals, they believed, could the objectives identified by the Virginia School of public choice be realized (Heffernan 1996: 77). Adapting the approach of the Heritage Foundation and the work of the Virginia School, they developed a series of policy-making techniques known collectively as "micropolitics" which Pirie would later describe as the "creative counterpart" of the public choice critique (Pirie 1988b).

From its apparently inauspicious beginnings in 1977, the ASI has sought to apply free-market ideas to the real world as "policy engineers" determined to translate theory into practice. As Cockett has explained:

> Whereas the IEA, or even the CPS, might establish the theoretical case for denationalizing British Steel, the ASI would provide the detailed, step-by-step proposals to show how this could be done in practice . . . Whereas the IEA had provided the general theory and principles, and the CPS had won a party political constituency for those principles, the ASI found a niche for itself as the "policy engineers" to develop practical policy proposals which could translate those principles into practice when the Conservative Government came to power. The *raison d'être* of these three "think-tanks" did, indeed, directly map the contours of the process of putting ideas into action. Hayek had always realized the need for such a progression from "ideas" to "practice" and the work of the ASI represented the final stage of that process whereby ideas came to be translated into practical policy proposals, to be implemented by a political party pledged to acting on those ideas (Cockett 1994: 283).

In Pirie's words, it is "engineers" who follow "pure scientists" to make the machines which alter reality. In *Micropolitics* he advances a new interpretation of the Heath Government's record. Rather than accepting the usual New Right criticisms – that Heath never really believed in economic liberalism, or that he was not tough enough to carry through a principled programme – Pirie claims that the government "lacked a coherent theory of policy application, and thought that the task of political leaders was simply to implement ideas" (Pirie 1988a: 52). Winning the intellectual battle of ideas, he argues, is not enough; methods must also be devised by which free markets can be secured in practice, not merely advocated in theory. The idea at the core of "micropolitics", then, is that "creative ingenuity is needed to apply to the practical world of interest group politics the concepts of free market theory" (Pirie 1988b: 267). Only through the application of "practical" ideas can real change be effected.

Although Pirie is more generous in his treatment of the Heath Government than most other New Right commentators, his account is no less eccentric; in opposition before 1970 Heath was attacked for putting policy technique ahead of ideology, and he entered government with a well-developed (some would say overdeveloped) programme for office. Hence Pirie's explanation for the failure of the Heath Government tells us more about the purposes of the Institute than about recent British history. Pirie had spotted a gap in the political market-place; since neither the IEA nor the CPS could reasonably be described as "policy engineers", the ASI would announce that this was by far the most important role which any think-tank could play, and present its credentials as the body best able to fulfill it. At the same time, however, Pirie knew that his clients in the Thatcher administration were unusually interested in ideas; hence when the purpose suits him he talks up the importance of ideas, which elsewhere he plays down. In several cases, Pirie argues, "the success of the policy has led to the victory of the idea rather than the other way around" (Pirie 1988b: 269). If driven towards its logical conclusion this remark implies that policy-makers interested in changing the climate of opinion should ignore initial unpopularity in the expectation that their measures will eventually find acceptance – exactly the mentality which lay behind the Poll Tax.

In his *General theory of employment, interest and money*, John Maynard Keynes famously suggested that the (political) world is ruled by the ideas of intellectuals:

> . . . the ideas of economists and political philosophers, both when they are right and when they are wrong, are more powerful than is commonly understood. Indeed, the world is ruled by little else. Practical men, who believe themselves to be quite exempt from any intellectual influences, are usually the slaves

of some defunct economist. Madmen in authority, who hear voices in the air, are distilling their frenzy from some academic scribbler of a few years back. I am sure that the power of vested interests is vastly exaggerated compared with the gradual encroachment of ideas . . . soon or late, it is ideas, not vested interests, which are dangerous for good or evil (Keynes 1936: 383).

This observation, mounted and framed, takes pride of place in the entrance hall of the IEA. At the same time, however, it is a statement of the relationship between ideas, interests and circumstances that finds less favour at the ASI, where the very reverse is believed to be the case. Pirie has written that ideas "may change our thinking, but they will not change the world" (Pirie 1988a: 52). As Heffernan has recently explained:

> In its own terms the [Adam Smith] Institute is not so much concerned with popularizing ideas (which may be defined as ends) as it is [with] seeking to communicate suitable methods (which could be defined as means) to enact designated ideas in practice . . . As a result, the [Adam Smith] Institute is more likely to mount and display the observation of Karl Marx that "philosophers only interpret the world, the point is to change it" than it is to endorse the Keynes quotation favoured by the Institute of Economic Affairs (Heffernan 1996: 77).

As we saw in Chapter 3, the IEA's long-established working method has been to popularize free-market ideas by publishing pamphlets and papers and organizing lectures, lunches and seminars targeted at Hayek's "second-hand dealers in ideas", or those "opinion-formers" (journalists, academics, writers, broadcasters and commentators) who are presumed to determine the political thinking of the nation as a whole. The ASI, on the other hand, operates with a different understanding of the relationship between ideas (theory) and events (practice). Ideally it tries to anticipate the future priorities of government, and either through the media, informal contacts or its own publications provide blueprints for reform which can be readily translated into legislation when ministers judge that the time is right. In short, the ASI would like to see its work as the concrete embodiment of the more abstract speculations published by the IEA.

Despite its small size and limited budget, the ASI has generated a considerable media profile compared to other think-tanks. In 1980, for instance, the ASI published *Reservicing Britain*, a paper (by Michael Forsyth) on contracting out local government services. While this received limited coverage in the national press, it was the subject of a detailed article in James Goldsmith's short-lived magazine *Now*. This article was then taken up by the head of Mrs Thatcher's Policy Unit in 10 Downing Street, Sir John Hoskyns, who arranged for copies to be circulated to Conservative-led local authorities throughout the country. This approach, based on the practice of the more aggressive US "advocacy tanks" (see Introduction), shows that large budgets and substantial staff numbers can be less important than imaginative marketing.

The ASI has long laid claim to the title of think-tank, its charter describing its role as furthering "the advancement of learning by research and public policy options, economic and political science and the publications of such research" (cited by Kavanagh 1990: 87). At the same time, the ASI remains a very different organization from (say) the PSI, the NIESR; or even the IEA; given the Institute's remarkable track record for the rapid production of policy ideas it is probably the best British example of an advocacy tank.

At the same time, however, political issues that are likely to cause dissent within the ASI are particularly frowned upon. Questions to do with Britain's relations with the European Union, for instance, are ones on which Institute insiders "claim strict neutrality, given the divisions [such issues] foster within conservative (and indeed other) political organizations" (Heffernan 1996: 82). In other words, if the ASI is a "political" think-tank, "politics" has clearly defined limits.

As we have seen, the ASI claimed in a report published in 1990 that more than a hundred of its ideas had made their way into public policy (Adam Smith Institute 1990: 1). More recently, Pirie and Butler have "privately claim[ed] that over 200 of the 624 proposals contained in the *Omega file* have been implemented by government and . . . that key elements of the 1988 Education Act were the result of their initiatives" (Heffernan 1996: 84). As Heffernan has argued, however, it is mistaken to suggest that think-tanks such as the ASI provided in themselves the ideas that gave intellectual weight to Thatcherism. Any direct impact such groups may have had, he argues, has been at the margin, rather than at the centre, of public policy.

> Determined outsiders, proud of their independence from government and of closed political circles, the Adam Smith Institute [has] certainly played a part in the New Right crusade to turn back the so-called collectivist tide. Keen supporters rather than involved participants, the impact of the Institute was that of a Thatcherite foot-soldier eager to make some contribution to the political work of the Conservative Government (Heffernan 1996: 82).

Unlike other British think-tanks of the New Right, the ASI did not distance itself from the Conservative Party after the fall of Margaret Thatcher, and after New Labour won the 1997 general election it was soon making friendly noises. As early as July, Madsen Pirie told a reporter that he was greatly impressed with the Blair Government. This might seem strange at first sight, because the reputation of the Institute during the 1980s was that of the most militant of the liberal think-tanks, with strong connections to the "No Turning Back Group" of hardline Thatcherites. In fact, this reputation was won largely through its aggressive marketing, and its association with what was seen as Margaret Thatcher's ideological flagship, the community charge or poll tax. While it has yet to stray from the confines of economic liberalism in its policy suggestions, its preference for practical measures over ideological purity means that it has built into its ethos an acceptance of the sort of pragmatic considerations which disillusioned more long-standing votaries of economic liberalism. It will do business with anyone prepared to give its message a hearing

A powerhouse of policies?

Several authors have described New Right think-tanks such as the ASI as part of the "outer circle" of the Conservative Party, organizations that, during the years of opposition prior to the election of the first Thatcher administration in 1979, fulfilled a purpose that was being inadequately served at that time by the Conservative Party's existing policy-making machinery in general and its Research Department in particular (Barnes and Cockett 1994). What is less clear, however, is the nature and extent of the "unique contribution" that such groups made to the political thinking and policies of the Conservative government after 1979. While Kenneth Baker, a one-time Heathite who became a loyal Thatcherite, has claimed in his memoirs that the think-tanks were "an influential powerhouse of ideas and policies for 1980s Conservatism", hard evidence of direct think-tank "influence" on government policy after 1979 is less forthcoming (Baker 1993: 162). This remark applies to the ASI as much as to other think-tanks of the New Right.

It has been suggested that the number of policy initiatives that can be attributed to New Right think-tanks is relatively small. Hames and Feasey, for instance, have argued that there is "virtually no example of any legislation on either side of the Atlantic that was entirely and uniquely due to one individual think-tank" (Hames and Feasey 1994: 231). While this is a very exacting (if not impossible) benchmark, it is more difficult than may appear at first sight to assess the specific motivations of the Thatcher and Major governments and more difficult still to identify the direct contribution an outside organization such as the ASI might have made to their respective endeavours. The behind-the-scenes image cultivated by the ASI (and other New Right think-tanks) has not always been acknowledged in the published memoirs of those leading decision-makers it sought to influence. The ASI is not mentioned at all in *The Downing Street years*, Margaret Thatcher's record of her period in power; the Institute is also ignored in the memoirs of other economic liberals in Mrs Thatcher's Cabinets, such as Nigel Lawson, Geoffrey Howe and Nicholas Ridley (Heffernan 1996: 83).

Yet unlike other organizations and actors, the ASI has claimed responsibility for the community charge, or poll tax. Pirie, in particular, has made much of the fact that he first advocated such a policy in the *Daily Mail* as long ago as 1981. That the invention of the Poll Tax has often been credited to the ASI has, however, been described as one of the great myths that have surrounded this subject. On the contrary, it has been suggested, the ASI was in no way responsible for this notorious policy failure (Crick and van

Klaveren 1991). Pirie's *Daily Mail* article appeared as officials were drafting a Green Paper on local government finance; in the final version a poll tax was considered, only to be dismissed as unworkable. Further discussions took place within the Department of Environment during 1984 and 1985, but the ASI's most important publication on the subject, Douglas Mason's *Revising the rating system*, did not appear until April 1985 – several months after the Whitehall enquiry began. Other non-governmental actors, Heffernan argues, were far more important in launching the poll tax flagship than any free-market think-tank. Among these was Christopher Foster from the accountancy firm Coopers and Lybrands and formerly at the LSE, who played a key role in the Department of Environment review. Foster was the co-author of a 1980 book which had discussed a poll tax as a plausible alternative to the rates. Advice was also sought from the Downing Street Policy Unit, and another, far less ideological think-tank, the Institute for Fiscal Studies (IFS) was involved in the detailed work; indeed, if the IFS had been properly heeded the experiment would have been either abandoned or at least tried out with more caution (Butler et al. 1994: 30–1, 286, 293).

In fact, there were plenty of other forces urging ministers on, notably the delegates to Conservative Party conferences of the late 1980s, who provoked the Thatcher Government's decision to introduce the tax at once rather than in stages as previously intended. The community charge now stands as testimony to the dangers of implementing a policy which looks very neat on paper before consulting all relevant interest groups; the ASI was obviously not directly responsible for this omission, but it probably helped to convince ministers that the idea was good enough to justify a high level of risk. Ironically, Adam Smith himself laid down as his first maxim for taxation that "the subjects of every state ought to contribute towards the support of the government, as nearly as possible . . . in proportion to the revenue which they respectively enjoy under the protection of the state" (Smith 1822: 255). Under Edward Heath the Conservative Party had been more faithful to Smith; when the October 1974 manifesto promised a search for an alternative to the rates, the ability to pay qualification was explicitly included. The Shadow Environment spokesperson responsible for this promise was Mrs Margaret Thatcher (Conservative Central Office 1974: 13). Elsewhere Smith stressed that "those local or provincial expenses of which the benefit is local or provincial . . . ought to be defrayed by a local or provincial revenue, and ought to be no burden upon the general revenue of the society" (Smith 1822: 239). Yet in an attempt to make the community charge more politically acceptable, the Thatcher Government vastly increased subsidies to local authority budgets through national taxes. It has been estimated that "at least £1.5 bn [of taxpayer's money] was wasted on setting up, administering, and replacing the community charge" (Butler et al. 1994: 180).

More recently, the ASI has claimed credit for the idea of "empowerment", a concept which underpinned John Major's Citizen's Charter launched amidst much publicity in 1991. As Sarah Hogg and Jonathan Hill, who played a significant role in developing the concept as members of John Major's Policy Unit, have observed, however, the ASI is only one of a number of think-tanks and other organizations to have claimed credit for this initiative; others include the IEA, the CPS and even the National Consumer Council (Hogg and Hill 1995: 103). Despite this, the ASI did invest a great deal of effort in fleshing out the initial proposals for this initiative and the Charter is something to which the Institute continues to lend its support. Madsen Pirie was for some time an enthusiastic member of the Citizen's Charter advisory panel. Unfortunately, while this initiative did not produce the same type of difficulties for Major that the poll tax caused for his predecessor, the most common response from the electorate was one of indifference.

Conclusion

As we have seen, any attempt to measure the influence of individual think-tanks encounters unavoidable problems. But if the record of any think-tank can be appraised with confidence, this should be true of the Adam Smith Institute. The ASI itself certainly seems to have thought so: in its publication *The first hundred*, those instances "where the Institute considers its research made a critical impact on the success of a proposal" are distinguished from those where it feels less certain (Adam Smith Institute 1990: 1). Some of these claims are remarkable; for example, even if the ASI was only "one voice in a chorus" which successfully called for a reduction in the highest rate of income tax from 60 to 40 per cent in 1988, the opposing chorus included the Prime Minister herself, who would have preferred a more cautious pruning. Whether or not the recommendations of the ASI played a part in overcoming her reluctance is unclear; certainly neither the Prime Minister nor the Chancellor Nigel Lawson credit the Institute with prompting such a radical step in their memoirs. In other cases the Institute certainly gained wide publicity for its stance, but hindsight still suggests slender grounds for self-congratulation; for example, the first of the ASI's "hundred" concerned cutting back on the number of quangos – an achievement which, according to the various definitions of such bodies, was either short-lived or non-existent. As Andrew Marr has recounted, a much-publicized blitz on quangos launched in the Thatcher Government's first year removed only 250 people from their posts; Philip Holland, MP, the ASI's quango-hunter in chief, identified around 2,500 of such bodies in 1981, but another independent group discovered 5,521 "non-elected bodies carrying out executive functions on behalf of the government" in the mid-1990s. Reforms which the ASI supported, notably those in health and education, have contributed to the rising trend of non-elected decision-makers (Marr 1995: 78). Other achievements include the selling of ITV franchises to the highest bidder – a policy for which Mrs Thatcher subsequently offered a heart-felt apology – and (achievement number 9) the poll tax.

If the ASI's list of policy "successes" were to be taken at face value it would constitute both a testimony to the potential influence of poorly funded think-tanks and a warning to future governments about the unfortunate consequences which can arise from paying undue attention to a body which, by its very nature, can have only a partial grasp of the difficulties involved in policy-making. In reality, such evidence must be approached with scepticism. If a think-tank proposes a policy, it might act as a stimulus to a minister who had never considered the subject before, or tip the balance for a wavering minister. The arguments might help to reinforce an existing governmental intention – or ministers might never bother to read the proposal, having decided to go ahead anyway. In all of these cases a think-tank might be able to argue that its arguments had been decisive, but strictly speaking it would only be justified in the first instance. The poll tax example has already been discussed; on the available evidence that could be classed as an instance of "policy reinforcement". A further random example (number 54) relates to a proposal to privatize Rolls Royce; yet when the aero-engines division was nationalized by the Heath Government in 1971, this was done as an emergency measure and the new company was formed explicitly with an eye to a sale to the private sector when conditions were right. Once the Thatcher Government had made its first tentative steps towards the privatization of other industries it hardly took a genius to point out that Rolls Royce could be a suitable candidate. Indeed, Cento Veljanovski (admittedly an author with strong IEA connections) has chided the ASI for its "euphoric" approach to the serious business of privatization – a policy which, on balance, became less popular the more it was associated with ideological fervour (Veljanovski 1987: 2).

The extent to which the ASI's claims to policy influence are overstated cannot be calculated with any real confidence until the Public Record Office releases the relevant documents – and even then the evidence will be open to contestation. However, case studies of the impact of ASI (and other New Right think-tanks) already suggest that the "policy engineers" have exaggerated their role (see Jordan & Ashford 1993). No-one can doubt that the general election of 1979 presented these groups with unprecedented access to policy-makers. Whatever circumstances led up to the Conservative victory, the opportunity was open to the think-tanks to foster a lasting free-market revolution. The three New Right think-tanks could be seen as complementary, not in competition; the IEA and the ASI were avowedly nonpartisan bodies, and were respectively ideological "keepers of the conscience" and practical policy advisers. As we have seen (Chapter 4) the CPS was handicapped by its peculiar brief; torn between intimate contact with the Conservative Party and independence, it arguably ended up achieving neither.

Although in much of the literature on the Thatcher years the New Right think-tanks tend to be lumped together, their aims and conduct must be distinguished. Of the three, the ASI was best placed to exert practical influence over government policy. It shared with the IEA the advantage of "deniability" – its independence meant that it could float ideas without fear of embarrassing ministers. In fact, it could perform the role of a useful foil to the government; thinking the unthinkable and ensuring wide publicity for its thoughts could be seen as a form of market testing (or softening up), after which policy could be developed in the expectation that anything less radical than the original ASI proposal would be received with a sigh of relief. This status was denied to the CPS, with its intimate links to the Conservative Party in general and Mrs Thatcher in particular. After spending years in the wilderness and developing a deep suspicion for the profession of politics the IEA had an understandable tendency to act as an ideological watchdog, judging whether the government was holding to its general course and acting more as a judge of existing policies than as an advocate for specific reforms. The ASI, by contrast, was set up after Mrs Thatcher had become Leader of the Opposition, and in September 1976 the Labour Prime Minister James Callaghan signalled that he was prepared to ditch Keynes. From the outset, therefore, the ASI believed that its task was not to change the tide of opinion so much as to swim with it, and to focus not on overall strategy but on individual measures over a wide range of policy areas. Unfortunately for the ASI, we have seen in earlier chapters that its assumptions about a favourable climate of opinion were either the product of wishful thinking, or derived from the further assumption that the only climate worth worrying about was the thinking of a few well-placed policy-makers (see Chapter 7 for further discussion on this point).

Given its unique advantages, is the ASI's somewhat brash presentation of its successes justified? The main problem here is to find an appropriate definition of success. The publicity released by the ASI strongly implies that only the implementation of a policy counts as a success; that having one of your ideas adopted is an end in itself. While this approach is perfectly understandable, it neatly avoids the question of outcomes – an aspect which is far more relevant for the policy engineers at the ASI than for the more abstract thinkers of the IEA (despite the suggestion in Pirie's letter to Fisher, see earlier). The most obvious point here relates to the future of the think-tank itself; if it is identified as the main source of a policy which misfires, it will find its influence reduced in future (see also the discussion of the CPS in Chapter 4). In these instances an independent think-tank becomes an ideal scapegoat, and short-term success over specific issues becomes the best way of ensuring long-term decline. In the case of the ASI the other relevant factor is the fate of the ideology it was set up to serve, however much it might claim to deal in policies rather than ideas. The Institute's identification with the poll tax, for example, led some people to regard the incident as something more than a public relations embarrassment for the government; instead it could be regarded as evidence for the chaos which results from the rigid application (or misapplication) of economic liberalism. There was another respect in which the poll tax was a set-back for the ASI. At the time that the legislation was being enacted, Pirie was congratulating the Thatcher Government for showing "acute sensitivity to that which is politically acceptable". In *Micropolitics,* he proceeded to claim that think-tanks had "learned how the political system worked, and how to solve the problems it posed to would-be legislators" (Pirie 1988a: 51, 65). In writing these words, Pirie clearly overlooked the warning of the right-wing academic, Maurice Cowling, who cautioned against the notion that "those who write but do not rule would be rather better at ruling (if they had a chance) than those who do" (Cowling 1963: 1). Yet it could be argued that the example of the poll tax shows that neither the government nor the think-tanks understood how to implement policies – or that no amount of policy-making expertise can overcome the problem of implementing a policy which an overwhelming majority of the public finds distasteful. It seems, indeed, that the poll tax was not deeply unpopular when the idea was mooted – which, in view of later developments, strongly implies that policy-makers failed to explain it sufficiently in advance, and later suffered the consequences of the omission (Gilmour and Garnett 1997: 343).

The ASI's main mistake during the 1980s was to claim that it was "clearly the prime source" of government policies on numerous occasions and to have been "hugely influential in shaping events". It would have been far more advisable to present itself as "only one voice in a chorus", even if this meant sacrificing some immediate impact in its sales-pitch to potential clients. If the creative thinkers at the Institute were fully capable of generating ideas, they lacked the resources (and, it appears, the inclination) to gauge their likely impact. Regrettably it seems that this rather cavalier approach to policy-making spread to the Institute's allies in government (some of whom, of course, had enjoyed first-hand experience of the ASI's methods). In too many cases the result was legislation which quickly had to be revised or scrapped.

It is a cliché that imitation is a sound measure of success, and on these grounds the ASI's record is remarkable. Many of the new think-tanks which sprang up in the 1980s have clearly followed the advocacy tank model of which the Institute is probably Britain's best example. For these bodies, as for the ASI, to thrive is to win media coverage. Potential demand, from features editors anxious for lively comment to fill their pages, is large, but competition (not least from rival advocacy tanks) is fierce. Staff members can always contribute their reflections on the political scene, but a better form of publicity is to win coverage of their policy ideas from other newspaper pundits. This necessitates the high-speed production of pamphlets on topical themes; even if the ideas enshrined in such publications are well thought-out, only cursory attention can be paid to their likely consequences. Ironically, the current vogue for advocacy tanks constructed on similar lines to the ASI raises the prospect that the think-tank tradition in Britain, which was originated by enthusiasts concerned to help governments in their long-term thinking, will end up promoting government by gimmick and sound-bite – if only as part of a chorus which includes the far more powerful voice of technological innovation (see Conclusion).

CHAPTER 6

After the New Right

The period since the late 1980s has seen the emergence of a plethora of new think-tanks in Britain, some of which have already won a high media profile. One reason for this development is the assumption that New Right groups such as the IEA, the CPS and the ASI succeeded, at least to some extent, in transforming the substance of political debate in Britain during the 1970s and 1980s. As Richard Cockett has noted, whereas only a generation ago bodies such as the IEA were widely seen as a refuge for cranks and eccentrics, it is now "almost *de rigeur* for all political parties, let alone individual politicians, to have at least a couple of think-tanks under their wing to demonstrate any pretensions to intellectual and political vitality"; the proliferation in think-tank numbers that has occurred in Britain since the late 1980s also means that "any new think-tank, of whatever ideological hue, now has to operate in a very crowded field" (Cockett 1996: 87). Most importantly, whatever success the think-tanks achieved was gained at very little expense; unlike the situation in the United States, the possibility opened up that in Britain one could win media prominence with nothing more than one or two creative minds, an eye-catching name, and a typewriter.

Whether this state of affairs will continue, however, is uncertain. As we have seen in all the examples cited here, the fortunes of think-tanks, like other institutions, are contingent on historical circumstances; while they may flourish under certain conditions, they can just as rapidly fade and decline when political and economic circumstances change. As we have seen, it is difficult to predict in advance which developments will help or hinder; few would have

175

thought, for instance, that after two Conservative election victories the Thatcherite Centre for Policy Studies would be afflicted by passionate arguments about its future role.

It was, however, always likely that the downfall of Margaret Thatcher in 1990 would witness the emergence of several new think-tanks on the right of the political spectrum in Britain to delineate the way forward for Thatcherite conservatism in the 1990s and beyond. The first of these, the European Policy Forum (EPF), emerged in 1992, partly as a consequence of the internal disputes within the IEA in the late 1980s (see Chapter 3), but also because Europe – an issue which the New Right think-tanks had generally avoided – was now regarded as perhaps the most important policy area for Britain, and was an obsession for members of the governing party at all levels. The record of the third Thatcher Government revealed that, like the uneasy marriage between economic liberalism and social authoritarianism (see Chapter 4), developments in Europe forced Conservatives into awkward choices which the think-tanks found equally difficult to tackle. The resignations in rapid succession of Nigel Lawson and Geoffrey Howe from the third Thatcher Government involved many factors, including personal grievances, but at root they can be traced to the fact that both Howe and Lawson saw the trappings of national sovereignty as less important than what they regarded as Britain's economic and strategic interests. In pushing through the Single European Act (1986), Margaret Thatcher seemed to agree with them, but as the EC moved towards deeper economic and monetary unity she dug in her heels. Most disturbingly for economic liberals, both sides to this dispute were able to conduct a bitter and damaging row while arguing that they were acting in perfect accordance with their shared ideology. Howe and Lawson could claim that rational economic activity is impossible without a stable currency, whereas Mrs Thatcher was adamant that "you can't buck the market" – currencies, like other commodities, should be allowed to find their own price level. During this destructive row Mrs Thatcher's main champion was Sir Alan Walters, who had been chosen as her special economic adviser at the prompting of Sir Alfred Sherman after a fruitful association with both the IEA and the CPS.

The EPF was launched in 1992, with Graham Mather (later to be elected as a Conservative member of the European Parliament) as its president and Frank Vibert (formerly Mather's Deputy Director at the IEA) as its vice-president. The EPF was set up to provide a voice within the European debate which was "constructive, market-led and decentralist"; from the start it hosted talks by prominent figures across the full range of attitudes to Europe (EPF: 1997). Unfortunately, as early as 1992 divisions within the government were so wide as to be irreconcilable; the known views of the impressive list of speakers during the Forum's first year (including Lord Howe, the president of the EU Commission Sir Leon Brittan, and the Euro-sceptic Chancellor Norman Lamont) only shows that, at best, it was set up too late to solve the problem while the Conservatives remained in office.

More recently, the European Foundation, under the chairmanship of Bill Cash MP, has been established to articulate an aggressively anti-federalist policy in respect of the European Union, while a more senior Euro-sceptic, John Redwood, has founded Conservative 2000 to "continue his leadership election bid of the summer of 1995 by other means" (Cockett 1996: 88). Thus the silence of the New Right think-tanks on Europe has been replaced by a number of jarring voices, many of which are more concerned to promote particular individuals than to advance public debate (such bodies have been dubbed "vanity tanks"). On paper, at least, of these bodies, the EPF would seem to offer the greatest hope of a constructive contribution; its main handicap is the fact that positions on Europe in all parties tend to be impregnable to the kind of informed discussion which it promotes.

The divisive impact of Europe on the New Right is well known, but it has not been the only cause of fragmentation among the think-tanks. In February 1996, yet another new (and ostensibly Thatcherite) think-tank, Politeia, was launched. This was set up by Sheila Lawlor, formerly a leading figure in the CPS and a regular contributor to political broadcasts such as the BBC's *Question Time*, to cover social and economic issues. Backed by senior Conservatives including Lord Parkinson (who became honourary treasurer), and with an early list of contributors including the ministers Peter Lilley and Stephen Dorrell, Politeia was seen as a potential rival to the CPS; established as an independent foundation, it was likely to avoid the kind of questions about status which have dogged the Centre. Its income for the year ending November 1996 was reported as £121,042, most of which came from donations (*Labour Research* 1997). At least Politeia

177

was set up in good time to conduct its own inquest into the Conservative defeat of May 1997; whether this will eventually consider the role which ideology (and the think-tanks themselves) played in producing that result must be doubted. An early contributor to this debate, Maurice Cowling, once attributed the Thatcher revolution to the influence of "about fifty people"; in his pamphlet for Politeia in the wake of the Conservative defeat he still had no doubts that the New Right had won "the battle of ideas" (Cowling 1990: xxxvi; Cowling 1997). Whether or not there is any truth in this assertion, its constant repetition 18 years after the 1979 general election can only act as a deterrent for those Conservatives who want to engage in creative thinking now that the party is back in Opposition.

In 1992, the former CPS Director of Studies, David Willetts, became Conservative MP for Havant; he was subsequently appointed a Government whip and Paymaster-General in the Major administration. Following the General Election of 1992, Willetts also joined the board of the Social Market Foundation (SMF) and became involved in its work (he would later join the Advisory Council at Politeia). The SMF had arisen during the last years of the Social Democratic Party (SDP). David Owen, who took over the leadership of the party after the 1983 election, was determined to drive it closer to the free-market ideas of the Conservatives, and hoped that an associated think-tank would act as an SDP equivalent of the CPS. Significantly Owen preferred to work with a new body, rather than existing organizations associated with other senior SDP figures, such as PSI (see Chapter 2) and the Institute for Fiscal Studies (which the then Labour MP Dick Taverne had helped to set up in 1969). In 1989, Robert Skidelsky (the historian and biographer of Lord Keynes) and the SDP peer Lord Kilmarnock set up a rudimentary think-tank operation, run from Kilmarnock's personal premises in the House of Lords and Regent's Park Road. The SMF soon acquired charitable status, requiring at least formal independence from the SDP. Its initial aims were to "research, publish and gain acceptance for policies based on the concept of the Social Market". Its first publication was Skidelsky's pamphlet *The social market economy*. This appeared in 1989 and contained a series of responses to Skidelsky's paper from across the political spectrum.

The phrase "social market economy", Skidelsky argued, signified a choice in favour of the market economy. This did not, however, imply a minimal conception of the state. The "social" part of the label, for Skidelsky, implied that the state should create and maintain an appropriate legal framework for market exchange, limit and supplement the market where necessary and "ensure that the market is politically acceptable" (Skidelsky 1989: 7). Certain market outcomes, he argued, "may be efficient and yet be socially unacceptable, and thus weaken the system which produces them" (Skidelsky 1989: 13). Skidelsky went on to flesh out certain areas of justifiable state activity. The National Health Service (NHS), for instance, could be defended on the grounds of "market failure" in dealing with insurance. Skidelsky also displayed some concern for equality, and wrote approvingly of John Rawls's theories of justice. Subsequent papers issued by the SMF, on a European single currency, the NHS, education and telecommunications, sought to apply social market thinking to each of these policy areas.

Between 1990 and 1992, however, the SMF remained a think-tank in search of a role. On the face of it, Skidelsky's pamphlet seemed a genuine attempt to forge a new Middle Way in a polarized political climate – unlike the previous use of the phrase social market in the 1970s, which in hindsight seemed little more than a temporary cloak of warm words wrapped around the economic liberalism that in practice had caused mass unemployment and, in some areas, a situation approaching social breakdown (see Chapter 4). But this middle way was precisely what the existing government did not want, so the fate of these ideas depended crucially on the support of a powerful moderate party. Apart from the usual handicaps faced by third parties, the SDP project suffered from personality clashes, and indeed the foundation of the SMF reaffirmed the disastrous split between Owen and other senior members of the SDP who wanted either to merge with the Liberals or else to continue an intimate alliance. The Owenite SDP collapsed in 1990, and the SMF was left in political limbo. Towards the end of 1991, an internal review concluded that, while there was no future in an organization looking backward to the SDP, there was "a core commitment of former members to the values outlined by Skidelsky of a market economy underpinned by social consent and institutions" (Baston 1996: 65).

After the 1992 general election, the SMF was relaunched and moved into new offices close to the House of Commons, at 20 Queen

Anne's Gate, Westminster. The Conservative victory and the prospect of five more years of Conservative Government encouraged the SMF to drift further in the Thatcherite direction favoured by Owen (who had not been a candidate at the election and soon entered the House of Lords). For the first time, the SMF acquired a permanent staff, with Danny Finkelstein as director and Roderick Nye editor. The statement of aims was revised to read as follows:

> The Foundation's main activity is to commission and publish original papers by independent academic and other experts on key topics in the economic and social fields, with a view to stimulating public discussion on the performance of markets and the social framework within which they operate (in Baston 1996: 66).

In 1993, the SMF issued papers by, among others, David Willetts on pensions, Evan Davis on schools and Sir Peter Kemp (a former adviser to the Thatcher Government) on the future of the civil service. These papers followed the publication in 1992 of a paper written by Howard Davies, the director-general of the Confederation of British Industry (CBI), on the management of public services. In 1994, the SMF published two contrasting statements about the effect of market institutions on modern society. In *The undoing of conservatism*, John Gray argued that markets were destroying the very interests and institutions that were the basis of conservatism, while the prolific David Willetts, in *Civic conservatism*, suggested that the increased role of the market would actually lead to a revival of "civic" values (Gray 1994; Willetts 1994). These were intelligent contributions to a key debate, but taken together they only proved that despite the efforts of Lord Skidelsky the concept of a social market remained as problematic as ever; it was still open to critics to claim that society and the market were incompatible, and that those who used the phrase would always choose the market whenever the clash arose in practice.

The appointment of Danny Finkelstein to the post of director of Conservative Research in the summer of 1995 appeared to demonstrate that SMF principles were still favourably regarded at high levels in the Conservative Party. Yet to describe the SMF as a Majorite think-tank is to oversimplify matters. Of the four patrons of

180

the SMF in 1995, Lord Chandos was a Labour spokesperson in the House of Lords and David Sainsbury has expressed sympathy for Tony Blair's positions. Despite its vagueness, the guiding concept of the social market still has the potential to attract New Labour. But with so many think-tanks contesting for space in the post-Conservative era, the SMF has serious handicaps; notably, unlike other former members of the SDP who went unnoticed for some years before resurfacing in Blair's circle, the SMF arguably committed itself too far to the Conservative cause in the years after 1990. However, there is every reason to suppose that it will survive the change of administration – indeed, it is probably best placed to do so of all the think-tanks associated with the New Right. Over the 12 months to February 1996, it declared an income of £337,216 (*Labour Research* 1997: 10).

Think-tanks and New Labour

A more obvious source of inspiration, if not policy innovation, for New Labour is the Institute for Public Policy Research (IPPR), established in 1988 to "take a new look at the state and its relationship with the market" in the light of experience since the late 1970s (Cornford 1990: 23). The interesting question here is why it took Labour so long to respond to the perceived success of the New Right think-tanks. Presumably a full answer would have to refer *inter alia* to the civil war within the party after 1979, and shell-shock induced by successive defeats. According to James Cornford, its first director, the IPPR was perceived by its founders as "going to have influence in a very short period of time, five years maximum. It was not involved in an intellectual revolution, but was trying to accelerate the process of change and thought in the Labour Party on the modernising side". Cornford, a former academic with long experience of independent research bodies memorably described think-tanks as 'the performing fleas of the body politic', but believed that they had had an impact during the 1980s "and set an example worth following" (Cornford 1990: 22). Later he argued that the key to success would be the Institute's mode of operation, rather than its core beliefs. With a small staff and little money, Cornford thought, one could still mobilize a lot of external resources. The secret to

this was "to act as a secretariat for a much larger network of interested people"; by 1988 Labour could draw on a fairly wide body of
scholars and journalists willing to volunteer their services, as the
fragmentation of the early 1980s began to be replaced by a conviction that differences should be buried in the fight against the Conservative Government (interview quoted in Ruben 1996: 67).

In 1988, the IPPR employed just three people, with only one
room to work in. The Institute later expanded to 25 employees,
either full-time, part-time or working on specific projects for a fixed
period; extra staff were taken on to help with the Commission on
Social Justice set up in October 1992. Although personnel levels
inevitably fluctuate, the IPPR normally accommodates about 20
people, including five administrative staff and an outreach officer
who helps in public relations, organizing seminars and conferences
and developing contacts with donors. The deputy director, Anna
Coote, heads the Social Policy Unit, which is concerned with health
and welfare rights; Coote also directs the Institute's media and com-
munications programme, having previously worked as a senior
lecturer in media and journalism at Goldsmiths College, University
of London and a member of the editorial board of the *New Statesman*. There are also smaller units surveying human rights, education
and the environment.

Having been set up with a provisional budget of just £200,000,
the IPPR's resources increased during its first few years. Income
was just under £500,000 in 1991, and in excess of £1 million in
1995. While resources have increased significantly, however, little
of this money is committed from one year to the next and the lack
of core funding, in particular, remains a constraint on the Institute's
activities and growth. Originally the IPPR was heavily dependent
on individual donations (and Cornford's skill in prising money from
unlikely sources). More recently the Institute was beginning to con-
form to a contract research model, with more than half of its resources earmarked to specific research projects.

Since 1988, the IPPR has acquired a reputation for solid research.
Cornford has observed that, during his time as director, the IPPR
was more involved in "a kind of revival of morale of people on the
left than influential in detail on the policy of the time" (quoted in
Ruben 1996: 77). After another defeat at the polls in 1992, however,
the notion that Labour could fight its way back to power without a

fundamental overhaul of the party and its principles was rejected by party officials. Initiatives with which the IPPR was most intimately associated – notably the much-publicized Commission on Social Justice – were designed to exploit Labour's image as a caring party. Since the death of John Smith (a strong supporter of the Commission) there has been a tendency for Labour to take this compassionate reputation for granted, and the main thrust of party activity has been directed towards the task of convincing the business community and specific target voters that Labour could be trusted with the economy. To this end, in April 1995 a Commission on British Business and Public Policy was established; in January 1997 Michael Heseltine launched a well-publicized "gate-crashing" raid on a conference on this subject held under IPPR auspices. The IPPR was also an early participant in the debate over the regulation of the utilities privatized by Conservative governments after 1979.

Although the IPPR has from the outset been identified with the modernizing wing of the Labour Party – attempting, among other things, to generate more sympathy within the party towards the free market – this process has now moved so far that the Institute seems beached on a sandbank of yesterday's preoccupations. In a 1990 article, James Cornford expressed the view that "Setting your own agenda and saying what you think – speaking truth to power – are essential conditions and justifications for the existence of think tanks" (Cornford 1990: 27). He wished to avoid a hand-in-hand relationship with Labour – possibly remembering the complications which arose from the CPS's unsatisfactory mixture of independence from, and involvement with, the Conservatives. During the course of the Commission on Social Justice there was a moment when the same kind of trouble loomed. Although the Commission was deliberately set up in a form which ensured that its conclusions could be denied by the Labour leadership, John Smith was embarrassed when he was questioned on the BBC *Today* programme about the possibility that the Commission might recommend the abolition of child benefit. In fact, the idea had been discussed and then rejected by the Commission (McSmith 1994). Yet this incident did ·not set a precedent, and instead of being hand-in-hand with Labour the IPPR has generally been kept at something more than arm's length.

Ironically, the Labour Party victory which its members craved has turned out to be a serious blow to the IPPR, since the landslide

is judged to have been secured by concessions to a political programme which the Institute was specifically set up to combat. Since
the election of May 1997, rumours of the IPPR's demise (or at least
a serious crisis) have circulated; the Institute looked especially vulnerable since staff members closest to the new government (notably
Patricia Hewitt and David Miliband) had already left. The dynamic
Cornford had departed in the summer of 1994. In September 1997
the Institute's chairman, Lord Eatwell (former economic advisor to
Neil Kinnock), was driven to tell the *Financial Times* that the newspaper was wrong "to suggest that IPPR's ideas are not having a
profound effect on government policy". He pointed out three instances – green taxes, a University for Industry, and competition
policy – where the IPPR's advice had been taken, and hinted that
"there is more in the pipeline" (Eatwell 1997). Whether or not this
stout defence will work in the long term is open to serious doubt;
those businessmen who hedged their bets by offering funds to
the IPPR will have noticed that other bodies, notably the revived
Fabian Society and Demos, enjoy more favoured status with the new
regime. In its attempt to attract thinking people of all parties and
of none, New Labour also set up an "independent ideas network",
Nexus (mainly based in academia), in 1996. This is a worrying development, since the IPPR in its early days seemed to be a marriage
between the rigorous research methods of the "contract research
organisations" NIESR and PSI and the media skills of the ASI, whereas
almost all the other think-tanks which have been set up recently
are based on a fairly uniform advocacy tank model. Despite its current problems the IPPR might have a healthy future as an independent think-tank, yet the forging of a new identity will probably take
some time given the original impression that the Institute represented
Labour's belated fight-back against the New Right.

Demos is the most media-friendly among the new think-tanks.
It was established in the spring of 1993, and arose from discussions
between Martin Jacques, the former editor of *Marxism Today* and
Geoff Mulgan, formerly a research assistant to the present Chancellor, Gordon Brown. Mulgan and Jacques were impatient with what
they regarded as outdated ideological labelling – a sentiment shared
by many people who had once been attracted to the Marxist theories which were widely discredited by the collapse of Eastern European Communist states at the end of the 1980s. The founders decided

that Demos should avoid too close an identification with the political left, and agreed that it should concentrate on matters which had been neglected by existing bodies. In practice this meant that Demos would try to keep away from the subjects which had traditionally formed the basis of partisan conflict – notably economics.

Demos has won considerable attention from the press, particularly since Black Wednesday in September 1992, after which disillusionment with the Conservative Government became endemic and alternative views gained more of a hearing. In December 1995 its income for the previous 15 months was almost £400,000; funders included British Telecom and some local councils (*Labour Research* 1997: 10). Its small staff are all young, which seems to encourage the media to talk about the individuals as much as their ideas. Some of its work is reminiscent of the kind of study undertaken by PEP in the 1950s and 1960s – notably a well received inquiry into the use of public spaces – but the typical Demos project is based on surveys of social attitudes among even younger people. Like New Labour, it is very fond of gathering information through focus groups. The subjects it explores tend to coincide with immediate public concerns, such as drugs, gender relations and political apathy; almost invariably its findings are presented in the broadsheets as challenges to the established thinking of older people.

Surveys like these are not only of great interest to a media which is obsessed with the concerns of youth – no less important is their effect in validating Demos's post-modern outlook, which supposedly eschews ideology. Among its recent authors is Alan Duncan, the radical libertarian Conservative MP (Duncan 1993). Nevertheless, Demos is undoubtedly closer to the Labour Party at present than to any other. Indeed, it could claim to have played some part in influencing Labour since 1993, even if such influence is more easily detected in its discourse or rhetoric than in the detail of policy:

The overall theme, for instance, in recent Labour Party pronouncements . . . has been on the need to combine rights with responsibilities – a rhetoric that is more than reminiscent of the communitarian ideas of American academic Amitai Etzioni, whose growing – if not entirely undisputed – reputation in this country Demos has done a great deal to foster. Etzioni's work on the so-called "parenting deficit" has been published in Britain

185

by Demos and the think-tank also helped sponsor some of his London lectures in the Spring of 1995 (Bale 1996: 30).

The association of Demos with Etzioni's ideas provides an instructive echo of the New Right's approach; like much of recent New Right thinking promoted by the think-tanks, communitarian ideas originated outside the social and political context of contemporary Britain, which raises the immediate question of their precise relevance here. "Communitarianism" is also reminiscent of "social market"; it is a word which lends itself to partisan rhetoric, but can mean almost anything. In Britain, to assert that one believes in community seems to have become a short-hand way of saying that one is not a Thatcherite; but since Mrs Thatcher's famous denial that there was such a thing as society has been interpreted by opponents out of its true context the use of the word community can become an easy way of avoiding difficult questions about how sociality can really be restored in contemporary Britain. Whether Demos, for all its energy and good intentions, will bring much more clarity to this debate must be doubtful.

Although it is too soon to make a firm judgement, the election of New Labour in May 1997 can be seen as a distinctly mixed blessing for Demos. Its fixation with media exposure is highly reminiscent of the ASI, but unlike that group it lacks a distinct ideological inspiration – indeed prides itself on its freedom from such antique obsessions. Demos was initially highly attractive to the media after years of New Right domination in the think-tank world, but at the time of writing (October 1997) it has begun to operate under a highly popular government whose policies are designed to cater to perceptions of the public mood. This was the role which Demos was playing before the 1997 general election; significantly, since the change of government, Geoff Mulgan has been drafted into the Downing Street Policy Unit.

An associated danger is that Demos is now so closely linked to the rather rootless mood of the mid-1990s that it will suffer when this trend disappears. Before the election there was a hint that the reaction against Demos might come sooner because of its brash style and its reliance on jargon rather than clear prose; a *Guardian* article in February 1997 reported with some incredulity Demos' claim to be "the nation's leading authority on women" (Freely 1997). A piece in *The Economist* of October 1997 claims that "many of the themes and statistics Mr Blair has been citing of late seem to have been lifted straight from a recent Demos pamphlet on rebranding Britain" – a view which is highly reminiscent of the sort of thing which used to be written about the New Right groups and the Conservative Party, and which indicates that if and when New Labour falls from public favour Demos will also be accused of having run out of ideas. Indeed despite its technical independence of all parties Demos is in danger of too close identification with Tony Blair; the *Economist* article suggested that Demos has a "taste for grandiose pronouncements which fall apart on closer inspection", and even if New Labour continues in office for many years it is unlikely that Blair's successor will have the same rhetorical preferences.

Conclusion

By the summer of 1997, think-tanks were a well-established part of the British political scene, although the fortunes of particular bodies were changing. The attachment of the label "think-tank" to a report by any organization was apparently a guarantee of media attention; the BBC was even running a discussion programme under that name. However, the prospects for the British groups were uncertain. There were increasing signs that think-tanks were being regarded by the major parties as little more than useful sources of political recruits; new and high profile "think-tankers" elected in 1997 included Stephen Twigg of the Fabian Society and Patricia Hewitt of the IPPR, and despite his peripheral involvement in the sleaze scandals which marred the last days of the Conservative government, David Willetts was clearly on the fast track to promotion within his party. The other worrying development was a definite tendency for think-tanks to concentrate on anticipating subjects of media interest, rather than more contentious (or less trendy) issues for policy reform. For example, in 1997 the Fabian Society, which once had ambitions to effect radical changes across the board of government activity, was winning media publicity through a report on the future of football. In short, while on a superficial view, developments since 1990 have brought think-tanks even closer to the centre of public debate, more detailed analysis reveals that this could turn out to be dangerous to them and of limited value to public debate in Britain. These suggestions will be developed further in our concluding chapter.

CHAPTER 7

Conclusion: Think-tanks, politics and democracy

1: A brief history of British think-tanks

Clearly British think-tanks are not new, even if they are more prominent now than ever before. The present volume is necessarily selective in its treatment, but from our survey a history of their activities and its context can be sketched.

The first wave

The history of outside policy advice in Britain can be traced back to the Fabians and beyond. As we have noted, the Fabians emerged against a background of growing economic malaise in Britain, when existing government institutions were seen by a number of energetic thinkers as inadequate to meet the challenges of a mass industrialized democracy. However, for the present purpose, the history begins in the 1930s, when a more discernible pattern emerged.

In response to the global economic crisis which began with the Wall Street crash, a number of talented individuals with backgrounds in government service, academia and journalism (in some cases, like that of Keynes, a combination of all three) reached the conclusion that expert advice was necessary for the successful conduct of economic policy in an increasingly complicated and interdependent world. At the same time, a demand began to be heard that the whole range of government activity should be placed on a more systematic basis – that Britain, like other European countries, should embrace the concept of planning, as opposed to what was perceived as its traditional *ad hoc* and amateurish approach.

At this point difficulties arose which had a crucial effect on the story of think-tanks to date. While the economists agreed that the government needed help, they could not agree on the advice which ought to be given. The Economic Advisory Council (EAC) set up by the Labour Government of Ramsay MacDonald in 1931 was riddled with internal differences over issues such as free trade versus tariff reform; the centre of controversy then (as, arguably, it has been ever since) was the figure of J.M. Keynes. In addition the EAC faced powerful opposition from the Treasury, not only because it contained advocates of unorthodox remedies, but also because it threatened to end Whitehall's privileged position as a source of government advice. The natural conclusion was that a body should be set up outside the machinery of government, but given the internal quarrels within the economic profession the National Institute of Economic and Social Research did not emerge until 1938.

The origins of Political and Economic Planning point to a slight variation on the same theme. Here the early difficulty hinged on the word "planning". Just as orthodox economists were deeply uneasy about Keynes' developing plans for hands-on government management, even those who were attracted by Max Nicholson's ideas were dubious about such a radical departure from established practice. Again, the result was a delay in setting up PEP, and as with the NIESR its statements of intent reflected an uneasy compromise.

As the 1930s progressed, and especially during the course of the war, it was generally accepted that Keynes and Nicholson were at least working on the right lines. The British war effort undoubtedly benefited from a great influx of experts, many of whom were closely associated with the think-tanks, and together with officials and politicians they created a managed society unique in British history (Cromwell's Major-Generals might have had more restrictive purposes, but lacked the technology to carry out their designs).

After the war it was acknowledged by all but a handful of economic liberals that things could never be the same again, but even a Labour Government committed on paper to planning soon acknowledged a public demand that life should be as close to normality as possible. Harold Wilson's "bonfire of controls" was the most spectacular illustration of the government's desire to retreat from the detailed direction of economic activity; much more important was the mass exodus of experts from Whitehall. But for some people – especially those in the generation which had no personal experience of pre-war conditions, and could therefore harbour illusions about a golden age where the ration-book was unknown – the government could not move fast enough to dismantle the elaborate apparatus of controls. Friedrich von Hayek's *The road to serfdom* was a vividly written and closely argued Bible for such people, who overlooked the fact that its gloomy message was originally inspired by events in countries with very different political cultures from that of Britain, with its deeply ingrained individualism (see Chapter 3). This rising generation of economic liberals focused their attention on the Attlee Government's nationalization programme when arguing that freedom was in danger. The fact that the new state industries were almost all run by non-socialists – and, more importantly, that the government showed little interest in developing a coordinated economic strategy on the basis of those industries – was ignored.

Although the return to peacetime conditions might have seemed like "glad confident morning" to some of the enthusiasts at the NIESR and PEP, the supposed hegemony of collectivism has been much exaggerated. Rather, a compromise was established, well exemplified by the record of the Churchill Government. The wartime controls finally disappeared, as did those aspects of Labour's haphazard nationalization programme which ministers judged inappropriate on the grounds that market competition could work (e.g. steel and road haulage). More seriously, in economic matters the government established the post-war trend of only heeding the advice and forecasts of outside experts when they coincided with narrow political considerations; Keynes' views were now better represented in Whitehall, but the presiding spirit in Downing Street was a "bastardized" version, geared primarily to the winning of elections. Planning in anything but its most superficial form was almost impossible in this context. Whatever the ambitions of their founders, in practice PEP and the NIESR were content to work within the compromise or broad consensus of the early post-war period; what they could not approve was the fact that governments often ignored all their statistics and factual analyses, taking the expedient rather than the long-term view. However, they must accept a share of the blame for this outcome, in that governments could only expect to prosper from

191

risking long-term prospects for present gain if the electorate remained ignorant of what was really happening. The NIESR and PEP did attempt to reach a wider audience with their findings, but never developed the necessary communication skills; one might say in their defence that they never could, because reality is complex and almost by definition impossible to convey in a media-friendly fashion.

Unlike the NIESR and PEP, the Institute of Economic Affairs was never prepared to change tactics in order to win political influence; instead of bowing before what its supporters saw as the prevailing climate, the Institute vowed to change it. Yet the above account shows that the economic liberals who formed the IEA were fighting something of a straw doll: one which could only appear life-like to them because they saw politics as a battlefield of ideas, where their own apparent defeat could only mean victory for the other side. The IEA's mistake was to overrate the power of ideas at a time when Britain's economic position had become so weak that policy-makers were at the mercy of outside events to an extent unknown in the nineteenth century – that golden era for the Institute's supporters. Just as they were uncompromising in their attachment to the free market, they could see no possibility of accommodation with their straw doll, which they called collectivism or socialism depending on their mood or immediate polemical purpose.

This analysis was mistaken. The war-time consensus was just such an accommodation, although the word "consensus" has been skewed by some to stand for complete agreement. The ends of full employment, an effective welfare state and economic growth were agreed by most senior politicians, but of course the preferred means were different for Labour and the Conservatives. While radical spirits in each party shared the IEA's view that there could be no compromise, until 1975 the leaders were unanimous in their opposition to all-or-nothing politics. The economy would remain mixed in terms of ownership, even though the mixture might differ from time to time, and no government would either abandon the welfare state or move to the other extreme of taking responsibility for everything. Even in the 1960s, when Macmillan and Wilson responded to Britain's relative decline by pushing for more systematic planning, the experiment foundered, partly through a lack of political will but also because of the institutional apparatus of British government, where the Treasury still reigned. Despite (qualified) successes such as race relations legislation, the enthusiasts of the first wave had hardly progressed further in influencing government policy than they had in the days of the EAC. In the extent to which the think-tanks had succeeded in taking the detailed arguments in favour of the consensus to the wider electorate, the record was no better. In view of subsequent events, they would be justified in claiming no more than that they had helped a clear majority of voters to think that at times of economic trouble governments should do some-thing; but while post-war prosperity lasted this feeling was buried under a complacency which would be shattered in the early 1970s, when the events which had previously directed government pol-icy more subtly took the driving seat in a way that no-one could disguise.

The second wave

Although it was founded in 1955, the IEA is more conveniently classed in the second wave of British think-tanks. The second wave arose in response to the oil shock of 1973–74, which brought to an end the period of British post-war history which is usually described as the era of consensus. As we have seen, the ideas of John Maynard Keynes were deployed with an eye to winning elec-tions rather than as a tool for long-term economic management; the Conservative victory of 1979 brought to office a government which at times seemed to pursue economic policies because they ran directly counter to Keynes' teaching. The IEA, set up to oppose what it saw as increasing state interference based on the ideas of Keynes, and other planners (whom they usually lumped together under the umbrella word socialists), had expected some sort of crisis for 20 years. When events finally moved its way it continued to expound the free-market message which was taken up by other second wave organizations; the most notable change was a new tendency to crow about its part in the downfall of the consensus, and in this respect it emphasized its differences from the first wave groups, which tended to exaggerate their influence but could never be accused of triumphalism.

193

We have seen that there were significant differences between the IEA, the Centre for Policy Studies (1975) and the Adam Smith Institute (1977), but all three denounced the British post-war experience from the same ideological stand-point. The British economy, they argued, had been swamped by controls and cruelly damaged by well-meaning but wrong-headed and ham-fisted followers of Keynes. This analysis was characterized by accounts of post-war history which were as sweeping as they were readable. Yet few counter-arguments were heard at the time; not only were the advocates of the post-war compromise re-examining their beliefs in the light of calamitous events, but those who continued to hold responsibility for government were forced by the International Monetary Fund to adopt at least some of the programme of the second wave think-tanks. In their plight the politicians were reluctant to blame themselves for the poor economic decisions of the past; in the most significant and misleading speech of the 1970s, the Prime Minister James Callaghan blamed Keynes. In these circumstances the new members of the second wave, the CPS and the ASI, had no need to conduct the kind of in-depth research favoured by the NIESR and PEP to prove their case; events had apparently done that for them. While the older bodies conformed broadly to the model of contract research organizations (see Introduction), the groups in the second wave are properly regarded as advocacy tanks. Despite frequent protestations that the first wave groups avoided policy prescriptions in the findings they were commissioned to produce, their preferences were usually lurking amid the wealth of detail. By contrast, the typical second wave production was a hard-hitting pamphlet in which argument featured more strongly than research.

The hopes of the first wave think-tanks had been disappointed after 1945 because governments were reluctant to commit themselves to full-scale planning. Economic liberals in the mid-1990s are still torn between boasting about their success in the war of ideas, and bemoaning the same pragmatic considerations which prevented the Thatcher Governments from establishing a *laissez-faire* Utopia. In fact, despite the significant advantage of intimate access to key decision-makers, the second wave (or New Right) project suffered from the same kind of handicap as its predecessor. While the extent of the changes introduced by these governments cannot be denied, many economic liberals, rightly or wrongly, were worried that the full-blooded implementation of a systematic programme would meet opposition from the conservative majority within the body politic. Like the suggestions of the first wave, the ideas of the economic liberals were only implemented when they chimed in with the government's own purposes, and although that clearly happened more frequently during the 1980s than ever before, for most of the period there were still defined limits. As in the case of planning, we can never know whether the instinctive caution of ministers was well-founded; it is possible that the economic counter-revolution might have enjoyed popular support if it had been pushed to the limit. However, the experience of the poll tax, when the Thatcher Government itself began to act as if it were a New Right think-tank, suggests that the politicians were in fact correct.

The third wave

A discernible third wave of think-tanks began in the late 1980s, and is still continuing in the late 1990s. This wave was clearly inspired by the perceived success of the second one; the Institute for Public Policy Research (1988) was founded to give the Labour Party its own CPS, and the Social Market Foundation (1989) emerged to do the same job for the Social Democrats. Apart from organizations like Conservative 2000 – small groups devoted mainly to serving the interests of individual politicians, aptly described as vanity tanks – the other new bodies, such as Politeia (1996) and the European Policy Forum (1992) have arisen either because of splits in the second wave institutions or in response to problems which the second wave groups failed to address. At present, the most salient characteristic of the new bodies is their lukewarm (or avowedly non-existent) ideological inspiration. Both the IPPR and the SMF were overtaken by events, in that the IPPR quickly established a "soft-left" identity (in the image of party leader Neil Kinnock) which was superseded when Tony Blair became leader, and the SMF soon lost the party it was designed to serve. Demos had obvious links to Labour through Geoff Mulgan, but whereas the other new think-tanks seemed to be in search of a clear line Demos rejoiced in its lack of one; it posed as a forward-looking think-tank in a post-modern, post-ideological world.

Whether or not the present fashion of decrying the labels left and right will continue for long, it is possible to claim that the third wave think-tanks are inherently unstable because their lack of ideological glue – the lack of any feeling of us against them – makes them seem hollowed out versions of the New Right groups. After the New Right, one could have expected a return to the painstaking research of the first wave groups, but members of the new bodies have been deeply impressed by the success of the second wave think-tanks in achieving their objective of saturation media coverage. With so many groups now competing for attention it is crucial to keep up a steady barrage of eye-catching publications; this demands very rapid work, and in order to attract media attention sound-bites are prized more highly than sustained argument. Rather than complementing and informing major parties, the best-known of the new think-tanks are now duplicating their functions almost exactly, in that they tend to court the media with policy ideas which focus on problems of current, short-term vogue; in most cases, interestingly, they also avoid questions of fierce political controversy (such as Europe), while the old, more objective think-tanks felt no such restraint (see especially Chapter 1). In 1995, for example, the new-look Fabian Society helpfully published pamphlets For and Against a single currency. In view of this pragmatic approach it is no accident that particularly since the mid-1970s, think-tanks have been regarded by all major parties as invaluable recruitment-areas. In terms of personnel, at least, this ensures that the third wave of think-tanks will be highly unstable.

We began this volume with an attempt at definition. Recent developments have made this task – difficult enough to start with – almost impossible. A definition which applied to first wave think-tanks would be difficult to sustain in the context of the third wave, and yet since PEP (now PSI) and the NIESR are still performing the same kind of functions as they did at the outset, the problem cannot be solved by saying that a wholly new definition is appropriate. Rather, anything like a satisfactory definition would have to become more complex almost every year. At the same time the exclusion of bodies normally called pressure groups, such as Greenpeace, seems increasingly arbitrary; after all, environmental questions arise in connection with a wide range of public policies, and in its battles with transnational companies and governments Greenpeace requires a substantial research effort. There clearly remains at least one relevant difference; as yet think-tanks have not dug tunnels at road-building sites, or occupied oil rigs. Yet like Greenpeace, advocacy tanks are aggressive campaigning organizations; if they begin to perceive that writing pamphlets is a lot less effective in winning media attention than more direct action, the kind of people who are attracted to the third wave bodies are likely to be tempted into a change of tactics before long.

2: Think-tanks, pluralism, and the climate of opinion

The existence of think-tanks in Britain throughout the present century, and the recent increase in their number, might be regarded as evidence for a healthy pluralist society. On this argument, public debate is enhanced by diverse inputs from a range of groups – the more of them there are and the more they disagree, the better for everyone (Stone 1996: 27–8). In this way democracy is sustained. Pluralists might be dismayed that the IEA found it so difficult to win a serious hearing in the 1950s, or that it took so long for contrary voices to combat the New Right in the 1980s, but even if those periods could be seen as regrettable interludes of ideological hegemony, they are now over and we can look forward to free and fair competition in ideas for the immediate future at least.

This view suffers from at least one serious drawback. The recent bumper crop of think-tanks reflects the evident success of the New Right bodies in winning media exposure and elite attention without incurring significant costs. These developments are likely to be enhanced by technological changes, such as the advent of the Internet. A pluralist would be expected to welcome this, as a sign that almost anyone can set up a think-tank and hope to win notice (Stanfield 1990: 551). There is insufficient space here to examine the counter-argument that this view is naïve, because opinions which threaten vested interests (especially the interests of newspaper proprietors) will never get attention – this is an interesting starting-point for a debate which can never be resolved. For us the more immediate question is whether the recent proliferation of think-tanks will lead to a more *educated* electorate.

197

When examined from this perspective recent developments are a source of concern, not a cause for congratulation. As we have seen, the first wave of think-tanks worked on the assumption that facts speak for themselves, and although they had mixed success in reaching the wider public with their deluge of statistics and analysis, the supply was there if people had been sufficiently interested. The NIESR and PEP never considered that they were involved in a war of ideas; although they were certainly not free from bias, they avoided polemics when presenting their findings. The IEA's purposes were very different; from the start the Institute was concerned to counteract the alleged influence of socialism on people broadly like its own supporters – not only policy-makers and civil servants, but also journalists and academics. These were the opinion-formers through whom the remainder of the electorate (according to Dicey and Hayek) was bound to be influenced. Once it had been taught that socialism was a road to serfdom, the public would create a virtuous, instead of the prevailing vicious, circle, and successive new generations would be introduced to the philosophy of freedom. Only governments which recognized the truth of economic liberalism, and the dangers of collectivism, could then hope to be elected.

The problem with this attitude is that it envisaged an essentially passive electorate, and it was an important first step towards assuming that converting the opinion-formers was all that mattered – in other words, that if policy could be changed through reaching the key people, it might not matter after all if voters did nothing more than acquiesce in the results. Given that the model for the IEA was the Fabian Society, rather than the less ideological first wave groups, this was not a surprising outcome. In a lengthy assault on collectivism in general and the Fabians in particular, W.H. Greenleaf has scoured the works of Shaw and the Webbs in search of quotations which reveal them as having regarded the electorate as stupid at worst, and at best in need of direction from a group reminiscent of Thomas Carlyle's "Aristocracy of talent" (Greenleaf 1983: 163). Hayek's stated views on the enlightened intellectual (see Chapter 3) are rather more subtle than Shaw's remarks, but they tend in the same direction. Indeed, they imply an attitude which, from the democratic point of view, is even more worrying. The Fabians might have regarded the electorate as standing in need of guidance, but they were writing at a time when a large number of workers could genuinely be regarded as politically passive, since they had only recently been given the vote. The problem for the IEA in the mid-1950s, as they saw it, was that the electorate had developed the settled habit of voting the wrong way – i.e. for socialism in its various guises. In short, where the Fabians saw the new democratic electorate as innocent, the economic liberals regarded it as full of sin, and in need of reprogramming from the top. In a characteristic phrase (which opens the chapter in his volume *Capitalism* entitled "Indoctrination against capitalism"), Arthur Seldon has illustrated this attitude. He writes of an "unrelenting barrage of argument against capitalism" which had lasted "for a century" (Seldon 1990: 21). Amazingly, Seldon's book was written more than 30 years after the IEA had started its own counter-barrage, and a decade after many other economic liberals had begun celebrating their victory in the Battle of Ideas. Given Seldon's powerful conviction that his ideas were right, and his undoubted skills in presenting them, it is understandable that he should lash out in this way in the face of continuing evidence that they were still unpopular; even so, his outburst implies deep contempt for those who remained unconvinced by the case for capitalism.

During the 1980s this extreme (if half-conscious) elitism was reinforced in the most dramatic way. According to Maurice Cowling, only "about fifty people" fired with a zeal for economic liberalism were able to carry through what Richard Cockett calls a "counter-revolution" (Cowling 1990: xxxvi; Cockett 1994). The claim that a great deal was accomplished by so few may be an exaggeration even in a country which continues to suffer from what is arguably the most centralized political system in the developed world (see Introduction), but even when qualified it implies a *coup d'état*, rather than a response to a widely expressed public demand. In 1978 Hayek complained that a "free constitution" now apparently meant "*a licence to the majority in Parliament to act as arbitrarily as it pleases*"; after the Conservative victory in the following year this lament would not often be repeated by the spokespeople of economic liberalism (Hayek 1978: 70, italics in original). Yet most journalists and academics – especially those on the left – spoke as if there had really been a change in public attitudes, and they often expressed this by reference to a phrase associated with the New

Right think-tanks – the "climate of opinion". This, it was alleged, had shifted in favour of Mrs Thatcher's brand of Conservatism, just as it had moved towards Labour in 1945 and again in the mid-1960s. What went unnoticed in these accounts was the electoral evidence; Alec Douglas-Home's Conservative Party (supposedly the victim of an adverse shift in the climate of opinion) won 43.4 per cent of the vote in 1964; only in 1979 did Mrs Thatcher's Party achieve a higher share (43.9 per cent), even though it was supposedly in tune with the climate (see, for example, Kavanagh 1987: 17–21). As we have seen, the Labour Party gained a higher percentage of the vote when subsiding to defeat in 1951 (when it was allegedly running out of ideas and its ministers were tiring) than it received in its landslide of 1945 – or, for that matter, than in 1997. This apparent confusion arises because in a democratic polity commentators tend to use the phrase climate of opinion as if it refers to significant numbers of people, if not a clear majority. In most cases, however, when such commentators come to outline the opinions in question they turn out to be the ideas held by the relatively few people who have a significant impact on the preparation of legislation at a given time: in Dicey's words, "a small number of men . . . who happened to be placed in a position of commanding authority". Dicey's instances of places where legislation had been guided in this way were the Russia of Peter the Great and Bismarck's Prussia – not normally seen as models for a democratic state (Dicey 1914: 4–5).

The phrase the "climate of opinion" thus figures even in academic literature as a rationalization for change in a democratic polity, whether it reflects opinion in the wider electorate or just ideas expressed within the charmed circle of government and echoed by cheerleaders in the press. Those with a more personal interest in political events tend to be most sensitive to claims about the "climate". Writing for the right-wing Monday Club's journal *Monday World* in 1972, Jonathan Guinness claimed that "there are growing signs that our attitude on many questions is closer to that of ordinary people than is the 'climate of opinion' so-called, that the 'climate' is not that of the great outdoors but of a sedulously air-conditioned penthouse" (Guinness 1972: 5). In 1976 Sir Keith Joseph's lecture delivered at Preston in the previous September was published under the title "Inflation: the climate of opinion is changing". The only specific evidence in the speech which lent any support to the title was the claim that "Mr Wilson and Mr Healey have come closer to my views to judge by their deeds, their words and, not least, by their silences" (Joseph 1976: 9–17). That the silences of two people – albeit the Prime Minister and the Chancellor of the Exchequer – could in any way constitute a change in the climate of opinion would seem rather a wild exaggeration even by normal political standards; and the worst enemies of the two men would have hesitated before claiming that their deeds had been shaped by a real conversion to Joseph's way of thinking.

Perhaps the best-known example of misuse of the concept, if not the precise phrase, was provided by a politician looking for an alibi – James Callaghan, as he contemplated defeat during the 1979 general election campaign. He told his policy adviser Bernard Donoughue that "there are times, perhaps every 30 years, when there is a sea-change in politics . . . There is a shift in what the public wants and what it approves of. I suspect there is now such a sea-change – and it is for Mrs Thatcher" (Donoughue 1987: 191). Although he did not use the phrase, Callaghan was clearly referring here to what others have called the climate of opinion. Yet of all the winning percentages in post-war elections to that point, Mrs Thatcher's Conservatives achieved the third lowest – only Labour, in the two 1974 general elections, performed less impressively. During the election campaign Mrs Thatcher largely succeeded in restraining her New Right rhetoric; even so, voters preferred Callaghan by a wide margin. Although there can never be a simple explanation for an election result, that of 1979 must be attributed above all else to a widespread rejection of a government which seemed too incompetent to solve Britain's problems, not a general, well-informed feeling that the post-war consensus as a whole had failed, or that there was now a radical alternative which promised to work better. Callaghan's rationalization of his government's defeat may have been an innocent mistake – possibly he mistook the views of leader-writers in Conservative-supporting newspapers for a wider public feeling – but it has only stuck because it was convenient for so many eloquent commentators on both the left and the right, who welcomed this apparent endorsement of their own wishful view that the voters had grown heartily tired of the consensus which both ideological factions despised. The fact that a biased verdict has slipped into the academic literature on the past 20 years can only be attributed to laziness.

In the abstract, the significant extent to which the New Right think-tanks helped to create the impression that the wider climate of opinion (as opposed to the temperature in an air-conditioned penthouse) had changed can be seen as a remarkable achievement. In reality, it must be considered an alarming development for believers in pluralist democracy. Of course, leading decision-makers have always surrounded themselves with *cliques*, and these have usually been dominated by non-elected advisers – one only has to think of Churchill with Beaverbrook and Cherwell, among many examples. However, in the late 1980s this tendency was taken to a new extreme; instead of acting as an informal brake, a source of expert advice or a conduit for public opinion, Margaret Thatcher's advisers (among whom members of think-tanks were especially prominent) apparently tried to insulate her from manifestations of a public hostility which at best they regarded as the temporary, dying spasms of the old consensus mentality. This does not imply any conscious design among the right-wing think-tanks; having convinced themselves that they had won the battle of ideas (and clearly talk in the media and academia about a new climate of opinion helped them to reach this view), there was really no other conclusion open to them. Indeed, the argument advanced here is that, insofar as this assumption encouraged them to mistake the implementation of policies which they generally favoured for a widespread public conversion to New Right ideology, the second wave think-tanks were damaged by it as much as anyone. Such a view was bound to tempt the think-tanks into triumphalism in spite of the weight of evidence showing that real enthusiasm for the economic counter-revolution in the wider public was skin-deep. Since the ultimate goal of all the think-tanks was policy change, they can be forgiven for failing to take proper account of the fact that instead of provoking a change in the climate of opinion which in turn leads to legislative reforms, they had tended to take the alternative, short-cut route outlined in the Introduction, and concentrated on helping to bring about legislative measures in the vague hope that public opinion would eventually respond. They certainly were at least partly responsible, however, for fostering the atmosphere in which all opponents of the government's ideology were regarded as enemies. To this mood can be traced the tendency of governments since 1979 to take decisions without full discussion, even within Cabinet, and the corresponding sense that policy-makers are out of touch with the views of voters. This tendency became so pronounced that in early 1998 even the newly retired Cabinet Secretary lamented that "things are moving too much away from democratic account- ability" (Norton-Taylor 1998).

The final irony is that the habit of rationalizing a change of government by referring to a shift in the climate of opinion, whatever the real evidence, encouraged the media to accuse the New Right groups of going stale even before the predictable Conservative defeat in the 1997 general election – whereas despite their factional splits they were as keen as ever on market liberal ideas, and were constantly showing how their ideology could be applied in new policy areas. One newspaper article in 1993 – compiled by a very sympathetic observer of New Right think-tanks, and, significantly, consisting of short, crisp phrases rather than detailed analysis – claimed that the IEA's "influence peaked in the 1980s", while the CPS was assumed to have "lost its radical cutting-edge" (Cockett 1993).

The premiership of John Major represented something of a lull; free-market reforms were pushed further than ever, but Major himself was at most a career Thatcherite whose desire to present his policies as pragmatic decisions led him to avoid close identifica- tion with any one think-tank. But since the 1997 general election the conditions of the late 1980s have returned. The only significant changes from the think-tank perspective have been the identity of the monarch and his courtiers – and an even greater obsession with news-management. This led in November 1997 to the announcement of a new Central Strategic Unit (CSU) which, like the old CPRS, was to co-ordinate the work of departments – the difference being that instead of co-ordinating policy like the think-tank, the CSU was to ensure that stories favourable to the government were properly presented. Newspaper articles quickly acknowledged the situation by revealing who was "in" and who was "out" of government favour; naturally a significant proportion of the identified favourites were think-tankers, who were either still working for the institu- tions which had brought them to notice or had joined the govern- ment team as back-benchers and members of the Downing Street

Policy Unit. Since claims to direct policy influence have been exaggerated, groups like the CPS seem in hindsight to have been most important during the 1980s as sources of "ideological fellowship" for government ministers. Instead of wanting to join a community of believers, think-tanks are now queuing up to provide a new and rootless regime with intellectual credibility. Winning and retaining favour depends on a quick response to every passing trend, which in turn must lead to over-hasty work. Thus the "credibility" now offered by most think-tanks is more apparent than real.

The most likely result of this continuing trend is that the think-tanks inside the charmed circle will become transmission belts for news and advice which pleases the government. More seriously, they could be used as a means of defeating democratic accountability. Ideas which the government wishes to float can be published as if they originated outside Whitehall, in the think-tanks; if they cause an outcry they can be disowned without much political cost – or implemented to see if the public will acquiesce, then blamed on the think-tanks if it does not. This might seem fanciful, but it is not so far removed from what happened in the case of the poll tax. Since then the media has raised the profile and prestige of think-tanks even further, and it is not implausible to suggest that before long the government publicity machine might try to excuse a policy disaster by claiming that the idea was backed by the climate of opinion – that is, a large number of newspaper stories about a think-tank proposal.

New Labour has apparently derived the same lessons from the 1980s as the think-tanks themselves. It behaves as if it is convinced that the climate of opinion changed in 1979, and that the New Right groups played a significant role in bringing this about; the landslide result in May 1997 is attributed to its ability to adapt to this alleged climate. Given the traditions of the Labour Party its best chance of presenting its policies to its core supporters would be to plead that events have left it with no alternative, but like the previous Conservative governments, it is determined to talk up the vitality of its thinking. In short, New Labour has a vested interest in purveying an "intellectualist fallacy", which asserts that ideas are more important than events in shaping policy (Garnett 1996b). Yet, having restricted its room for manoeuvre through pre-election promises it has to hope that slogans are more potent than new ideas; its own predelictions reinforce the tendency for think-tanks hoping to win favour to concentrate on media-friendliness, not intensive research. As long as the right "fifty people" are happy with the service provided by think-tanks, the state of knowledge among the public at large will remain in policy-making circles as irrelevant as it was during the 1980s. Even the cursory glance at the post-war British experience which the scope of this volume permits shows that New Labour has inherited many of the false premises adopted by its predecessor in power. Yet unless scholars approach the subject of think-tanks with suitable scepticism, future historians will continue to identify the climate of opinion with whatever a government does, and since its actions will broadly coincide with the proffered suggestions of the think-tanks, they will happily record the success of these bodies in influencing government policy. "We do not like the complexity of real history", Ralf Dahrendorf has written. "The authors of ideas prefer to think that they are directly responsible for realities which correspond to their speeches or writings, and the rest love simple causal explanations, not to say conspiracy theories" (Dahrendorf 1995: 40).

References

Adam Smith Institute 1990. *The first hundred*. London: Adam Smith Institute.

Addison, P. 1977. *The road to 1945: British politics and the Second World War*. London: Quartet Books.

Addison, P. 1992. *Churchill on the home front, 1900–1955*. London: Jonathan Cape.

Bailey, R. 1981. The second post-war decade: 1951–64. In *Fifty years of political and economic planning: looking forward 1931–1981*, J. Pinder (ed.), London: Heinemann.

Baker, K. 1993. *The turbulent years: my life in politics*. London: Faber & Faber.

Bale, T. 1996. Demos: populism, eclecticism and equidistance in the post-modern world. In *Contemporary British History* 10(2).

Barnes, J. & R. Cockett 1994. The making of party policy. In *Conservative century: the conservative party since 1900*, A. Seldon & S. Ball (eds), Oxford: Oxford University Press.

Baston, L. 1996. The social market foundation. *Contemporary British History* 10(1).

Bellerby, J. 1943. *Economic reconstruction*. London: Macmillan.

Blackaby, F. (ed.) 1978. *British economic policy 1960–1974*. Cambridge: Cambridge University Press.

Blackstone, T. & W. Plowden 1988. *Inside the think-tank: advising the cabinet, 1971–1983*. London: Heinemann.

Blundell, J. 1990. *Waging the war of ideas: why there are no shortcuts*. Washington, DC: Heritage Foundation.

Bosco, N. & C. Navari (eds) 1995. *Chatham House and British foreign policy*. London: Lothian Foundation Press.

Bradley, I. 1981. Intellectual influences in Britain: past and present. In *The emerging consensus . . . ?* A. Seldon (ed.), London: IEA.

Brittan, S. 1964. *The treasury under the Tories 1951–1964*. Harmondsworth: Penguin.

Brittan, S. 1968. *Left or right: the bogus dilemma*. London: Secker & Warburg.

Brittan, S. 1973. *Is there an economic consensus?: an attitude survey*. London: Macmillan.

Brogan, C. 1947. *Our new masters*. London: Hollis & Carter.

Budd, A. 1978. *The politics of economic planning*. London: Fontana.

Burnham, J. 1945. *The managerial revolution*. Harmondsworth: Pelican.

Butler, D., A. Adonis and T. Travers 1994. *Failure in British government: the politics of the poll tax*. Oxford: Oxford University Press.

Butler, E., M. Pirie and P. Young 1985. *The omega file*. London: Adam Smith Institute.

Cairncross, A. 1985. *Years of recovery: British economic policy 1945–51*. London: Methuen.

Cairncross, A. 1996a. *Managing the British economy in the 1960s*. London: Macmillan.

Cairncross, A. 1996b. The Heath government and the British economy. In *The Heath government 1970–74*. S. Ball & A. Seldon (eds), Harlow: Longman.

Callaghan, J. 1996. The Fabian society since 1945. *Contemporary British History* **10**(2).

Carr, W. & A. Hartnett 1996. *Education and the struggle for democracy: the politics of educational issues*. Buckingham: Open University Press.

Centre for Policy Studies 1974. *Sherman Papers*. University of London.

Centre for Policy Studies 1975a. *Objectives and style*. London: Centre for Policy Studies.

Centre for Policy Studies 1975b. *Why Britain needs a social market economy*. London: Centre for Policy Studies.

Centre for Policy Studies 1985. *Whither Monetarism?* London: Centre for Policy Studies.

Centre for Policy Studies 1987. *The welfare challenge*. London: Centre for Policy Studies.

Centre for Policy Studies 1989a. *Aims and achievements*. London: Centre for Policy Studies.

Centre for Policy Studies 1989b. *Exertion and example*. London: Centre for Policy Studies.

Clarke, P. 1996. The Keynesian consensus. In *The ideas that shaped post-war Britain*. D. Marquand and A. Seldon (eds). London: Fontana.

Cockett, R. 1993. A brief history of the think-tank. In *Independent on Sunday* 24 Jan.

Cockett, R. 1994. *Thinking the unthinkable: think-tanks and the economic counter-revolution, 1931–1983*. London: HarperCollins.

Cockett, R. 1996. Afterthoughts. *Contemporary British History* **10**(2).

Cole, M. 1963. *The story of Fabian Socialism*. London: Heinemann.

Congdon, T. 1989. *Monetarism lost, and why it must be regained*. London: Centre for Policy Studies.

Conservative Central Office 1974. *Putting Britain first* (manifesto for general election of October 1974).

Cornford, J. 1990. Performing fleas: reflections from a think-tank. *Policy Studies* **11**(4).

Cosgrave, P. 1985. *Thatcher: the first term*. London: The Bodley Head.

Cowling, M. 1963. *The nature and limits of political science*. Cambridge: Cambridge University Press.

Cowling, M. 1990. The sources of the new right. Preface to *Mill and liberalism*. Cambridge: Cambridge University Press, 2nd edn.

Cowling, M. 1997. *A Conservative future*. London: Politeia.

Crewe, I. 1989. Values: the crusade that failed. In *The Thatcher effect: a decade of change*, D. Kavanagh & A. Seldon (eds). Oxford: Oxford University Press.

Crewe, I. & A. King 1995. *SDP: the birth, life and death of the social democratic party*. Oxford: Oxford University Press.

Crick, M. & A. van Klaveren 1991. Mrs Thatcher's greatest blunder. *Contemporary Record* **5**(3).

Culyer, A.J. 1981. The IEA's unorthodoxy. In *The Emerging Consensus . . . ?* A. Seldon (ed.). London: IEA.

Dahrendorf, R. 1995. *LSE: a history of the London School of Economics and Political Science, 1895–1995*. Oxford: Oxford University Press.

Daniel, W.W. 1989. PSI: a Centre for Strategic Research. *Policy Studies* **9**(4).

Denham, A. 1996. *Think-tanks of the new right*. Aldershot: Dartmouth.

Denham, A. & M. Garnett 1994. Conflicts of loyalty: cohesion and division in conservatism, 1975–1990. In *Contemporary Political Studies 1994*, **1**, P. Dunleavy & J. Stanyer (eds). Exeter: Political Studies Association.

Denham, A. & M. Garnett 1995. Rethinking think-tanks: a British perspective. In *Contemporary Political Studies 1995*, **1**, J. Lovenduski & J. Stanyer (eds). Exeter: Political Studies Association.

Denham, A. & M. Garnett 1996. The nature and impact of think tanks in contemporary Britain. *Contemporary British History* **10**(1).

Desai, R. 1994. Second-hand dealers in ideas: think tanks and Thatcherite hegemony. *New Left Review* **203** (January/February).

Dicey, A.V. 1905. *Lectures on the relation between law and public opinion in England during the nineteenth century*. London: Macmillan.

Dickson, P. 1971. *Think-tanks*. New York: Ballantine Books.

Donoughue, B. 1987. *Prime Minister: the conduct of policy under Harold Wilson and James Callaghan*. London: Jonathan Cape.

Dow, J.C.R. 1965. *The management of the British economy 1945–60.* Cambridge: Cambridge University Press.

Duncan, A. 1993. *An end to illusions.* London: Demos.

Durbin, Elizabeth 1985. *New Jerusalems: the Labour Party and the economics of democratic socialism.* London: Routledge & Kegan Paul.

Durbin, Evan 1949. *Principles of economic planning.* London: Routledge & Kegan Paul.

Dye, T.R. 1978. Oligarchic tendencies in national policy-making: the role of private planning organisations. *Journal of Politics* **40** (May).

Eatwell, Lord. 1997. Letter to *Financial Times.* Monday, 15 September.

EPF 1997. European Policy Forum publicity brochure.

Foot, P. 1998. Man from the ministry of daft ideas. *Guardian,* Monday 12. January.

Franks, O. 1947. *Central planning and control in war and peace.* London: London School of Economics.

Freely, M. 1997. So just who is Helen Wilkinson?. *Guardian,* G2, February 27.

Friedman, M. 1986. Has liberalism failed?. In *The unfinished agenda,* M. Anderson (ed.). London, IEA.

Gamble, A. 1981. *Britain in decline.* London: Macmillan.

Gamble, A. 1983. Liberals and the economy. In *Liberal party politics,* V. Bogdanor (ed.), Oxford: Clarendon Press.

Gamble, A. 1996. *Hayek: the iron cage of liberty.* London: Polity Press.

Garnett, M. 1996a. *Principles and politics in contemporary Britain.* London: Longman.

Garnett, M. 1996b. Treatises and sound-bites: theorists, practitioners and the climate of opinion. Paper delivered to Political Theory Conference, Oxford, January.

Gilmour, I. & M. Garnett 1997. *Whatever happened to the Tories?.* London: Fourth Estate.

Goodman, R. 1981. The first post-war decade. In *Fifty years of political and economic planning,* J. Pinder (ed.). London: Heinemann.

Gray, J. 1994. *The undoing of conservatism.* London: Social Market Foundation.

Greenleaf, W.H. 1983. *The British political tradition. vol II: the ideological heritage.* London: Methuen.

Griffiths, B. 1985. *Monetarism and morality.* London: Centre for Policy Studies.

Guinness, J. 1972. The club today. *Monday World,* Spring issue.

Halcrow, M. 1989. *Keith Joseph: a single mind.* London: Macmillan.

Hall, R. 1969. Introduction. *National Institute Economic Review,* 50th issue.

Hames, T. & R. Feasey 1994. Anglo-American think tanks under Reagan and Thatcher. In *A Conservative revolution?: the Thatcher-Reagan decade in perspective*, A. Adonis & T. Hames (eds). Manchester: Manchester University Press.

Harris, M. 1996. The Centre for Policy Studies: the paradoxes of power. *Contemporary British History* **10**(2).

Harris, R. 1956. *Politics without prejudice: a political appreciation of the Rt. Hon. Richard Austen Butler*. London: Staples Press.

Harris, R. 1986. *Morality and markets*. London: Centre for Policy Studies.

Harris, R. 1994. *No, prime minister! Ralph Harris against the consensus*. London: IEA.

Harris, R. & A. Seldon (eds) 1977. *Not from benevolence . . . twenty years of economic dissent*. London: IEA.

Harrison, R. 1965. *Before the Socialists: studies in labour and politics, 1861–1881*. London: Routledge & Kegan Paul.

Harrison, R. 1993. The Fabians: aspects of a very English socialism. In *Defending politics: Bernard Crick and pluralism*, I. Hampsher-Monk (ed). London: British Academic Press.

Hartwell, R.M. 1995. *A history of the Mont Pelerin Society*. Indianapolis, Indiana: Liberty Fund.

Hayek, F.A. 1962. (ed) *The road to serfdom*. London: Routledge & Kegan Paul.

Hayek, F.A. 1967. *Studies in philosophy, politics and economics*. London: Routledge & Kegan Paul.

Hayek, F. 1978. Will the democratic ideal prevail? In *The coming confrontation*, A. Seldon (ed.). London: IEA.

Heath, E. & A. Barker 1978. Heath on Whitehall reform. *Parliamentary Affairs* **31**(4).

Heffernan, R. 1996. Blueprint for a revolution? The politics of the Adam Smith Institute. *Contemporary British History* **10**(1).

Hellebust, L. 1996. *Think-tank directory: a guide to nonprofit public policy research organisations*. Topeka, Kansas: Government Research Service.

Hennessy, P. 1990. *Whitehall*. London: Fontana edition.

Hennessy, P. 1992. *Never again: Britain 1945–1951*. London: Jonathan Cape.

Hennessy, P. & S. Coates 1991. Little grey cells: think-tanks, governments and policy-making. *Strathclyde Analysis Papers* **6**.

Hennessy, P., S. Morrison & R. Townsend 1985. Routine punctuated by orgies: the Central Policy Review Staff 1970–1983. *Strathclyde Papers on Government and Politics* **31**.

Higgott, R. & D. Stone 1994. The limits of influence: foreign policy think-tanks in Great Britain and the USA. *Review of International Studies* **20**(1).

Himmelfarb, G. 1987. *Victorian values and twentieth-century condescension*. London: Centre for Policy Studies.

Hobsbawm, E.J. 1964. The Fabians reconsidered. In *Labouring men: studies in the history of labour*. London: Weidenfeld and Nicholson.

Hogg, S. & J. Hill 1995. *Too close to call: power and politics – John Major in No. 10*. London: Little Brown.

Hoover, K. & R. Plant 1989. *Conservative capitalism in Britain and the United States: a critical appraisal*. London: Routledge.

Howe, G. 1994. *Conflict of loyalty*. London: Macmillan.

Isserlis, A. 1981. Plus ça change . . . In *Fifty years of political and economic planning*, J. Pinder (ed.). London: Heinemann.

James, S. 1986. The Central Policy Review Staff 1970–1983. *Political Studies* **34**(3).

James, S. 1993. The idea brokers: the impact of think-tanks on British government. *Public Administration* **71**(4).

Jenkins, P. 1989. *Mrs Thatcher's revolution: the ending of the socialist era*. London: Pan.

Jones, A. 1973. *The new inflation: the politics of prices and incomes*. London: Andre Deutsch.

Jones, K. 1988. Fifty years of economic research: a brief history of the National Institute of Economic and Social Research. *National Institute Economic Review* (May).

Jordan, G. & N. Ashford (eds) 1993. *Public policy and the impact of the New Right*. London: Pinter.

Joseph, K. 1975. *Reversing the trend: a critical reappraisal of Conservative economic and social policies*. London: Barry Rose.

Joseph, K. 1976. *Stranded on the middle ground: reflections on circumstances and policies*. London: Centre for Policy Studies.

Joseph, K. 1987. Escaping the chrysalis of statism. *Contemporary Record* **1**(1).

Kavanagh, D. 1987; and 2nd edition, 1990. *Thatcherism and British politics: the end of consensus?* Oxford: Oxford University Press.

Keegan, W. 1984. *Mrs Thatcher's economic experiment*. London: Allen Lane.

Keynes, J.M. 1936. *The general theory of employment, interest and money*. London: Macmillan.

King, A. (ed.) 1976. *Why is Britain becoming harder to govern?* London: BBC.

King, D.S. 1987. *The new right: politics, markets and citizenship*. London: Macmillan.

Labour Research 1997. New brains behind the scenes **86**(11).

Lamb, R. 1995. *The Macmillan years 1957–1963: the emerging truth*. London: John Murray.

Lawson, N. 1992. *The view from no. 11: memoirs of a Tory radical*. London: Bantam Books.

Lawton, D. 1994. *The Tory mind on education: 1979–94*. London: Falmer Press.

Layton-Henry, Z. 1992. *The politics of immigration*. Oxford: Blackwell.

Leruez, J. 1975. *Economic planning and politics in Britain*. London: Martin Robertson.

Levitas, R. 1986. Competition and compliance: the utopias of the new right. In *The ideology of the new right*, R. Levitas, Cambridge: Polity Press.

Lindsay, K. 1981. PEP through the 1930s: organisation, structure, people. See Pinder (1991).

McBriar, A.M. 1966. *Fabian socialism and English politics 1884–1918*. Cambridge: Cambridge University Press.

Mackenzie, N. & J. Mackenzie 1977. *The first Fabians*. London: Weidenfeld & Nicholson.

McSmith, A. 1994. *John Smith: a life 1938–1994*. London: Verso.

McSmith, A., D. Marquaud & A. Seldan (eds) 1996. *The ideas that shaped post-war Britain*. London: Fontana.

Marquand, D. 1997. *The new reckoning: capitalism, states and citizens*. Cambridge: Polity Press.

Marr, A. 1995. *Ruling Brittannia*. London: Michael Joseph.

Marwick, A. 1964. Middle opinion in the thirties: planning, progress and political agreement. *English Historical Review* **79** (April).

Middlemas, K. 1979. *Politics and industrial society*. London: Andre Deutsch.

Morgan, K. 1984. *Labour in power 1945–1951*. Oxford: Oxford University Press.

Muller, C. 1996. The Institute of Economic Affairs: undermining the post-war consensus. *Contemporary British History* **10**(1).

Nicholson, M. 1940. *How Britain's resources are mobilized*. Oxford: Clarendon Press.

Nicholson, M. 1967. *The system*. London: Hodder & Stoughton.

Nicholson, M. 1981a. The proposal for a national plan, in Pinder, J. (ed.) *Fifty Years of Political and Economic Planning*.

Nicholson, M. 1981b. PEP through the 1930s: growth, thinking, performance, in Pinder, J. (ed.) *Fifty Years of Political and Economic Planning*.

Norton, P. 1993. The Conservative Party from Thatcher to Major. In *Britain at the polls 1992*, A. King (ed.). New Jersey: Chatham House.

Norton-Taylor, R. 1998. Plagued by leaks and lack of trust. *The Guardian*. Monday 5 January.

Oakley, R. 1989. Privatized policy-making for the Tory right. *The Times*, 17 February.

Pinder, J. (ed.) 1981. *Fifty years of Political and Economic Planning: Looking forward 1931–1981*. London: Heinemann.

Pirie, M. 1988a. *Micropolitics: the creation of successful policy*. Aldershot: Wildwood House.

Pirie, M. 1988b. *Privatization: theory, practice and choice*. Aldershot: Wildwood House.

Prince, M.J. 1983. *Policy advice and organisational survival: policy planning and research units in British government*. Aldershot: Gower House, 1983.

Pugh, P. 1984. *Educate, agitate, organise: 100 years of Fabian socialism*. London: Cape.

Ramsden, J. 1980. *The making of Conservative Party policy: the Conservative Research Department since 1929*. London: Longman.

Ramsden, J. 1995. *The age of Churchill and Eden, 1940–1957*. London: Longman.

Ranelagh, J. 1992. *Thatcher's people*. London: Fontana.

Ricci, D.M. 1993. *The transformation of American politics: the new Washington and the rise of think tanks*. New Haven: Yale University Press.

Richards, H. 1993. Dry as wind-blown dust. *Times Higher Education Supplement*, 19 Feb.

Richter, M. 1964. *The politics of conscience: T.H. Green and his age*. London: Weidenfeld and Nicholson.

Ricketts, M. & E. Shoesmith 1990. *British economic opinion: a survey of a thousand economists*. London: Institute of Economic Affairs.

Rivlin, A.M. 1992. Policy analysis at the Brookings Institution. In *Organisations for policy advice: helping government think*, C.H. Weiss (ed.). London: Sage, 1992.

Robinson, A. 1988. The National Institute: the early years. *National Institute Economic Review*, May.

Rose, E.J.B., N. Deakin, M. Abrams, V. Jackson, M. Peston, A.H. Vanags, B. Cohen, J. Gaitskell & P. Ward 1969. *Colour and citizenship: a report on British race relations*. London: Oxford University Press for the Institute of Race Relations.

Roskill, O. 1981. PEP through the 1930s: the industries group, in Pinder, J. (ed.), *Fifty Years of Political and Economic Planning*.

Rothschild, Lord 1977. *Meditations of a Broomstick*. London: Collins.

Ruben, P. 1996. The Institute for Public Policy Research: policy and politics. *Contemporary British History* **10**(2).

Russel, T. 1978. *The Tory party: its policies, divisions and future* (Harmondsworth: Penguin Books).

Sandford, C.T. 1972. *National Economic Planning* (London: Heinemann).

Seldon, A. (ed.) 1981. *The emerging consensus . . . ? Essays on the interplay between ideas, interests and circumstances in the first 25 years of the IEA*. London: Institute of Economic Affairs.

Seldon, A. 1986. *The riddle of the voucher*. London: IEA.

Seldon, A. 1990. *Capitalism*. Oxford: Basil Blackwell.

214

Shearmur, J. 1995. The Centre for Policy Studies (Unpublished paper).

Sherman, A. 1979. CPS programme of activities 1979–84. Sherman papers, University of London.

Sherman, A. 1988. Discourses on ten stepping stones of John Hoskyns (Unpublished paper).

Skidelsky, R. 1989. *The social market economy*. London: Social Market Foundation.

Skidelsky, R. 1992. *John Maynard Keynes, Vol II: The economist as saviour 1920–1937*. London: Macmillan.

Skidelsky, R. 1996. The fall of Keynesianism. In *The ideas that shaped post-war Britain*. D. Marquand & A. Seldon (eds). London: Fontana.

Smith, A. 1822 edition. *An inquiry into the nature and causes of the wealth of nations*, Vol.III (London).

Smith, D. 1987. *The rise and fall of monetarism*. Harmondsworth: Penguin.

Smith, J.A. 1991. *The idea brokers: think tanks and the rise of the new policy elite*. New York: Free Press.

Stanfield, R.L. 1990. The Golden Rolodex. *National Journal*, 10 March.

Stephenson, H. 1980. *Mrs Thatcher's first year*. London: Jill Norman.

Stevenson, J. & C. Cook 1977. *The slump: society and politics during the depression*. London, Cape.

Stewart, M. 1972. *Keynes and after*. Harmondsworth: Pelican.

Stewart, M. 1978. *Politics & economic policy in the UK since 1964*. London: Pergamon.

Stone, D. 1991. Old guard versus new partisans: think-tanks in transition. *Australian Journal of Political Science* **26**(2).

Stone, D. 1996. *Capturing the political imagination: think-tanks and the policy process*. London: Frank Cass.

Stone, D., A. Denham & M. Garnett (forthcoming), *Think-tanks across nations: a comparative approach*. Manchester: Manchester University Press.

Thatcher, M. 1995. *The Path to Power*. London: HarperCollins.

Thomas, W. 1979. *The Philosophic Radicals: nine studies in theory and practice, 1817–1841*. Oxford: Clarendon Press.

Thompson, P. 1967. *Socialists, Liberals and labour: the struggle for London, 1885–1914*. London: Routledge and Kegan Paul.

Todd, M.J. 1991. The Centre for Policy Studies: its birth and early days. *Essex Papers in Politics and Government* **81**, Department of Government, University of Essex.

Veljanovski, C. 1987. *Selling the state: Privatisation in Britain*. London: Weidenfeld & Nicholson.

Veljanovski, C. (ed.) 1989. *Privatisation and competition: A market perspective*. London: IEA.

REFERENCES

Wade, D. & J. Picardie 1983. The Omega Project. *New Statesman* **106**.
Waldegrave, W. 1978. *The binding of leviathan: conservatism and the future*. London: Hamish Hamilton.
Wallace, W. 1990. Chatham House at 70: to the 1990s and beyond. *The World Today* **46**(5).
Wallace, W. 1994. Between two worlds: think tanks and foreign policy. Hill, C. & P. Beshoff (eds), *Two worlds of international relations: academics, practitioners and the trade in ideas*. London: Routledge and London School of Economics.
Weaver, R.K. 1989. The changing world of think-tanks. *PS: Political Science and Politics* (September).
Weiss, C.H. 1992. Introduction: helping government think: functions and consequences of policy analysis organisations. In *Organisations for policy advice: helping government think*, C.H. Weiss (ed.). London: Sage.
Whitehead, P. 1985. *The writing on the wall: Britain in the 1970s*. London: Michael Joseph.
Whiteley, P., P. Seyd, J. Richardson & P. Bissell 1994. Thatcherism and the Conservative Party. *Political Studies* **42**(2).
Wiener, M. 1985. *English culture and the decline of the industrial spirit 1850–1980*. Harmondsworth: Penguin.
Wildavsky, A. 1979. *Speaking truth to power*. Boston: Litte Brown.
Willetts, D. 1987. The role of the Prime Minister's policy unit. *Public Administration* **65**(4).
Willetts, D. 1991. *Happy families: four points to a Conservative family policy*. London: Centre for Policy Studies.
Willetts, D. 1992. *Modern conservatism*. Harmondsworth: Penguin.
Willetts, D. 1994. *Civic conservatism*. London: Social Market Foundation.
Williamson, P. 1992. *National crisis and national government*. Cambridge: Cambridge University Press.
Wright, T.R. 1986. *The religion of humanity: The influence of Comtean positivism in Victorian Britain*. Cambridge: Cambridge University Press.
Young, M. 1981. The second world war. See Pinder (1981).
Young, H. 1989. *One of us: a biography of Margaret Thatcher*. London: Macmillan.
Young, H. & A. Sloman 1986. *The Thatcher phenomenon*. London, BBC Publications.

Primary sources

1. References in the text to CAP and PREM refer to government files held at the Public Record Office, Kew, London.

216

2. LCC refers to minutes of the Leader's Consultative Committee, held in the Conservative Party Archive, Bodleian Library, Oxford.
3. Pamphlets referred to in the text but not listed in the References will be found in the pamphlet holdings of reference departments of university libraries.

British think-tanks

Adam Smith Institute
23 Great Smith Street
London SW1P 3BL
Website: http:\\www.cyberpoint.co.uk\asi

Centre for Policy Studies
57 Tufton Street
London SW1P 3QL
Website: http:\\www.cps.org.uk

Demos
9 Bridewell Place
London EC4V 6AP
Website: http:\\www.demos.co.uk

European Policy Forum
20 Queen Anne's Gate
London SW1H 9AA
Website: http:\\ourworld.compuserve.com\homepages\epfltd

Fabian Society
11 Dartmouth Street
London SW1H 9BN

Institute of Economic Affairs
2 Lord North Street
London SW1P 3LB
Website: http:\\www.iea.org.uk

Institute for Public Policy Research
30–32 Southampton Street
London WC2E 7RA
Website: http:\\www.ippr.org.co.uk

REFERENCES

National Institute of Economic and Social Research
2 Dean Trench Street
London SW1P 3HE
Website: http:\\www.niesr.ac.uk

Policy Studies Institute
100 Park Village East
London NW1 3SR
Website: http:\\www.psi.org.uk

Politeia
28 Charing Cross Road
London WC2H ODB

Social Market Foundation
11 Tufton Street
London SW1P 3QB
Website: http:\\www.smf.co.uk

INDEX